Hesitant Martyr in the Texas Revolution
James Walker Fannin

Gary Brown

Republic of Texas Press

Library of Congress Cataloging-in-Publication Data
Brown, Gary, 1945-
    Hesitant Martyr in the Texas Revolution: James Walker Fannin / Gary Brown.
        p. cm.
    Includes bibliographical references and index.
    ISBN 1-55622-778-7 (pbk.)
    1. Fannin, James Walker, 1804?-1836.   2. Soldiers--Texas--Biography.
    3. Texas--History--Revolution, 1835-1836.   4. Goliad Massacre, Goliad,
    Tex., 1836.   5. Texas. Army--Biography.   I. Title.
    F390.F23 B76 2000
    976.4'03'092--dc21
    [B]   99-462160
                                                                            CIP

Republic of Texas Press is an imprint of Wordware Publishing, Inc.
No part of this book may be reproduced in any form or by
any means without permission in writing from
Wordware Publishing, Inc.

Printed in the United States of America

All inquiries for volume purchases of this book should be addressed to Wordware
Publishing, Inc., at 2320 Los Rios Boulevard, Plano, Texas 75074. Telephone
inquiries may be made by calling:

(972) 423-0090

Contents

Contents

Preface

In the early days of 1804 or 1805, an illegitimate child was born of a distinguished veteran U.S. Army officer of the War of 1812 and a woman from his neighboring plantation in Georgia. That child would, after a difficult and sometimes troubled childhood, become involved in the Texas Revolution of 1835-1836 and become a martyr—although somewhat tarnished in reputation.

During his short lifetime, he used several names. He also espoused the values and culture of the American south in the early 1800s—honor, chivalry, an attachment to military tradition, and courage.

But in his personal life he did not always practice those values he advocated. He was a slave trader who dealt in human misery for profit; he sacrificed his personal honor at times in pursuit of personal ambition; his "code of chivalry" at times placed the lives of his men in danger; and he pursued the dream of a brigadier generalship only to become commander of an army he found he no longer wanted to lead.

But, in the tragic and disastrous end of his life and military command, his personal courage never faltered.

And he was one of the best field officers revolutionary Texas could place on the battlefield against the Mexican army in 1835 and 1836.

As a Texas hero, he has not been treated kindly with the passage of time. His place in Texas history has always been relegated to a footnote for the Alamo martyrs and the victory at San Jacinto. Unfairly, he is remembered as the commander who lost twice as many men as were killed at the Alamo and San Jacinto combined.

Texas has not been willing to forget him, but historians have not hesitated to label him with negative terms: Blind ambition, indecision, lack of strategy, underestimation of the enemy, reliance upon "councils of war," and lack of attention to crucial details quickly come to mind.

But much of this criticism is undeserved. Neither Travis nor Houston was forced to struggle under the kinds of hardship that this officer endured in the south Texas plains in 1836. Each of the three commanders faced separate and distinctive burdens, but this leader in the end found neither Travis' exaltation nor Houston's victory.

Like virtually every other Texan leader in 1835 and 1836, he had flaws of character and elements of his background that were best left behind in his native United States. But, looking closely at the man and his command, it is apparent he has been in many ways judged unfairly.

His name was, at the time of his death, James Walker Fannin Jr.

Section I

Southern Roots in Mexican Texas

Chapter One

Georgia, West Point, and the Formative Years

In the early days of 1805—some historians claim 1804—an illegitimate child was born in Georgia, the son of Major Isham S. Fannin and the daughter of an employee on his brother's plantation.

While among the landed Southern gentry in the early 1800s such an event was certainly not unheard of, it did create problems socially. The child was sent away.

The Fannin family, although prominent and financially secure in Georgia, had a touch of scandal in its past and just enough skeletons in the family closet to make this illegitimate birth more than embarrassing to Isham Fannin.

The family name had originally been Fanning and Isham's father, James W., had dropped the "g" to disassociate himself from the clan's severely tarnished role in prerevolutionary America.

The first Fannings arrived in the colonies in the mid-1600s. By the time of the revolution, the family was well established in colonial society and immediately took a prominent role in the Revolutionary War—although on the British side.

In North Carolina, a lawyer named Edmund Fanning married the daughter of the Tory Governor Tyron, who was particularly hated by the colonists. After the Revolutionary War, Edmund Fanning moved to Canada and for nineteen years was governor of Prince Edward Island and a lieutenant general in the British army.[1]

Edmund's brother, James W. Fanning, adopted the independence cause and fought on the colonists' side of the revolution. After the war, he immigrated to Georgia and became a successful and wealthy planter. To disassociate himself from his despised Tory brother, James dropped the "g" from the family name and for the rest of his life identified himself as "Fannin."

In Georgia, James W. Fannin continued to prosper and grow. James Fannin died in 1803, leaving a successful plantation and several children including one son named Isham.

Isham, who continued using the abbreviated family name "Fannin," had served as a major of militia in the War of 1812. But before that, in 1805, he had the illegitimate child. In 1809 he married Margarett Potter and they later had a daughter whom they named Eliza.

When Isham died on April 26, 1817, he called to his bedside his two children. His young daughter, whom he was raising at home, was brought to him in these final hours. His young son, whom he had neither accepted nor raised, was also summoned to his deathbed. In his final moments, he whispered something to the children. Exactly what was said remains unknown, but its impact was profound—especially on the young boy.

Years later the boy would recall that moment in a poignant letter to his sister, but some unnamed family censor clipped the passage from the correspondence, leaving us with no indication what was said that day.

After Isham's death, daughter Eliza remained with her mother. The son, however, went back to the family that had adopted him—the family of his true mother, who was named Walker.

That boy was named James Fannin Walker, but in his lifetime he would change his name—occasionally even re-adding the "g" to Fannin. But, in the end, he adopted the given name of his paternal grandfather.

His childhood experiences followed him throughout his adulthood. Until the final day of his short life, despite his intense personal ambition, he often appeared uncomfortable with himself. He is remembered in Texas history today as James Walker Fannin Jr.

Little is known of his early years. Eliza's mother appears to have encouraged the siblings to maintain contact with each other. In later years, James referred to her in favorable terms. Some reports claim his maternal grandfather adopted him, and it appears the two had a close and comfortable relationship.

It is also apparent that Isham Fannin maintained at least some relationship with his son—a fact emphasized by his dying request to talk with the boy. In later years, James would write favorably of his father, ". . . what he done for me, (which but few fathers would have done)."[2]

So it appears that as socially stigmatizing as his birth circumstances might have been in Southern society, he was not overly traumatized by it. Growing up on the plantation of his true mother, he probably also visited the home of his sister and stepmother.

There are no records of his attending school during the early years, but it can be assumed he at least participated in "plantation schooling" common in the American South during that period of his life.

Somehow he managed to obtain a position at West Point while still a young teenager. The service records of his father in the War of 1812 and his grandfather in the Revolutionary War may have been a factor in his selection, but his academic preparation obviously was not.

U.S. Army records indicate he enrolled at West Point at age fourteen years and six months on July 1, 1819—still using the adopted name "James Fannin Walker." At the time of his admission, his guardian was listed as Abraham B. Fleming of Savannah, Georgia.[3]

Little is known of his physical stature and appearance. In later years, there would be descriptions of him as a grown man including one by historian Harbert Davenport, quoting unnamed sources, in which he describes Fannin as ". . . more than six feet tall. My recollection is that Fannin was described as being dark, with military bearing, and a studious cast of countenance—the thought that occurs to me being that he was neither of the flashing coal black type of Bonham, nor the ruddy haired and gray-eyed, as was Travis, but of complexion somewhat between the two."[4]

Documents from West Point indicate that Fannin, under the name "Walker," completed his Fourth Class Year (freshman) ending June 1820. Of eighty-six classmates, he finished sixty-second in mathematics, fifty-seventh in French, and sixtieth in "Order of

General Merit." It was obvious from the beginning of his military career that academics would not be a strength.

By January 21, 1821, he was failing French and had been remanded back to the Fourth Class. By June of 1821 his grades had improved, but he was still struggling. Of seventy-four class members, he ranked twenty-third in mathematics; twenty-eighth in French, and twenty-seventh in Order of General Merit.

By October 29 of that year he was listed as "absent with leave," and on November 1, 1821, the superintendent of West Point wrote, "I have the honor to enclose the resignation of Cadets James F. Walker of Georgia and Cyrus Canon and recommend that they be accepted to take effect on the 30th of November."[5] In addition to having an academic problem in French, his conduct record was not the best. He was liberally punished or assigned extra duty for absences or tardiness for roll calls, classes, and formations.

One of the reasons for these unexcused absences may have been to visit his cousin Martha Fannin, who was attending a girls' school in Philadelphia.[6] Martha Fannin would later marry Dr. Tomlinson Fort after, as she allegedly claimed, being courted by Mirabeau B. Lamar in Columbus. But she was also the same age as her cousin James, and the two appear to have felt close enough to have shared their thoughts during this period.

Exactly what happened to James Fannin between October 29 and November 20 of 1821 will probably never be known, but it effectively put an end to his preparations to become a military officer. The story has been reported in several history books that he got into a fight with another cadet—supposedly over a comment derogatory toward the South. He is listed simply as "Resigned to take effect 20 November 1821," which was actually ten days before the superintendent's recommendation.

There are no records to substantiate the theory that he resigned after a fight, or perhaps even a duel, rather than accept punishment by army authorities. In fact, West Point archives contain a document that suggests his departure from the academy was the result of an entirely different personal situation.

That document is a letter from Fannin's cousin addressed to him at the academy and dated October 3, 1821:

> Greenboro, Greens County
> Georgia Oct 3rd 1821

Dear Cousin
    By the request of your Grandmother & Mother I forward you this & hope you will not delay in returning home for they are very low indeed & are not expected to survive many months & if you do not come shortly it is probable you will never see them again for your Grandmother has entirely lost the use of one side by the dead Palsey & the old Gentleman as you know has the shaking Palsey & so very bad that he cannot carry anything to his mouth. I presume I need not say anything more at present as you are not ignorant of their extreme old age So be in haste & gratify your relations for they are all very anxious for your return & do not delay as you observed in your last letter untill June go immediately on the reception of this to the Superintendent and inform him of these things & I have no doubt but what he will permit you to return. Your Uncle Fannin passed by here a few weeks since on his way to [unintelligible] for his health & he will return to Savannah as soon as the sickly season is over & he recovers his health

> With Respect & Great
> Esteem I am your relative
> (DWalker)[7]

For whatever reason he resigned his position at West Point—duel or family emergency—James Fannin Walker wrote the superintendent three weeks after his cousin's letter:

West Point
Oct 25th 1821

Sir

Circumstances not admitting my longer stay at the Milty Acdy I hereby offer this as my resignation of the Appointment of Cadet in the U.S. Army.

I remain Sir
Your Obs.
James F. Walker[8]

From the records, it is obvious James Fannin did not "take" to military regimen nor did he fare well in his studies. He did not learn advanced military tactics, theories of warfare, or even histories of previous battles. Although he attended the academy in the years immediately following Andrew Jackson's victory at New Orleans, Fannin never later referred to that or any other battle in an informed way.

While his stay at West Point lasted a little over two years, it should be remembered that he was remanded back to the beginning class so he cannot be considered to have "completed" two years at the academy. He almost certainly had no advanced training in fortifications, logistics, transportation, or intelligence gathering.

While at the academy he chose not to exercise personal discipline, and his unexcused absences reflect disdain for following orders. His problems cannot be attributed to lack of prior schooling—his letters in later life reveal him to be a literate and analytical man—but as a youth he was wild and irresponsible, and it resulted in his leaving the United States Military Academy an untrained and undisciplined young man, who never gave up his dream of a military command.

After dropping out of the academy, Fannin returned to Georgia, residing successively in Twiggs and Troup Counties but removed, in 1828, to Columbus, in Muskogee County, where he became a merchant. He was also secretary of a Temperance Society and a division inspector of the Georgia militia.[9]

James Walker Fannin Jr.

Photo source: *The Dallas Historical Society*

He began developing an interest in politics and was reported in a 1988 article by *The Victoria Advocate* to have been elected as judge of the Muscogee County Court in 1830 only to be disqualified for having fought in a duel.[10] He also later served as a representative to the state convention in 1833 from Troup County, Georgia.

With regards to the disqualification for dueling, there appear to be no records in Georgia of such a legal action taken, and the article did not elaborate on the circumstances of the duel. Much mystery remains concerning his departure from West Point: Many sources claim he left the academy after a fight with another cadet but, again, offer no specifics. There is some speculation he was asked to leave—an action roughly comparable to today's discharge "for the good of the service." Dueling would have been a discharge offense at West Point, but the scanty records of Fannin's service there contain no mention of a duel or expulsion for fighting.

While he attempted to reconstruct his life after West Point, it appears he became interested in settling down and becoming financially secure. He married Minerva Fort, and on July 17, 1829, their first daughter, Missouri Pinkney, was born.

He also appears to have maintained some contact with his step-mother and half-sister. After Isham's death, Margarett married J.H. King, who became Eliza's stepfather. After Eliza had gone to finishing school in Salem, Margarett wrote her in 1829 that James had sent news of his baby daughter.

During this period it was customary for established and wealthy plantation owners to send daughters to northern "finishing" schools since there were few public education facilities available for girls. After two years of boarding school at Salem, it was determined that Eliza should go to finishing school in Connecticut.

On October 27, 1830, James Fannin wrote his half-sister a long and very personal letter. She had at that time returned home from Salem and was preparing for her trip to Connecticut.

He was then twenty-five years of age and eleven years Eliza's senior, and his letter was filled with brotherly advice. Eliza kept the letters, which were handed down among family members over the years and in 1931 made available to Clarence Wharton, who published excerpts:[11]

> James tells Eliza reproachfully that he has heard from others that she is now with her mother and among her former friends, and that he would like to consider himself her "dearest relative." "We have always been separated from

each other, but you will not suspect me of selfishness or the want of that fraternal feeling incident to our relationship.

Little is known about James Fannin during this period of his life, and this letter is significant because, in it, James Fannin reveals a great deal about himself. But even here, historians are robbed of information about a crucial facet of Fannin's background and thinking during this period.

Wharton continues:

After this passage he begins the discussion of some personal family matter and tells her "you are now of an age to know," but some careful hand has with knife or scissors neatly cut from the letter what she is now "old enough to know." After the blank left by the censor's scissors, the letter continues for four pages and refers to his "long silence and peculiar situation." "If you can not see this in all its true bearings, ask mother or Mr. King [her stepfather]."

Like Wharton, we can only speculate what matter of importance, or secret, he felt he needed to share with Eliza. Some have speculated the censored passage had to do with the illegitimate circumstances of his birth while others have suggested he may have used the suffering he had endured because of those circumstances to encourage his young sister to not make the same mistake his own mother had.

He may have suggested unknown family circumstances that had resulted in the two of them being separated all their lives. Or he may have confessed personal feelings about being sent away from his father and adopted. It was the first but not the only time he wrote Eliza of his "peculiar situation." It was something that very obviously weighed heavily upon his mind.

We do not know who the censor was: if Eliza decided to remove it before she saved the letter, or if Margarett intercepted the correspondence and clipped the passage to prevent her daughter from reading it.

At the conclusion of the letter, according to Wharton, Fannin " . . . grows eloquent in the description of his baby daughter, whom Eliza has never seen. "To praise our little daughter would be useless. If you wish to see or know anything of her, come and see her. I can not visit my friends until after the next year, when I hope to save enough money to buy a carriage, as we will then have too many to go any other way, and tho' we do live down near the Indian border, we still have some pride."

This passage also reveals something about James Fannin in 1830: He is struggling with finances and self-image problems. In 1830s Georgia plantation society, finances and personal pride no doubt were closely intertwined. While Eliza was living with her mother and a stepfather, who could afford the considerable expense of sending her to a northern finishing school, he was struggling to purchase a carriage for his wife and daughter.

Throughout his life, James Fannin would exhibit love and affection for his immediate family. Later, in a Texas society that included men and leaders whose pasts were certainly suspect with regards to marital relationships and parental responsibilities, James Walker Fannin Jr. would never once be accused of anything but complete devotion to Minerva and his two daughters.

About this time, he writes of his daughter again: "She is a real Fannin and I do not say too much when I assert that she is one of the finest children in Georgia. She is all life, never cries, is always laughing."[12]

Shortly after this letter, Eliza moved to New Haven, Connecticut, and began school. In 1832, while Eliza was still enrolled, James Fannin applied for, and received, lottery lands from the former Cherokee Territory located in northwest Georgia.[13]

He was beginning to obtain land in his name, but his quest for financial security continued to elude him. In response, he began to consider alternative, and more risky, business endeavors.

Early in 1832 his second daughter, Minerva, whom he may have nicknamed Eliza, was born—a fact he mentioned in a letter to his sister in April of that year. At the time he wrote the letter, he was in Charleston, South Carolina, preparing to sail for Havana, Cuba, purportedly for a cargo of sugar.

Clarence Wharton again affords us a glimpse into Fannin's thinking and feelings in this letter to his sister:

> He chides her for two pages for not having written often and then such brief letters. "Writing, my own dear

but truant sister, is not only a relaxation from severe studies, but an amusement to the tired, worn-out mind—like a
mile walk after a day's ride. It supplies the joints and sin-
ews, makes many things vigorous and elastic. But my dear
Eliza will not think that her only paternal brother is one of
those crusty, crabbed old crones who wishes to monopo-
lize the whole of her time, etc."[14]

Wharton records that he then tells her he "left her sister,
Minerva, and her nieces, Missouri Pinkney and Eliza [Minerva],
quite well, but does not pause to comment on the personality of
the little daughters, though we hope he still regarded them the finest in Georgia."

The reason for this lack of comment may have been by painful
design: Baby Minerva had been born severely retarded.

A month later he writes his sister again, this time from Havana
where he is lonely and homesick. "Feelings which seemed quite
dormant yesterday are today in their zenith—Nay, as warm as the
tropic of Cancer will admit. I love my old friends with a holy love.
No wonder then that I love my only sister a little."

Wharton then reports that Fannin again refers to his "peculiar
situation" and describes his final moments with his father:

Can I (remember my peculiar situation) ever recur to
the never to be forgotten April 26, 1817, and see our common parent in the last death struggle, and hear him calling
for both of us, and you a helpless infant, unconscious of
your loss, held in his dying arms; can I, who known a
father's anxieties and witnessed this scene, remember this
and what he done for me (which but few fathers would
have done), not feel some solicitude for the object nearest
his heart? The full overflowing heart of a true Fannin
responds in feelings of deepest gratitude—in love the most
lasting and indelible.

He is again vague about the nature of his business—mention-
ing that he is going for a cargo of sugar and will keep a vessel in the
trade. The "cargo of sugar" was, in reality, a cargo of slaves. By
mid-1832 James Fannin had become a slave trader. Although U.S.

law allowed the practice of slavery, it did ban the importation of new slaves from Africa.

Because of the nature of the business and the penalties for conviction, little is known about his activities during the next two years. By 1834, however, the so-called "no man's land" on the Sabine Lake between Louisiana and the Mexican province of Texas was quickly becoming an importation point for illegal slaves introduced into the United States.

Texas was also becoming a promising land for American immigrants who wanted free or cheap land and a new start in life. Stephen F. Austin's small colony near the mouth of the Brazos River was quickly growing, and stories reached the American South of unlimited crop and stock-raising potential there. Although illegal in Mexico too, slaves would be in great demand by the American planters there.

It is not known when Fannin first visited Texas, but on May 26 of 1834 he was back in Havana. There he made a contract with Harvey Kendrick for the purchase, from a man named Thompson, of the schooner *Crawford* for five thousand dollars, for which he drew a draft on E.W. Gregory of New Orleans.[15]

The manifest of the ship indicated that it was sailing from Havana on June 12 for the Brazos River in Texas with a cargo of sixteen free Negroes. This Fannin swore before the United States consul in Havana and to the fact that the ship would be continuing on to New Orleans where payment for the boat would be made. Because of Mexican laws banning the import of slaves, this oath was necessary for permission to sail to Texas.

No reason is cited for the stop at Velasco, but Wharton claims the sixteen "free Negroes" were no doubt unloaded there and that Fannin failed to realize enough cash in the transaction to pay for the boat in New Orleans. On August 22, 1834, he was in Mobile requesting that Thompson grant him an extension on the payment for the boat based upon another planned trip to Havana.

By then he had established himself as a resident in Austin's Colony in Texas and was operating a plantation along the San Bernard River in conjunction with Joseph Mims.

For better or worse, James Walker Fannin Jr. had placed his and his family's future in the Mexican province of Texas.

1   Wharton, Clarence, *Remember Goliad* (Glorieta, New Mexico: The Rio Grande Press, Inc., 1931), reprinted 1968, pg. 21.

2   Ibid., pg. 25.

3   Sheila Biles, Library Technician for Special Collections and Archives Division, United States Military Academy to Gary Brown dated June 14, 1999.

4   Rosenberg Library Archives, Galveston Texas, "Letter from Harbert Davenport to Miss Winnie Allen, Archivist, University of Texas Library," dated February 26, 1936.

5   United States Military Academy archives, National Archives Microfilm Publication 688, *U.S. Military Academy Cadet Application Papers*, 1805-1666.

6   Martha Fannin would later write her memoirs including an account of her time at finishing schools in Elizabethtown, New Jersey, and at Philadelphia. In 1953 many of her papers were made available by her great, great niece, Mrs. Ernest C. Reed, in Fort Worth. In one, she reveals that James Fannin used to travel to Philadelphia to visit her during the period he was at the academy. Deen, Edith, "1818 Girl Tells of College Life," *Fort Worth Press*, August 13, 1953.

7   United States Military Academy archives, National Archives Microfilm Publication 2047, *Engineer Department Letters Received Relating to the U. S. Military Academy*.

8   Ibid.

9   Davenport, Harbert, "Notes from an Unfinished Study of Fannin and His Men, Brownsville, Texas, 1936," Barker Texas History Center, University of Texas at Austin, pp. 193-4.

10 Harsdorff, Linda, "Fannin's Watch Returns," *The Victoria Advocate*, Sunday, April 10, 1988.

11 Wharton, pg. 22.

12 Ibid.

13 Smith, James F., *The 1832 Cherokee Land Lottery of Georgia* (New York: Harper and Brothers, 1838), pg. 351.

14 Wharton, pg. 22.

15 Ibid., pg. 25.

Chapter Two

Cotton Fields and Slave Ships

James Walker Fannin Jr. was expected to arrive at Austin's Colony sometime in 1834.

By that time, Joseph and Sarah Mims had been living and farming in Texas for a decade and were only beginning to appreciate the hard and dangerous land they were occupying. As part of Stephen F. Austin's "Old Three Hundred," the Mims had received title to a choice piece of land fronting the San Bernard River—only a few miles south of the Brazos River and near the Anglo community of Brazoria.

The land was good earth for growing cotton and corn. It had been claimed that Texas earth was "so fertile all you had to do was kick some dust on the seed and let nature take its course." That of course had been stretching the truth, but the land was productive, especially near the river.

Flooding enriched the bottomlands with silt and nutrients, but as the Mims had learned the hard way, rains to the north also created devastating flooding. They had arrived in Texas in 1824, and the first bad flooding had occurred four years later. Another bad flood had occurred in 1833, and they were just recovering from it. But in between, the land was producing more and more cotton, and the burgeoning markets in New Orleans were creating quick wealth to those tough enough to live here and manage the land.

The Anglo homesteading was also extending culture from the American South into Mexican Texas. Small farmers made up the majority of white homesteaders in the Austin Colony in 1834, and most homes were "dogtrot" log houses "chinked" with mud—called dogtrot since the houses consisted of two log rooms connected by an open and covered breezeway that was the favorite place for sleeping dogs in the summertime.

Around 1830 the economy had developed to the point that elegant homes were also being constructed and taking on the appearance of Southern plantations. As the cotton crops continued to expand, so did the need for labor, and another Southern institution—slavery—began to emerge in Texas.

Slavery was not new to Texas in 1834. Despite Mexican laws prohibiting the introduction of slaves into Mexican Texas, American slaves were brought into the area from Louisiana—often legally as "indentured servants" but more often than not illegally by slave ships from Cuba and the Caribbean.

Just downstream from the Mims home was a spot along the banks of the San Bernard River that had come to be known as "African Landing." Where an ancient giant oak tree had fallen along the bank—creating a natural landing pier—slave ships entered the interior of Austin's Colony and docked with relative impunity.

One hundred years later the *Houston Chronicle* reported that "At African Landing they were taken ashore and hastily groomed for sale to buyers who drove down in carriages from their plantations and pinched, thumped and measured the human commodities while their body servants fanned the flies away."[1]

The article continued, "the naked negroes were hurriedly given a course in wearing clothes, for there was much readier sale for those who gave an impression of being civilized. The poor frightened creatures, with their hoodoo charms and tribal marks, rolled their eyes in dismay while they walked around stiffly in their pants and skirts. The bodies of the blacks were greased from head to foot to give an illusion of youth and health."

Not all Anglos—as the Texans were calling themselves—favored slavery, and many openly opposed the importation of Africans into the area. Still, on nearly every colonized piece of land in Austin's Colony in 1834, slaves were apparent. But slave importation was illegal under Mexican law, and the settlers were now legally Mexican citizens.

In pledging their loyalty to Mexico City, the Anglos had promised to become Catholic, pay Mexican taxes, follow Mexican law, and adapt to Mexican cultural values. If fact, almost none had done so. Few bothered to learn Spanish, and the conversions to Catholicism were largely done with crossed fingers behind the back. Protestant ministers from the United States traveled throughout the colonies and performed services and "unofficial" marriages.

Mexico made occasional attempts at taxing the settlers and even had established a customshouse and fort not far to the northeast of Mim's land where the Brazos River emptied into the sea at a hamlet called Velasco. But the Mexican government officials were lax and corrupt, and few customs were ever collected. Smuggling had become so rampant that it was considered respectable by most of the Anglos. And the smuggling now included the wholesale importation of slaves from the United States and Cuba.

But in 1834 there had been a change in Mexican politics at Mexico City, and the new Centralist administration under General Antonio Lopez de Santa Anna was now vowing to start collecting the taxes and had begun dismantling many of the civil liberties promised under the Mexican Constitution of 1824. Trouble had been brewing for some time.

Two years earlier, in June of 1832, several men from the Austin Colony had attacked the fort at Velasco, forcing the Mexican military garrisoned there to withdraw. Shortly thereafter Colonel Mexia was dispatched with his fleet to Velasco for the purpose of investigating the disturbance. Accompanied by Stephen Austin, who had been attending the legislature at Coahuila and Texas, Mexia proceeded to Brazoria, where he was honored at a reception at the tavern of Mrs. Jane Long, the widow of the already legendary filibusterer Dr. James Long. Toasts were exchanged and good will was again established between the colonists and the Mexican government.

But 1833 had been a bad year in other ways. The flood had been devastating, and in its wake, a thick layer of silt emitted a sour stench. Mosquitoes bred by the millions. By summer the flood had crested, but cholera spread and became epidemic.[2] Still the plantations and the communities continued to grow and expand.

It was in 1833 that Stephen Austin had taken petitions for reforms to Mexico City only to find that the cholera epidemic had caused Mexican officials to abandon that city. In frustration he wrote a letter to contacts in San Antonio, urging Anglo Texans to consider separation from the Mexican federation. That letter was intercepted and resulted in his arrest in January of 1834. He would be detained in Mexico City for another year and a half.

While Austin was in Mexico City from July 1833 to July 1835, President Santa Anna changed from a Republican Federalist to a Centralist dictator. The change was due to popular outcry against reforms that lessened the privileges of the church and the military and a fear that the United States was trying to annex Texas. Essentially, Austin was held as a hostage for the good behavior of the Anglo Texans.

But Santa Anna had problems in areas of Mexico besides Austin's Colony. He led the army against a Federalist uprising in Zacatecas in which the Federalists were brutally crushed. He named his brother-in-law, Gen. Martin Perfecto de Cos, commandant general of the northeastern frontier that included Coahuila and Texas.

General Cos would become a name soon recognized by virtually every settler in Austin's Colony and the rest of the Anglo settlements in Texas.

When Cos occupied the capital of Coahuila in May 1835, the governor and some legislators fled to Texas. Among those legislators were some "observers" from the United States and Texas who had just received very lucrative—and suspicious—land grants to develop large tracts of territory in Coahuila and Texas.

One of those observers was a Scotsman—James Grant. His would also be a name that would become readily recognizable throughout Texas as the rebellion spread.

By 1834 the constant upheavals within the Mexican government had led to a renewal of tensions and had created divisions among the white immigrants themselves. Longtime settlers like Joseph Mims, with large land grants, tended to advocate peace with the Mexican government, but the younger newcomers, some with no land grants, felt little loyalty to Mexico and sided with those advocating annexation to the United States.

That summer season in 1834 Joseph and Sarah Mims had occasion to look back over the previous decade in Texas. Life had been hard: Indians, floods, disease, and a foreign culture had been difficult obstacles. But life had also been good: They had survived the elements and hostiles and had prospered.

And soon, a young newcomer from Georgia was coming to help them farm the plantation. James Walker Fannin Jr. was scheduled to arrive by ship with his family. Unknown to Joseph and Sarah Mims, James Fannin had little intention of farming and even less intention of obeying and adapting to Mexican laws and culture. But his arrival at the Austin Colony would help change the course of Texas history forever.

---

1   "Fannin Was Wealthy Man For His Time; Had Big Plantation," *Houston Chronicle*, Sunday, April 19, 1936.

2   Creighton, James A., *A Narrative History of Brazoria County, Texas* (Waco: Texian Press, 1975), pg. 80.

Chapter Three

Texan Émigré

James and Minerva Fannin arrived in Texas with their two daughters to discover a land of contrasts—politically, economically, and culturally. He almost certainly arrived in Texas with very few assets. A letter of introduction by Edward Hanrick to Samuel M. Williams, sent from Montgomery and dated August 28, 1833, suggested, "I believe he is an enterprising man and from What I can learn he is Worth nothing and perhaps as we say wuse [worse] than nothing, and his case is desperate, for he has nothing to lose and all to gain."[1]

The debt Fannin owed Thompson for the schooner *Crawford* was only one of many that followed him to Texas in 1834. According to Clarence Wharton, "He had a leaky pen when he came to signing notes and drafts, and when he located in Texas in 1834-5 he left a trail of such obligations all the way from Georgia."[2]

But, broke or not, Fannin arrived in Texas with something desperately needed by the plantation owners in Austin's Colony in 1834: the ability and connections to provide slave labor. The cholera epidemic had ended, the floods had subsided, and the political problems with Mexico were temporarily placated. The prices for cotton had soared, and the market in New Orleans was quickly purchasing all cotton produced in Texas.

Joseph and Sarah Mims had arrived in 1824 among the earliest of Austin's colonists and had endured the hard times in log cabins. By the 1830s, however, as Texas plantations developed they included barns, stables, warehouses, storage facilities, gardens, and slave quarters. But these facilities could only be maintained by the increased production of cotton and only with the means of additional free labor.

A decade after his arrival in Texas, Joseph Mims was successfully established but struggling to expand his profitable plantation near Brazoria. He needed additional labor, and James W. Fannin Jr. represented the potential for obtaining more slaves. Mims and Fannin agreed to a partnership, and Fannin's role in the agreement appears to be the importation of slave labor for Mims and other farmers in Austin's Colony.

Fannin's correspondence and the letters of others in the colony verify that he immediately established himself as a slave trader upon arriving in Texas. In fact, his slave trading reputation preceded his arrival. Edward Hanrick's letter of introduction to Samuel Williams also included the reference to Fannin as "one of the persons that was to be engaged in the Negroe Speculation."[3]

Slavery, while economically necessary in Austin's Colony, was already a controversial political topic. Constitutionally illegal under Mexican law, exemptions had been granted to the immigrants, and slaves had been imported into Texas from the American South through questionable "indentured" certificates that listed them as house servants and field hands.

Such practices were not unusual in Mexico itself, which for decades had used a similar form of debt peonage to force peasants to work the owners' lands. In Austin's Colony, the black "indentured servants" would "x" an indenture contract, which legally allowed them to be imported into Texas under Mexican anti-slavery laws.

A more disturbing and controversial aspect of Texas slavery during the 1830s involved the importation of slaves directly from Africa—usually through Cuban ports. The United States Slave Trading Act of 1820 defined participation in the African trade as piracy, with a mandatory death sentence. In this respect, American and Mexican laws were very similar, and even the lax regulations on importation of domestic servants were scheduled to end by 1840—legally abolishing all forms of slavery in Texas.

Importation of African slaves into Texas was already a well-established fact by the time Fannin arrived. James and Rezin Bowie were legends, partially due to their slave importing exploits in the province.

The illegal importation of these Africans—easily distinguishable by their tribal scars, tattoos, and dialects—was usually achieved by having the "blackbirders" (the ship captains) sail their vessels up the mouth of the Sabine River dividing American Louisiana and Mexican Texas. In this "no-man's area," the captains could then safely unload their cargoes—usually at a location in Sabine Lake.

James Fannin, however, planned a more direct route up the San Bernard River to the location known as African Landing. The location was ideal—but risky—for the importation of African slaves into Austin's Colony.

Immediately upon arrival in Texas, James and Minerva Fannin and their two daughters took up residence on the Mims Plantation. Later, an old Mims slave, Jerry Johnson, whose father was blacksmith on the Mims Plantation, stated that Fannin never lived in the Mims residence. Instead, he stayed in a smaller house nearby.[4]

Joseph Mims located his home on the eastern portion of his grant and farmed over three thousand acres and operated a ferry on the San Bernard. Although James Fannin only lived in Austin's Colony a little more than one year, the inventory of his property after his death indicates he prospered very quickly. That posthumous inventory listed three thousand acres of land, thirty-nine Negroes, two hundred twenty bales of cotton, sixty head of cattle, five horses and mules, and three yoke oxen.[5]

But slavery and economics were not the only controversial issues that Fannin found when he landed in Texas. Politics in Mexico City and the Centralist movement being led by General Antonio Lopez de Santa Anna had created concern in Austin's Colony and resulted in division among the settlers themselves.

Revisions of the Mexican Constitution of 1824, with its federal structure and guarantees of civil liberties, have often been listed as the basis for the Texas Revolution. In fact, Mims, Fannin, and other farmers in Austin's Colony were profiting and living freely under the constitution. The Old Three Hundred and other newcomers were alarmed about two basic changes being advocated by the Centralist government and Santa Anna: total abolition of slavery in Texas and the enforcement of tariffs and taxes.

The Texan immigrants had long been subject to tariffs and taxes levied by Mexico City but in practice had been basically immune from paying them. Geographical distance, corrupt governmental officials, and lack of military enforcement had resulted in the farmers of Austin's Colony enjoying virtually free trade with New Orleans and other American ports.

But in 1830 Mexico had decided to start sharing the profits that the successful cotton farmers in the colony were earning from American trade. This shift in Mexican policy was also fueled by concern that the United States was attempting to annex Texas through encouraging Anglo immigration and rebellion. President Andrew Jackson had openly attempted to purchase eastern Texas including Austin's Colony, causing Mexico to send troops and ban further Anglo American immigration, a ban quickly circumvented by the settlers in Austin's Colony through a technicality.

The Mexican troops, however, were a constant irritant and threat in the eyes of Mims and the other colonists. A decree was issued on April 6, 1830, authorizing forts and Mexican garrisons near the colonies at Anahuac and Velasco. Fort Velasco, in particular, threatened the Austin Colony settlers since it posed the most immediate danger to their lifestyles and cotton profits.

Historian Keith Guthrie, in Volume II of his anthology titled *Texas Forgotten Ports*, describes the garrison:

> Fort Velasco was built about 150 yards from the Gulf of Mexico and overlooking the Brazos River. Two concentric circles were formed by sinking rows of posts in the ground six feet apart and extending about ten feet in the air. After sand was packed into the space between the posts, a formidable wall was in place. A customs house office, housing for 120 soldiers, and a large cistern for water were built inside on the river side of the fort. In the middle a large mound of dirt was placed and topped with a nine-pounder cannon. The cannon was mounted on a circular track surrounded by a wooden parapet.[6]

Trouble had occurred first at Anahuac but quickly spread to Velasco. In June of 1832 several of the Austin Colony leaders including John Austin, Thomas Bell, W.H. Wharton, and Pleasant

McNell participated in an attack on the fort. It had included a naval bombardment and land assault, resulting in the death and surrender of some Mexican troops and eventual withdrawal of the garrison. As a result, those settlers advocating separation from Mexico became more open and challenging in their rhetoric. Known as the War Party, or War Dogs, they immediately began campaigning for independence for Texas.

Immediately after the Texan victory at Fort Velasco, however, politics was temporarily set aside as flooding and cholera devastated the colony in 1833. When James Fannin arrived in Velasco in 1834, the cholera epidemic had disappeared, the colony's economy was booming, and the War Dogs were once again agitating for independence from Mexico. He quickly joined them.

Amidst the political turmoil and intrigue he found upon arrival in Texas, Fannin also discovered a colonial culture whose leader, Stephen Fuller Austin, was imprisoned in Mexico City for allegedly inciting the same rebellion that the War Dogs around Brazoria were advocating.

Although drawn to the revolutionary rhetoric of his neighbors around the Mims Plantation, Fannin quickly addressed his most pressing need: the necessity of cash. In May of 1835 he bought one hundred fifty-two West Africans in Cuba and transported them to the Brazos River aboard the slave ship *Hannah Elizabeth*, arriving in June.

Fannin verifies this transaction in a letter dated September 15, 1835, addressed to Thompson. Again, Fannin requests an extension on the debt owed over the schooner *Crawford* and offers the excuse that he has nearly died from sickness. "I have since made a good trip, having brought for myself and others 152 negroes in May last [1835]," he informed Thompson, "but can not realize any cash for them until March or April, when you shall be fully paid every cent I owe you."[7]

Fannin reassures Thompson that the problems with the Mexican government provide "no serious danger for us"—probably referring to the slave trade. He concludes by informing Thompson, "I am settled on Caney Creek, midway between Brazoria and Matagorda."

This act of slave importation was not one of questionably introducing "indentured" servants into the colony from the United States: It was—under American and Mexican laws—an act of international piracy and subjected him to death by hanging should he have been caught on the high seas.

He was not caught, however, and he began to profit immediately from his venture. Many sources list Fannin as being a popular figure in the colony, and his subsequent election to positions of representation bear that fact out. His illegal slave trading, however, did not make him universally popular among the colonists.

One influential 1830 settler and Matagorda neighbor in particular, Samuel Rhoads Fisher, took exception to Fannin and his slave trading. It was to be an exception that would later explode into political bickering and the issuance of a challenge.

Fannin's slave-purchasing trip to Havana in June had had a sense of urgency to it. His considerable debts had continued to grow after his arrival in Texas.

He traveled to Havana again in January of 1835 where he negotiated a five-thousand-dollar draft from St. John & Leovans of Mobile—a debt that eventually was transferred to John A. Merle & Co. of New Orleans.[8]

In April 1835 Fannin traveled to New Orleans only to be arrested for a three-thousand-dollar debt owed a Theopholus Hyde and was released only after a bond for fifteen hundred dollars had been posted.

---

1 Edward Hanrick to Samuel M. Williams, Williams Papers, Rosenberg Library, Galveston, Texas.

2 Wharton, Clarence, *Remember Goliad*, pg. 26.

3 Edward Hanrick to Samuel M. Williams, Williams Papers, Rosenberg Library.

4 Platter, Allen Andrew, *Educational, Social, and Economic Characteristics of the Plantation Culture of Brazoria County, Texas*, Dissertation Presented to the Faculty of the College of Education, University of Houston, August 1961.

5 James W. Fannin Jr. estate inventory, Record of Wills, Inventories, Etc., Book A, Brazoria County Courthouse, p. 222, dated December 2, 1839.

6   Guthrie, Keith, *Texas Forgotten Ports Volume II* (Austin, Texas: Eakin Press, 1993), pp. 104-5.
7   Wharton, pg. 26.
8   Ibid.

Chapter Four

Revolutionary Rhetoric

Back in Texas, events were also taking a turn for the worse. In June 1835 a second incident took place in Anahuac. Angered over the arrest of a colonist there, several Texans including William Barret Travis captured the Mexican fort and customshouse and forced the evacuation of Mexican soldiers. The fighting did not have the popular support of most Anglo settlers, and Travis was later forced to apologize due to concerns about Mexican retaliation against Stephen Austin, who was still imprisoned in Mexico City.

The incident did, however, intensify the fears of the farmers in Austin's Colony and gave impetus to the War Dogs there, who by now included James Fannin.

On June 28, at Columbia, a "committee on resolutions" was appointed composed of both radical and peace parties, and they wrote a set of resolutions so moderate and well formulated that they later became a model for other municipalities: (1) a recommendation for the organization of the militia; (2) appointment of a committee of public safety and correspondence; (3) a recommendation that the Political Chief take steps to call for a public council to provide Texas a Provisional Government.[1] The committee, comprised of Austin Colony's prominent settlers, did not include James Fannin.

By July these resolutions had resulted in other Anglo colonies organizing and a general call for a consultation of all municipalities on July 14 at San Felipe.

At that meeting, the demand for a consultation of all Texans was defeated, and the general tone was conciliatory toward Mexican authorities. They did, however, call for two representatives to negotiate with Santa Anna's brother-in-law, General Martin Perfecto de Cos.

Four days later, back in Austin's Colony, the safety committee of the jurisdiction of Columbia recommended in the *Texas Republican* that subscriptions be taken up for the purchase of arms. It was also recommended that all men of military age, eighteen to fifty years old, assemble July 19 at Columbia, Brazoria, and Milburn's Plantation with the object of organizing three militia companies.[2]

Committees of safety and correspondence had been organized in Texas as early as 1832 to organize militias for defense against Indians. While they were not initially anti-Mexican, they soon became avenues for armed resistance against Mexican soldiers. By 1835 committees were active at Mina (Bastrop) and Gonzales. Austin's Colony formed a committee for the jurisdiction of Brazoria and Columbia on August 15, 1835. James Fannin's military career in Texas had just begun.

On August 20 Fannin, who had by now assumed the title of "Colonel," received the following letter:

> To Col. J.W. Fannin Jr.
> Sir
>   You are appointed as a confidential agent by the committee of safety and correspondence of the Jurisdiction of Columbia, to proceed to San Felipe and use your utmost exertions to persuade Wyly Martin and all other persons with whom you may have influence to co-operate with us in the call of a consultation of all Texas, through her representatives.
>   Velasco, 20ᵗʰ Augt 1835
>
> > B T Archer, Chrm.
> > Wm. T. Austin, Secy
> > Committee of Safety & Correspondence[3]

And so Fannin, after less than one year residency in Texas, found himself achieving two lifelong goals denied to him in his native American South: material wealth and military leadership.

He did not, however, depart immediately for San Felipe. He wrote a letter, dated one week later, August 20, 1835, that was to set the tone for his military bearing and direction in the coming months as a Texan commander. In that letter, addressed to a U.S. Army officer, he made the following observations and requests:

Velasco. Rio Brasos. Prov. Texas
27th August 1835

Major Belton
USA
Mobile Point

My dear Major... we should probably require from our friends in the U. States, & particularly from a few of the experienced officers. ...

The time is near at hand—nay has arrived, when we have to look around us and prepare, with our limited resources, for fight. ...

We now have the dread alternative presented to us, "of a tame submission to the subversion of our Constitutional rights and acquiescence to Military rule, or like men (& free born white men too) fight to the knife."

Will you authorize me to use your name at the approaching convention, or at any subsequent time, as an officer qualified & willing to command as brave a set of backwoodsmen as ever were led to battle?

"When the hurly burly is begun" we will be glad to see as many West Point boys as can be spared—many of whom are known to me, & by whom I am known as J.F. Walker—my maternal Grand-father's name, & by whom I was raised and adopted, & whose name I then bore. ...

Yr Friend & c
J.W. Fannin Jr.[4]

This letter is significant for several reasons. It shows that he saw the Texas Revolution in terms of an extension of American—United States—revolutionary tradition. The letter suggests that he had already determined that a fight with the Mexican army was going to take place and that the Texans would require help and assistance from the U.S. Army in the form of officers, men, and supplies.

But the letter is also significant in what it suggests about Fannin's thinking during this period. He had requested United States Army military assistance without authorization from any Texan leader at San Felipe. Acting without orders—or in defiance of orders—would become an accusation characteristic of Fannin's short military career in Texas. The brief mention of "free born white men" was also a precursor to later references of "white against brown" in the fight against Mexicans and one of the first examples of his transferring his Southern racism to Mexicans in Texas.

Fannin also discloses in this letter for the first time his belief that Texas required *professional*, not volunteer, soldiers. As his military duties would expand and he would assume greater command responsibility, this would become a litany complaint against the Texan military conduct of the revolution. And lastly, he directly addresses his own background with regards to his given name during his West Point experience.

On September 1 another incident occurred that brought Brazoria, Velasco, and Austin's Colony ever closer to war with Santa Anna and the Mexican military.

Responding to the disturbances at Anahuac, Cos had dispatched the ship *Correo Mexicano*, a well-armed revenue cutter. As the *Correo* moved north along the coast, it moved past the mouth of the Brazos at Velasco and Quintana only to discover the brig *Tremont* preparing to load cargo destined for Florida. The skipper of the *Correo*, Captain Thomas M. Thompson, ordered the *Tremont* to heave to. The captain of the *Tremont* was then ordered to board the *Correo* with his men while the crew of the Mexican ship then prepared to occupy the *Tremont*.

The crowd of colonists watching the action from land quickly boarded the steamer *Laura* and attacked the *Correo* and succeeded in reclaiming the *Tremont* and restoring the crew.

In the midst of this, another ship appeared on the horizon. Accosted by the *Laura*, the ship was discovered to be the *San Felipe* carrying Stephen Austin, who had just been released from house arrest in Mexico City and was returning to Brazoria by way of New

Orleans. After towing the *San Felipe* back to Velasco, the colonists and passengers exchanged ships with the *Laura,* escorting Austin and the others over the sandbar into Velasco. The colonists, under the command of Captain T.W. Grayson, manned the sailing ship. After nightfall, the *Correo* attempted to approach the *San Felipe* only to be driven back after a firefight. The next morning both ships were helpless in the windless waters off the coast. The colonists in the *San Felipe,* with the assistance of the steamer *Laura,* were towed within gunshot distance of the Mexican ship, which then surrendered unconditionally.

Again, as in Anahuac and Velasco, the colonists had confronted Mexican authorities and succeeded in defying Santa Anna's edicts. In the midst of all this armed confrontation, James Fannin's neighbors were becoming experienced veterans in opposing the Mexican military, but, again, Fannin himself had been absent from the action.

Austin's return had a rallying effect on the colonists at Brazoria and Columbia. On September 8 a banquet in his honor was held at the Brazoria tavern operated by Mrs. Jane Long, widow of filibusterer Dr. James Long. Austin was already a legendary figure in Texas, and his return was celebrated by over one thousand who paid seven dollars to hear his speech, which set the moral tone for the coming revolution.[5]

The event included virtually every prominent Anglo colonist in Texas—not just Austin's Colony—and began with an afternoon dinner followed by a dance that ended in the late morning hours. In his newly acquired role as representative and military leader, James Fannin Jr. was also in attendance.

The highlight of the dinner occurred when, after a keynote speech, Austin succeeded, at least temporarily, in uniting the colonial factions and called for a general consultation to consider future relations with Mexico. His speech, concluded with a toast, was electrifying in its effect. The news of Austin's pronouncement for a consultation spread rapidly throughout Texas. His stand for the Constitution of 1824 as opposed to the Centralist regime of Santa Anna was the one point on which both the peace and war parties could unite.[6]

Toast after toast was raised that afternoon and evening including one by Colonel James Fannin: "Union; may the people of Texas unite Roses white and red and their only emulation be who shall, who will do the most for the public good."[7] While the banquet celebrating Austin's release from Mexican custody solidified, at least briefly, the factions within the Anglo community, these activities further alarmed Mexican officials who were monitoring closely all separatist and revolutionary rhetoric.

Earlier, during August, Cos had rebuffed all proposals for negotiations and instructed the Mexican commander at San Antonio de Bexar, Colonel Domingo de Ugartechea, to issue arrest warrants for several prominent Texans including Travis. A clash of cultures seemed inevitable.

As a result of the *Correo Mexicano* capture, General Cos decided to move from his headquarters in Matamoros and reinforce Colonel Ugartechea in Bexar. Word of his plan to sail for Copano was received at Matagorda ten days after the Austin banquet. Sailing aboard the armed ship *Veracruzana*, Cos would be leading two additional ships transporting Mexican soldiers.

Among those spreading the alarm was James Fannin. In a letter to a Brazoria neighbor, David Graham Mills, Fannin reported:

Cana Creek Sept. 18, 1835

David Mills, Dr. Sir
    Letters have been recd. Express from citizens residing at or near Copano informing the citizens of Matagorda, that the armed vessel Vera Crusanna had arrived and was landing arms and ammunition and that they were to wait the arrival of two vessels with 400 troops, which are expected soon—Gen. Martin Perfecto De Cos is on board and I suppose the expected force with what is at Bexar is to form a small body-guard with which he purposes visiting San Felipe.

    We have determined here to raise a sufficient force to justify a reasonable belief that we can succeed, in an effort to secure at least the arms and ammunition and if to be found the troops . . . It is proposed to organize and collect the people of Cana [Caney] and Bay Prairie and rendezvous at Robertson

> Ferry on Colorado River on Monday 28 Inst and proceed from thence to James Carr's residence on the Lavaca when proper information will be recd. to guide our future perations [*sic*].
> . . . use your influence and accustomed diligence in collecting volunteers and spreading the intelligence as rapidly as possible . . . I am particularly anxious for some of the citizens to have an opportunity of confronting Genl. Cos. . . .
>
> J. W. Fannin Junr.[8]

The settlers, according to Fannin, planned to attack Cos and attempt to capture his arms and ammunition and take prisoners. Another person sent a warning was Edmund Andrews in nearby Brazoria, who, on the same date, responded that he had received Fannin's warning and was forwarding it to Velasco.[9]

This news was particularly alarming to the Austin Colony settlers since it confirmed their fears that Santa Anna was serious about using the Mexican army to suppress their petitions and enforce the tariffs and taxes against them.

To garner support for the expedition to confront Cos, the *Texas Republican* on September 26 published a list of persons subscribing five hundred dollars each to buy "arms and munitions of war" and prominently listing the name of James W. Fannin Jr. The article included a warning: "Let General Cos come. We will give him a warm reception."[10]

But in the end, despite the subscriptions and passionate calls to arms, the expedition against Cos did not materialize, and the Mexican general traveled undisturbed through Goliad to Bexar where he joined forces with Colonel Ugartechea.

The reason that Fannin and the proposed expedition fell through was that, throughout the Mexican state of Texas, events were unfolding at a violent and uncontrolled speed. The colonial resistance at Anahuac and Velasco was spreading, and Texas was literally on the eve of revolution. Another flash point between the Mexicans and colonists had arisen near the community of Gonzales.

The campaign against Cos fell through in the end because of the Gonzales confrontation. As suddenly as it was proposed it was dropped, and within a week Fannin had raised a small company called the Brazos Guards and was off to Gonzales to join the Patriot army and march with it to Bexar.[11]

James W. Fannin Jr. had been called from Brazoria to Gonzales with other prominent Texan leaders. His brief career as a Texas plantation owner, slave trader, and business partner of Joseph Mims was finished. His elusive dream of a military career and command were finally about to be realized.

Painting of James Walker Fannin by C.B. Normann,
courtesy the UT Institute of Texan Cultures at San Antonio

1   *Texas Republican,* July 4, 1835, quoted in Creighton, James A., *A Narrative History of Brazoria County, Texas,* pg. 97.

2   Ibid., July 18, 1835, pg. 98.

3   Jenkins, John H., Ed., *The Papers of the Texas Revolution 1835-1836 in Ten Volumes* (Austin: Presidial Press, 1973), 1:358-9. Hereafter cited as *PTR.*

4   Ibid., 1:371-3.

5   Guthrie, pp. 124-5.

6   Creighton, pg. 103.

7   Smith, Ruth Cumby, "James W. Fannin, Jr., in the Texas Revolution," *The Southwestern Historical Quarterly,* Vol. XXII, No. 2, October 1919, pp. 82-3.

8   Jenkins, *PTR,* 1:457.

9   Ibid., 1:455.

10   *Texas Republican,* September 22, 1835, quoted in Smith, Ruth, "James W. Fannin, Jr., in the Texas Revolution," pg. 83.

11   Wharton, *Remember Goliad,* pg. 27.

Section II

Rebel Against Santa Anna

Chapter Five
Arrival at Gonzales

Fannin organized the Brazos Guards and joined his Brazoria neighbors and other colonists at the rendezvous near Gonzales on the eve of yet another military clash between the settlers and Mexican authorities. From Bexar, Ugartechea was monitoring the events closely and dispatched one of his lieutenants, Francisco de Castañeda, to retrieve a small cannon that the Mexican army had loaned the colonists in the nearby settlement of Gonzales. The Anglo settlers balked, and a short stand-off ensued between the two groups. On October 2, 1835, the colonists attacked the Mexicans, and Castañeda was forced to withdraw to Bexar without the cannon.

James Fannin is surprisingly quiet about the events at Gonzales, but at least one source does place him at the scene during the outbreak in fighting. Marshall de Bruhl, in *Sword of San Jacinto*, states that "From the west bank of the river the Texans, among whom was James W. Fannin, taunted the Mexican troops on the opposite shore. They raised a white banner with the famous 'Come and Take It' legend over their little cannon. After a few rounds were exchanged and one death occurred, the Mexicans withdrew to San Antonio."[1]

By military standards the "Battle of Gonzales" was not really a battle but more of an armed skirmish. But this clash, in the interior of the colonies, differed from the previous fights along the coast. This time there had been casualties. Castañeda had lost one or two men killed and several wounded—hardly devastating but nevertheless a clear escalation in the hostilities. At Gonzales, it appeared the breach between the colonists and their Mexican government had been irretrievably destroyed. The Campaign of 1835 had begun.

Anglo colonists, who had been converging on Gonzales prior to the fighting, decided to pursue Castañeda back to San Antonio de Bexar and lay siege against Ugartechea's garrison there. A general call was spread throughout the colonies for men and arms. James Fannin, who had been preparing the assault against General Cos upon his arrival at Copano, abandoned those plans and instead remained with the Gonzales contingent.

Fannin was now a captain in command of the Brazos Guards and joined several of his neighbors in urging a call to arms and convergence on Gonzales. In a communiqué from an unlisted location, he joined in the issuance of the following declaration:

> Camp of the Volunteers
> Friday Night. 11 o'clock;
> October 2, 1835
>
> Fellow Citizens: -
>   We . . . urge as many as can be possibility leave their homes to repair to Gonzales immediately, "armed and equipped for war even to the knife.". . . If Texas will now act promptly; she will soon be redeemed from that worse than Egyptian bondage which now cramps her resources and retards her prosperity.
>
> J.W. Fannin, Jr. (*et al*)[2]

It appears the colonists had established efficient lines of communication throughout the Anglo colonies, which may have been speedy, but were also faulty: A postscript to the above letter erroneously added, "the Mexican Commander and several soldiers were slain. . . ."

The next recorded communication from Fannin occurs four days later, October 6. General Cos, unchallenged at Copano, had marched through Goliad where he left a small detachment of twenty-seven men before continuing on to Bexar on October 5. The October 6 letter, addressed to Austin in San Felipe, relays Fannin's and other Texans' concern about Cos' arrival in Bexar:

Gonzales October 6 1835
12 o'clock at night

Dr. Col

You will receive important dispatches by the Bearer that Col Ugartachea and probably Gen Cos—are now on their march here, with all their forces to take the Gun [Gonzales cannon] if it is not delivered—You will see by Ugartachea's letter to you, he proposes a sort of compromise. That will give us an opportunity to entertain him a little while, upon the Suggestion that you are sent for, until we can get in more ment [equipment]. We who subscribe this, request you earnestly to come on immediately, bringing all the aid you possible Can—we want powder and lead. Do all you can to sent on instantly as much as possible.

J.W. Fannin Jr. (*et al*)[3]

This letter reveals Fannin and the others were proceeding under several misconceptions involving General Cos. The Mexican general had not arrived in Bexar by October 6—he was still three days away—and Colonel Ugartechea had no intentions at that point of returning to Gonzales, with or without Cos, to retrieve the cannon.

The letter also suggests that while Ugartechea was "proposing a sort of compromise" the Texans had no desire to cooperate. In the communiqué, Fannin and the others urged Austin to come to Gonzales immediately with "powder and lead" and indicated they intended to use his anticipated arrival as a reason to postpone negotiations with Ugartechea.

But Fannin's signature on the correspondence indicates that he, at last, was at the scene of the action and finally becoming a participant, rather than just an agitator, in the coming revolution.

It was at this time that James Fannin met and developed a working relationship with a man he at least outwardly had very little in common with. The alliance would turn out to be beneficial for both men and advance Fannin's military standing in the eyes of the Texas leaders assembling outside Gonzales.

Much has been written about James Bowie, a complicated man even by Texas standards in 1835, with his swings between compassion and unbridled aggression, diplomatic temperance and drunken orgies, frontier crudeness and acceptance into "proper" Mexican society. His varied career as slave trader, knife fighter, dealer in land and mining, veteran of the battle at Nacogdoches in 1832, and member by marriage of the prominent Veramendi family in San Antonio made him attractive as a man familiar with Mexican society as well as with conflict.[4]

Fannin, on the other hand, arrived at Gonzales with high ambitions but lacking experience in fighting, commanding men, or any knowledge of Mexican culture or society. His single year in Texas had certainly not prepared him to understand or deal with the complexities of Texan, much less Mexican, politics. That he and James Bowie should form a personal alliance was unusual.

And yet, only three days after Fannin's first correspondence from Gonzales, on October 9, another letter was addressed to Stephen Austin, this time from Bowie:

At Camp above San Antonio, October 9, 1835

To General Stephen F. Austin:
    I have declined further action under the appointment given to me by yourself. This you will therefore look upon as my resignation.
    I will be found in Captain Fannin's company, where my duty to my country and the principles of human rights shall be discharged on my part to the extent of my abilities as a private.

Respectfully,
James Bowie.[5]

Austin apparently accepted Bowie's resignation—not that he really had any choice—but would later reinstate Bowie as the tactical commander of a joint command.

On the same date that Bowie and Fannin officially established their alliance, James Fannin's neighbors to the south were also actively establishing a military presence. When Fannin and the

Brazos Guards had given up the scheme to confront and arrest Cos at Copano, another group further south at Matagorda assembled under the command of George Morse Collinsworth. The group left around October 6 to intercept and attempt to kidnap General Cos at the old Spanish presidio La Bahia at Goliad where it was rumored he was bivouacking with a considerable payroll chest.

Over one hundred men had joined the expedition by the time they arrived at Victoria. It was there they learned that General Cos had left Goliad for San Antonio de Bexar and, upon departing, had left the presidio there guarded by only a skeleton crew of soldiers. On the evening of October 9, the same date Fannin and Bowie joined forces above San Antonio, Collinsworth and his men successfully confronted the Mexican garrison at Goliad and forced their surrender.

The implications of Collinsworth's actions at Goliad were staggering: Armaments and supplies were captured, the Mexican army and General Cos were deprived of communications and supplies from the coast, and Cos was completely isolated from Santa Anna and the Centralists save a long, difficult overland route from northern Mexico.

On October 11, outside Gonzales, Stephen Austin was elected commander of the Texan army, and the next day James Fannin and the others set out for San Antonio with the goal of laying siege to Ugartechea and Cos.

By October 20 the Texan forces had established Camp Salado to the east of San Antonio. Fannin and Bowie had already been campaigning with Austin to establish a base of operations to the south of Bexar, and on October 22 they were directed to "proceed forth with to the Missions of San Juan Espada and San Jose, for the purpose of gaining information in regard to the present condition of those places—the supplies of corn there—the disposition of the inhabitants. . . ."[6]

Austin appointed Bowie a colonel and placed him in joint command with Fannin, whom he appointed a captain, to lead "the first Division of the first Battalion."[7] Thus, James Fannin, who had previously only commanded the Brazos Guards in transit, was now in charge of Texan forces in a potential combat situation. While Bowie was clearly appointed as the tactical commander, Fannin did enjoy the distinction of sharing a joint command with a man most Anglo Texans and many Mexicans already considered legendary.

The missions referred to in Austin's communiqué were part of a series of mission/presidios that had been established by the Franciscan Friars from Spain. Beginning in the sixteenth century, missionaries—accompanied by a few soldiers—moved north out of the Valley of Mexico founding missions and forts. By 1718 this activity extended to the San Antonio River, helping form the nucleus of the future city of San Antonio. At the time of the Texan siege of Bexar in 1835, the five missions, all on the banks of the San Antonio River, had been secularized and abandoned to the Mexican families seeking shelter in the stone buildings.

South of Bexar, the Mission San Francisco de la Espada lay in ruins. Also in dilapidation to the north approximately one and one-half miles, Mission San Juan Capistrano; two and one-half miles further north, Mission San Jose y San Miguel de Aguayo— the largest and most developed of the Franciscan missions in

It was from this abandoned Franciscan mission, San Francisco de la Espada, that James Fannin and Bowie headquartered during the early days of the Siege of Bexar. From this location, they made their scouting patrol in which, against Stephen Austin's orders, they overextended themselves and initiated the Battle of Concepcion.

Fannin and James Bowie led Texans in a skirmish with a Mexican patrol near the abandoned ruins of Mission San Juan Capistrano. That skirmish alerted Mexican general Cos of their presence and precipitated the Battle of Concepcion.

Texas; another two miles the Mission Nuestra Señora de la Purisima Concepcion de Acuna. These four missions, forming a "trail" along the San Antonio River, ended in the city of Bexar itself with the fifth and final mission: the Mission San Antonio de Valero: otherwise known as the "Alamo."

With Cos and Ugartechea in a defensive posture inside Bexar and the Alamo, Fannin and Bowie had advocated taking possession of the four other missions for use as bases of operation.

As Austin continued to establish siege positions to the east and north of Bexar, Fannin and Bowie traveled south on October 22 to the southernmost mission, Espada, and reported by letter that evening that they had taken possession without serious resistance. They then reported to Austin that they intended to move northward the following morning and occupy the nearest point to town, which would have been Mission Concepcion, in an attempt to trap Cos and the Mexicans between the two Texan forces.[8]

The next afternoon, the twenty-third, they sent another message to Austin advising him that they had visited the missions and made a report of limited foodstuffs and water but possible billeting quarters for soldiers. Fannin also requested a fifty-man contingent and reported that the Mexicans were expecting reinforcements at any time. He also reported a lack of funds and that the men were "complaining that corn and other provisions are not furnished them—."[9]

45

Although there had been only limited contact with the Mexican army, the Texan siege was already creating shortages for the Mexicans inside Bexar, and Cos was sending out foraging parties to obtain food in the fields surrounding the city. Other groups of Mexican reinforcements were arriving overland to join Cos and Ugartechea, and by October 24 it is estimated the Mexican forces totaled around seven hundred fifty men.

It was on the twenty-fourth of October that Fannin reported his first military encounter with one of these Mexican army units. In a joint dispatch from Mission Espada dated at 7:00 A.M. Fannin reported that he and Bowie had just been attacked by about fifty Mexicans whom he believed to be part of a much larger force commanded by Colonel Ugartechea. The report also states that they felt they could fortify and defend Espada if they received the fifty reinforcements and the funds to purchase food and supplies.[10]

If Fannin's August 27 letter to Major Belton was indicative of his tendency to act without, or against, orders, this communiqué also reveals what would become a future trait of harping on issues he felt Austin and the other Texan leaders should consider important. In this instance, his issue was the need for reinforcements and money. In the future his complaints would include the need for a professional officer corps and the disciplining of volunteer soldiers including the abolition of elections. It would be a personality trait that would alienate him from his superiors and the men over which he exercised direct command.

What Fannin—and Bowie—could not have known that early morning hour was that Austin was already attempting to respond to the initial request. Later that same day Austin wrote back that he was dispatching the fifty men and that there was no money available. He instructed Fannin and Bowie to issue certificates or receipts for anything procured, and if the local population would not accept those, to follow the "Law of necessity" and take what was needed while maintaining an account of all impressed goods.[11]

But that early morning letter reporting the clash with the Mexicans also contained the strong recommendation that Austin initiate some form of movement to established headquarters closer to Bexar. "Permit us to again request—nay urge, the propriety—the necessity of some movement which will bring us nearer together, and shut in the enemy and either starve them out, whip them out, or dishearten and beat them. . . .," the two commanders wrote Austin.

A second letter, also dated the twenty-fourth, was issued by Fannin and Bowie, but the wording of this correspondence written at 4:00 P.M. suggests that Fannin was the author. In it, he reminds Austin that they have requested fifty men and a plan to surround Bexar from the north and south. Now, he reports, they are expecting an additional attack that evening and require one hundred fifty reinforcing Texans. In this message, Fannin becomes more assertive and demanding: ". . . say to us what you wish done, and when we may expect others—and whether we shall take a position near Bexar tomorrow. . . ."[12]

The conclusion of the letter, indicating it was written by Fannin and not Bowie, requests that "Should any other officer be chosen to supercede Col Bowie, will you allow [me] [Fannin] to suggest the names of Genl. Huston and col. Hall—Mr. Wharton will assign my reasons etc."

Austin, however, had more than Fannin's concerns to deal with back at the camp in Salado. Although the siege had just started, desertions by the Texans were already becoming a concern. Politically, the calls for a Consultation were renewed and Austin rescheduled the meeting in San Felipe for November 1.

Initially a Consultation had been set in October, but the events in Gonzales had led to a postponement. Some delegates had met on October 11 and organized, on paper at least, the Texan army with Stephen Austin as commander in chief serving under a "Permanent Council." While the November Consultation was obviously designed to establish unity and direction among the various Texas factions, the end results would prove divisive—caused in large part by one of the recently arrived delegates who left Bexar for San Felipe: Sam Houston.

Although denied, reports circulated throughout the Texan camps that Houston had attempted to wrestle command of the army away from the popular Austin in the camp outside Bexar. Other reports, also unsubstantiated, claimed Austin offered command to Houston, who declined because the men had popularly elected Austin.

Regardless, Sam Houston left for San Felipe, and Stephen Austin remained behind at Bexar to deal with the growing unrest among the Texans. On October 26 he ordered, based upon reports from Fannin and Bowie, the Texan camp to relocate south of the city near the old missions.

Austin rejoined the other wing of the army at Espada mission on October 27. He then sent Bowie and Fannin with their command forward to find a good defensive position that the entire force could occupy that evening.[13]

Captain James W. Fannin Jr., joint commander of the First Battalion of the First Division Texas army, was finally about to experience his first role in a combat situation.

---

1   de Bruhl, Marshall, *Sword of San Jacinto* (New York: Random House, 1993), pg. 168.

2   Jenkins, *PTR*, 2:16.

3   Ibid., 2:59.

4   Barr, Alwyn, *Texans in Revolt—The Battle for San Antonio, 1835* (Austin: University of Texas Press, 1990), pg. 17.

5   Jenkins, *PTR*, 2:75.

6   Ibid., 2:187-8.

7   Barr, pg. 18.

8   Jenkins, *PTR*, 2:190-2.

9   Ibid., 2:202-3.

10   Ibid., 2:206.

11   Ibid., 2:209.

12   Ibid., 2:210.

13   Barr, pg. 22.

Chapter Six

With Bowie at Concepcion

Of the four abandoned missions to the south of Bexar, Mission Concepcion was located nearest to General Cos and the Mexican army inside the city. The stone church, completed in 1755, was constructed of limestone and was so well designed it had never crumbled. The imposing structure featured twin towers and a large dome. The towers, with pyramid roofs and open windows on all four sides, made excellent lookout posts. Nearby, the San Antonio River provided a water source for the mission, which was secularized in 1792 and abandoned in 1813.

It was here at Mission Concepcion, some two miles from the Alamo and the twin plazas of Bexar and six miles from Fannin's camp at Espada, that Austin envisioned establishing Texan siege headquarters.

Austin dispatched Fannin and Bowie on October 27 to find a good defensive position from which Austin and the remainder of the forces could camp that evening. Once a suitable position was located, Fannin and Bowie were instructed to return early enough for the remainder of the Texans to rendezvous there.

With Bowie in tactical command and assisted by James Fannin, officially designated a captain, the ninety-man force was divided into four companies, each lead by an officer of captain rank.

Traveling north along the bank of the San Antonio River, the Texans inspected the ruins at San Juan and San Jose. Once dubbed the "Queen of the Bexar Missions," San Jose had been the largest and most developed of the Franciscan outposts—complete with an aquifer system, gristmill, and huge granary. In its dilapidated state in 1835, however, Fannin and Bowie opted to bypass it and continue on to Mission Concepcion. Along the way, they skirmished

It was near this abandoned mission, Nuestra Señora de la Purisima Concepcion de Acuna, that Fannin and Bowie initiated the Battle of Concepcion that resulted in an early Texan victory and impetus for the siege and later storming of Bexar.

briefly with Mexican scouts, who then retreated to Bexar informing Cos of the Texan movement.

Austin had been anxious to obtain a position favorable to launching an offensive action against Cos and Ugartechea inside Bexar, and it was here near Concepcion that Fannin and Bowie determined would be the ideal site to establish a camp that evening.

The San Antonio River at this point made a crooked path that formed a series of horseshoe bends approximately one-quarter mile from the Concepcion mission. The site they chose was in one of these horseshoe bends, angling away from the mission. Trees shaded both sides of the broad riverbottom that lay about six feet below the level of the rolling prairie nearby.[1]

Before Fannin and Bowie left that morning, Austin ordered them to range only that distance that would allow them to return to Espada in time to move the rest of the Texan forces north to the chosen encampment site. But the day's inspection of San Juan and San Jose and the skirmish with the Mexican scouts had slowed their advance along the banks of the river until they had proceeded too far from Espada to return in time to escort the main force. Bowie did not want to risk losing this choice ground even if it meant disobeying Austin's explicit instructions, so he dispatched a rider to Espada to inform Austin of his decision to stay the night.[2]

Austin's reaction was anger and for good reason. Despite claiming an excellent defensive position near Bexar, Fannin and Bowie had also divided the Texan forces—already numerically inferior to the Mexicans—and done so in a manner that positioned their small contingent in a vulnerable position nearer the Mexican garrison than to that of their own forces.

After the skirmish with the Mexican scouts and their subsequent disappearance toward Bexar, Fannin and Bowie must have known that Cos would be alerted. With their vulnerability so apparent outside Concepcion, the two commanders nevertheless decided to establish their positions and prepared to spend the night on the riverbank. Guards were posted and additional lookouts were stationed in the twin towers of the old mission building.

That Cos was aware of their position became obvious when, in the darkness of night, a Mexican cannon located in the tower of the

San Fernando Church in Bexar fired several rounds dangerously close to the Texan camp. The shots also alerted Austin and the other Texans at Espada, who prepared to advance at daylight. The next day Austin issued a strong reminder that officers who failed to follow orders would be removed and court-martialed.[3]

Cos, too, planned to advance on Fannin and Bowie at first light. Dawn, however, came slowly the morning of the twenty-eighth due to a heavy fog. Despite this, Colonel Ugartechea departed Bexar with about two hundred seventy-five soldiers transporting two cannon.

In early morning while the fog was still thick, Mexican scouts found the Texan sentries—probably by accident—and light firing and counterfiring commenced and continued for a couple of hours.

Fannin, whose company occupied the riverbank of the horse-shoe forming the southern line of defense, at last began to earn the combat experience he had so desperately sought since his arrival in Texas. Initially, however, the fighting was severely limited due to the weather conditions. To improve their field of vision, the Texans cut down undergrowth and dug out firing steps in the embankment from which they could drop down to reload.[4]

As the fog thinned, the Mexican cavalry and footsoldiers advanced onto the prairie in front of the Texan's position and surrounded them with their backs to the river. Despite intense Mexican rifle and cannon fire, Fannin and the other Texans remained safely secure behind the natural fortifications provided by the riverbank.

Then the Mexicans concentrated their attack on Fannin's position along the south bank. In response, Bowie ordered Captain Robert Coleman's company to reinforce Fannin's men, and the combined rifle fire stalled the Mexican advance.

Three times in thirty minutes the Mexicans charged the Texan positions only to be driven back, with the rebels' sharpshooters concentrating on the artillerymen manning the cannon. Finally, after the third assault stalled, the Mexicans retreated—abandoning their cannon, which the Texans then turned on them as they withdrew.

The Texans had won the "battle" of Concepcion, and James Walker Fannin Jr. had gained his first taste of combat. The Mexican dead were estimated at between sixty and eighty with many more wounded, while the Texan forces counted only one mortality.

It was the Mexican wounded left behind on the prairie that confronted the Texans as they began investigating the battle-ground. In various states of injury, the wounded began begging for their lives. It took Fannin and the other confused Texans a few moments before they understood what the Mexicans were fearing: They believed it was the policy of warfare that all prisoners be executed.

Fannin and the other Texans that morning of October 28 did not execute the wounded prisoners. Later, the Anglo-Americans would bitterly accuse the Mexicans of betraying the mercy that was shown them at the Battle of Concepcion.[5]

Stephen Austin would not arrive on the battlefield for another half-hour after the Mexicans had fled back to Bexar. During that period, no doubt the colonists took the opportunity to celebrate what had seemed to be an easy military victory over a numerically superior army. James Fannin probably had a few moments to review in his mind the lessons learned from his first combat experience.

Unfortunately, the lessons he may have learned at Concepcion may not have been tactically sound ones. Bowie had made several decisions that were not based upon established military proce-dures and could have easily resulted in disaster.

He and Fannin overextended their position by camping at a location in which they were nearer the Mexican enemy than their own reinforcements. Also, while the horseshoe bend in the river provided natural cover, it also geographically trapped the Tex-ans—a fact they were able to overcome through their superior firepower and marksmanship and with the natural protection of the depressed riverbank and tree cover. And finally, the Mexican army had broken and retreated under the intense fighting—a fact leading to the false belief that Mexican soldiers could not or would not fight when confronted by armed Anglo settlers.

These lessons that at least seemed apparent in the moments after the conclusion of the Battle of Concepcion. If so, they were also lessons that would lead James Fannin into disaster soon in a depressed area on the Plains of Coleto where over-extension of his forces, the lack of natural protective cover, and disdain for Mexican fighting ability would all negatively impact his first and only battle command as a senior officer.

At Concepcion, many of these flawed battle tactics had been overcome due to the natural instincts, aggressive command, determined focus, and decisive leadership of a battle-tested commander like James Bowie. Fannin, while a co-commander on paper, only played a minor role as company captain at Concepcion while Bowie actually led the fight. At Coleto, in a few months, James Bowie would not be around to assume leadership.

Austin and the main group of Texans arrived on the battle scene shortly after the fighting had ended. The reasons for the late arrival also held valuable lessons for the future—lessons that were almost certainly lost on James Fannin that morning outside Bexar. But then in the euphoria of the early victory—and Concepcion was one of what seemed to be a series of easy victories after Velasco, Anahuac, Gonzales, and Goliad—the lessons were probably lost even on the battle-wise Bowie as well.

The night before, Austin had ordered his officers and men to be prepared to leave early in the morning, and in fact the army had been up and preparing to advance before dawn. When a company of volunteers had left for home without authorization, however, a large body of guards had unsuccessfully attempted to bring the men back. That wait, followed by problems hauling artillery and wagons across the river, slowed the advance.[6]

The first problem here that would in the future plague Fannin and other Texan leaders including Sam Houston was that an untrained volunteer army would exercise what it saw as its democratic right to obey or refuse orders. If as charismatic a leader as Stephen Austin had problems getting men to follow orders, unpopular and nonelected leaders in the future would have even greater difficulties on the battlefield. Secondly, the problems of hauling artillery and wagons across rivers would be a hardship that virtually every Texan leader, including Fannin, would experience.

Texas in 1835 was almost completely undeveloped, even by Mexican standards. With a precious few established traces overland, any journey of distance would be confronted with rivers, bayous, and creeks and virtually no bridges with which to cross them. On the major trails such as the El Camino Real, La Bahia Road, or Atascosito Route, ferry operators would sometimes be available.

But in the coming months, warfare, weather, and panic would render these ferries inoperable. Transporting any wheeled vehicle, whether it be wagon or artillery, across these rivers would be nearly impossible. It was a lesson Sam Houston would learn during the Runaway Scrape, and it was also a lesson James Fannin Jr. would learn soon on this same San Antonio River that had on this day protected him so well at Concepcion.

Austin may have been furious with Fannin and Bowie the night before, but their success on the battlefield that morning gave the Texans needed momentum. As the last of the Mexicans retreated into Bexar, Austin urged the reunified Texan militia to pursue them and take the fighting into San Antonio itself. When his leaders, including Bowie, strongly counseled against an assault, Austin acquiesced.

The "Battle of Concepcion" was in reality little more than a skirmish between two ill-prepared military units. But while it may have been miniscule as a military operation, it would result in military postures by both sides that would set the tone for the coming month. As a result of the fighting at Conception on that October 28 morning, the Mexican army would retreat into Bexar and the Alamo and assume a defensive position while Austin and the victorious Texans would settle in for what would become a month-long siege strategy.

1	Barr, *Texans in Revolt—The Battle for San Antonio, 1835*, pg. 22.
2	Hardin, Stephen L., *Texian Iliad—A Military History of the Texas Revolution* (Austin: University of Texas Press, 1994), pg. 30.
3	Barr, pg. 22.
4	Ibid., pg. 24.
5	Long, Jeff, *Duel of Eagles: The Mexican and U.S. Fight for the Alamo* (New York: William Morrow and Company, Inc.), pg. 72.
6	Barr, pg. 25.

Chapter Seven
Siege of San Antonio

Captain James Walker Fannin Jr. emerged from the Battle of Concepcion with something he had been seeking: combat experience qualifying him as a military leader. Before Concepcion, he had always been the high-profile political firebrand who, unlike his neighbors, could not boast of having engaged the Mexican enemy.

At the Anahuac and Velasco disturbances he had been absent during the fighting. He had not been among his Austin Colony neighbors who had secured the first naval victory of the rebellion with the attack and capture of the *Correo*. He had been present during the clash at Gonzales and, as a result, had abandoned the planned assault on General Cos at Copano.

Now in November of 1835, the siege of San Antonio was established and even more Texans were joining the cause. From the East Texas colonies, more men arrived including veterans of the fighting around Nacogdoches.

While the rebellion had not reached the crisis stage of secession, Anglo Texas and particularly San Antonio was quickly becoming a population of colonists who could boast of armed fighting with the Mexican army. From the south, names like Collinsworth, Dimitt, Wharton, and Austin were prominent in discussions about the fighting. Sam Houston was now in Texas. James Bowie had drawn blood against Santa Anna's troops. Anglo Texas in November 1835 was full of men who could claim to be veterans of the short fighting. And James Fannin could now be counted among them.

His previous command of the Brazos Guards was finished, and he was now firmly established within the upper echelon of Texans at Bexar. On November 2 he attended a council of officers called by

Austin below San Antonio. The purpose of the council was to adopt or reject two resolutions set forth by Austin and the command staff of the Texans. At the meeting, Fannin was elected chairman and led the discussion and voting on the resolutions. The first motion involved whether or not the town of Bexar (San Antonio) should be stormed and was overwhelmingly defeated, with Fannin voting with the majority against the assault. The second resolution recommended that their group (Colonel Bowie's Division) immediately unite with the main army above Bexar. This time the vote was much closer but the majority, including Fannin, chose unification.[1]

Other than reporting the results of the voting on the two resolutions, this letter to Austin is unremarkable except for one thing: On the signature block, Fannin signs his name as "J.W. Fanning, chairman." This would be one of the few times that he would revert to the earlier spelling of "Fanning" but something he would sporadically continue to do throughout the coming months.

Four days later, from a location two miles above Bexar, Fannin addressed a letter to the "President of the Convention of Texas" in which he enclosed the response from Colonel F.S. Belton, whom he had approached the previous August about serving in the Texas army.

In that letter, addressed to "Colonel" Fannin at Velasco, Belton provided a conservative but sound assessment of the military situation and problems in Texas and hedged on accepting an officer's commission in the Texas army. Among other obstacles, Belton listed "time and permission to leave the U. States is clogged with forms and difficulties . . . a resignation too from our service on entering yours would be necessary . . . and many military responsibilities not easily shaken off, or settled up are pending."[2]

Belton, identified by Fannin as in command at Fort Morgan in Mobile, did offer to assist in procuring supplies and equipment in New Orleans. Fannin had approached Belton in an attempt to stimulate interest among regular U.S. Army officers to serve in the Texan conflict. By enlisting the aid of Belton and other American officers, Fannin also hoped to develop a base of support for the Texan cause among the general American public.

In this letter, Fannin also urged the Convention to forward immediate requests to Texan recruiting and subscription stations in New Orleans and Mobile for heavy artillery, mortars, and ammunition. Specific but unrealistic, in his request he recommended very heavy artillery: two each of twelve-, eighteen-, twenty-four-, and thirty-two-pounders.

Throughout the coming conflict, the Anglo Texans would struggle with the problem of artillery. Ironically, the problems would usually stem not from the lack of cannon, but the inability to transport what was often a surplus of ordnance. In the coming defense of the Alamo by the Texans, the surplus of ordnance would result in some tubes remaining unmounted. However, the inability to transport heavy artillery across land would also result in the defense of the Alamo being conducted with only one truly "heavy" cannon: the famous eighteen-pounder carried from New Orleans to Bexar.

Fannin's November 6 call for heavy ordnance up to thirty-two pound stemmed no doubt from the general assessment by Houston and himself that the city of Bexar could not be successfully stormed and occupied until heavier artillery were obtained. At the time of his letter, the Texans had a few pieces of artillery but probably nothing heavier than a twelve-pounder.

In addition to the heavy artillery, he also called for procurement of "2 to 500 Round Shot for each one," which would have required purchase and shipment of up to four thousand rounds of ammunition: something the bickering politicians at the Convention were incapable of even negotiating much less purchasing.

It is clear from the letter that Fannin envisioned establishing a Texan army on the model of the U.S. Army, in which he was at least somewhat familiar from his West Point days. Not only did he seek an officer corps based upon recruitment from the United States, but also similar equipment with which to supply the troops. His letter also added the recommendation for two to four mortars of twelve- to twenty-four-inch caliber and two to three hundred rounds each.

This letter is particularly useful since it helps analyze Fannin's military strategy for the coming fight. He claims that with as few as four heavy battering cannon, the city of Bexar could be taken in as little as six hours.

That accomplished, he suggests that the additional artillery, powder, ammunition, and supplies obtained from Bexar could then be used to "fortify every seaport town in Texas, and that well too, and every other fort the service may require—." This November 6 letter has been widely quoted by historians and is significant from several aspects. The most common reference to this correspondence concerns Fannin's perception of the need to act quickly and his claim of understanding the politicians' problems in obtaining funding and financing for the revolution and the equipment he was so urgently requesting. In the main body of the letter, he makes the offer:

> If you cannot get money or credit for them I hereby authorize & empower your body to raise a Committee, & sell, hypothecate or otherwise dispose of all my property in Texas, consisting of Thirty six negroes, now on Cany Creek & Brazos river, to meet the purchase of the same—Do not say, that when San Antonio falls, we are safe, and will never need these arms. Take the parting advice of the great Washington, and in times of peace prepare for war—but realy these are times of war—the ending of which we know not, nor can the wisest foretell the issue—
>
> If you do not succeed, at least let us not neglect any measure, which may in the least way contribute to a fortunate conclusion—I had much rather expend the last shilling I had on earth, & beggar myself & family, by nobly doing my duty in all respects, than fail, by laging back & withholding what small pittance, it may be my fortune lot now to hold.
>
> This property, and indeed any other, will not be worth owning, if we do not succeed. . . .[3]

In the short period from his arrival in Texas in the fall of 1834 until November 6, 1835, it appears James Fannin Jr. had, for the record at least, fully embraced the Texan cause—even to the point of beggaring himself and his family.

The letter concludes with Fannin informing the Convention that there were about six hundred men in the Texan camp, but he acknowledges desertions may soon become problematic if the requested ordnance and supplies do not arrive soon. Whether sincere or not, it was an offer no other Texan leader offered publicly to match.

On the issue of the necessity of heavy artillery, Fannin and Sam Houston were in complete agreement—one of the few times during the coming revolution that the two would be in consensus.

Although Austin was still extremely popular among the Texans assembled at Bexar, the political bickering had already begun to affect his ability to lead. Although he was legitimately the commander in chief of the Texan forces, rumors continued to circulate that Bowie was the leader.[4] These rumors probably were fueled by the elation and euphoria after the victory at Concepcion in which Bowie had been the commanding officer and he and Fannin had led what had been a *de facto* independent force and Austin had only served as a backup—arriving after the battle.

Within days—possibly even hours—of the victory, however, the Texans began leaving for home without bothering to gain permission or even give notice. The problem of commanding a volunteer force based upon the democratic principle of voting for military decisions was already apparent at this time.

The Consultation, which had originally been scheduled to convene on October 15, had been delayed because of the fighting, particularly at Concepcion, and had been rescheduled for November 1. The site of the meeting was moved from Washington-on-the-Brazos to San Felipe, but hardly more than half the delegates reported, meaning that much of Anglo Texas was not represented. Another problem was Austin's absence, which led his opponents to immediately divide the discussions and voting.

Also problematic to the delegates was the status of the Anglo minority in Mexico already divided by civil unrest. The Consultation took great care that its actions not antagonize and scare off the friendly Mexican Federalists and unite them with the Centralists of Santa Anna against Texas. An invasion by a united Mexico could put an end to the independence movement. The Declaration of November 7, 1835 was therefore purposely ambiguous. It stressed the restoration of the Constitution of 1824 and the fact that Texas was the victim of a despot.[5]

This declaration, issued the day after Fannin's November 6 letter, set the tone for the coming political infighting and bickering that would plague the Texan leaders throughout the conflict.

After the November 2 "Council of War" had voted against an attack on Bexar and for unification of the Texan forces, Austin had ordered the troops to bivouac above San Antonio at the site of an old mill.

On November 7 Edward Burleson was elected regimental colonel in a referendum in which James Fannin placed third while receiving thirteen percent of the five hundred seventeen votes cast. Bowie, who had resigned his command after the split vote on November 2 by the Council of War, was appointed adjutant general—a position he readily accepted.

Austin, in the meantime, remained commander in chief and, with his forces now unified in one location above Bexar, began dispatching small parties to scout the area around the city for Mexican activity and reinforcements. William Barret Travis, one of the Anahuac agitators, was ranging south of Bexar with a small group of Texans attempting to intercept Mexican supply parties and reinforcements.

On November 9 Austin sent a communiqué to Fannin reporting rumors of as many as six hundred Mexican reinforcements approaching Bexar. In the letter, he ordered "Captain" Fannin to recruit one hundred fifty men and search out Travis and unite with him. In addition to intercepting the Mexican supply party, he was also instructed by Austin to relay instructions to Mexicans living in the area not to deliver food supplies to or communicate with the besieged Mexicans in Bexar.[6]

Travis, unaware of the rumors or Fannin's dispatch to join him, had tracked a herd of horses some fifty miles south of Bexar and succeeded in driving away their Mexican guards, securing some three hundred badly needed horses and mules.

As Travis returned to Bexar with his bounty, Austin recalled Fannin who had been sent out to join him. Fannin arrived back at the army camp on the eighteenth after a sweep across the Medina River. He divided his forces, sending Lieutenant John York on a swing west with one company while his own troops checked the trails to the east as far as the Atascosa and the Frio Rivers. Both commands failed to find Mexican forces.[7]

Earlier, on November 13, the Consultation had established a provisional government known as the Organic Law. The Organic Law created a governing consortium with a legislative branch known as the General Council and consisting of a representative from each of the Anglo communities. The executive branch was placed in the hands of a governor, and Henry Smith—an advocate of independence from Mexico—was placed in power.

The Consultation also provided for militia organization while establishing a regular army with two-year enlistments and United States Army regulations. Fannin's urgent appeals to adopt an American-style military organization appear to have been heeded. To recruit soldiers—and dispel fears that they were only fighting to gain land for the politicians and land speculators—a system of land grants was established to reward military service.

On November 12 Sam Houston was placed in charge of the regular army and given instructions to organize and develop a professional military. The Consultation also provided for volunteer citizen militias, however, and Houston did not exercise direct—or even indirect—control over the bulk of the armed Texans around Bexar.

If this awkward arrangement did not place Houston in a difficult enough position, the Consultation further ordered him to establish his headquarters at Washington-on-the-Brazos, some fifty miles away from Bexar.

Amidst all this confusion and in-fighting, James Fannin Jr. continued to promote his West Point background, his political contacts, and his recently acquired military fighting experience around Bexar. His approach appears to have succeeded since Sam Houston almost immediately took notice of him.

On November 13 Sam Houston wrote Fannin a confidential letter from San Felipe in which he offered the Georgia native the post of inspector general of the regular army. In a very frank manner, Houston shared with Fannin his fears and concerns about the developments going on at Bexar and throughout Anglo Texas. Asking Fannin to accept the position of inspector general and join him at Washington-on-the-Brazos, Houston also warned him not to leave if his presence was necessary in the camp: to remain at his post if he felt it expedient to prevent the mass desertions occurring.

Houston also outlined his interpretation of the military situation: Heavy artillery could not arrive at Bexar before March (some four months away), and so long as the Mexicans could forage food and supplies a siege would be a waste of Texan manpower and supplies.

Instead, Houston recommended a minimal force of Texans be left in Bexar to harass and maintain a "nominal" siege while the rest fell back to Gonzales and Goliad, where Texans continued to man the captured fort.

Houston sent his regards to another Texan leader he clearly respected: James Bowie. "I hear our friend Col. Bowie is at the Head of the army," he wrote Fannin. He was probably referring to Bowie's appointment as adjutant general a week earlier. "Bid him God speed. I am Glad of it! I congratulate him and the army," he concluded.

Houston concluded his communiqué with the admonishment that the Texan army should never have crossed the Guadalupe River in pursuit of the Mexicans after the clash at Gonzales and stressed the importance of retreating back to that community and to Goliad. "Remember one Maxim," he warned James Fannin, "it is better to do well, late; than never!"[8]

Ironically, Fannin's adherence to this advice in the coming months, whether by design or defect, would define his place and role in Texas history.

Fannin probably did not receive Houston's confidential letter immediately because he was still in the field on his sweep across the Medina, Atascosa, and Frio Rivers. The day after Houston's letter, Austin also wrote Fannin *"donde se halle"* (where he may be found) informing him that the deliverer, D. Salvador Flores, had been dispatched to perform a scorched earth policy around Bexar in an attempt to deprive the Mexicans of food and animal fodder. Austin asked Fannin to provide Flores with men and horses and then to personally return immediately to Bexar. He also mentioned that "Some reinforcements have arrived. . .".[9] The reinforcements he was referring to were the New Orleans Greys, a unit of

American and European mercenaries with whom Fannin would soon become embroiled.

Another letter was posted to Fannin on November 15 from San Felipe—this time from one of his Caney Creek neighbors from the coast: Richard Royster Royall, another Southern U.S. émigré who had established a plantation in Matagorda County. Royall was chairman of Permanent Council at San Felipe, which had been given the authority to raise men, arms, and revenues for "the common defense of Texas."

Royall, addressing Fannin as "Major," briefly describes the events happening with the provisional government and then dives into a tirade against Sam Houston. The purpose of his letter was obviously an attempt to supercede Houston's recommendation to Fannin that the Texans retreat to Gonzales and Goliad and wait for heavier artillery. The Consultation had been divided over whether to maintain the siege or even launch an assault on the city as opposed to waiting for more men and artillery—as both Fannin and Houston had counseled.

Royall, who would be confrontational and disruptive throughout the revolution, pled his case to Fannin in this letter:

> Your army certainly has been badly conducted we have forwarded all things even to Recruits so far as has been called for—and several wagons have been dispatched which have not been called for—and yet we are pubicaly complained of If your commander or his staff could see 2 inches from their Noses and Order supplies in time the country has means men all that is necessary.[10]

Royall informs Fannin that he plans to return to Matagorda and states that if the giant eighteen-pounder cannon transported by the New Orleans Greys is still there, he will make sure it is sent to Bexar. He is referring here to the cannon transported by Captain Robert Morris' unit of the Greys from New Orleans aboard the *Columbus* but without ball ammunition. Without the ammunition, the Greys left the cannon at Velasco where it was later shipped to Matagorda aboard the *San Felipe* but was lost in the gulf during a shipwreck. Salvaged by McKinney and Williams, the giant piece was being transported across country to Bexar.[11]

That Royall and Fannin were close acquaintances, if not friends, is evidenced in the remainder of the letter in which Royall discusses a financial proposition Fannin had evidently extended earlier.

> You write me & Mr. Newell relative to your negroes and the purchase of my Land. I wish you to be more definite as If I sell I must have half the amt. In March or April next either in cash or Negroes this will be necessary as we don't know how long we may be detained in public service and in the mean time I must as well as you Keep my Negroes employed to an advantage But any service I can Render to you In your absence will be done to the utmost If you advise me to buy a place for you or any thing else you may Request it shall be promptly complied with But for the present I will have your Negroes collected and as soon as you write me I will do as you desire—.[12]

It would appear from this correspondence that Fannin, while offering to sell his slaves and land to support the revolution, was also speculating in the purchase of additional or other land in Texas at the same time.

Fannin had earlier requested Royall obtain a coat and pair of pants for him, and the chairman concludes this November 15 letter by informing Fannin that no clothes were to be found at that time.

October and November of 1835 had been a period of critical and positive growth in the political and military stature of James W. Fannin Jr. During that period he had joined the Gonzales rebellion, marched to Bexar, participated in the Battle of Concepcion, scouted the southern perimeter of Bexar, and developed political ties with the leaders of the Texan revolt. As the month of November drew to a close in 1835, the siege of Bexar was quickly dwindling and James Fannin's role was about to change. But first he wanted to return home to Brazoria and his wife and daughters.

On November 18 he wrote three letters from his camp near Bexar. One, addressed to Stephen Austin, describes his scouting missions as far south as the Frio River and his unsuccessful attempts to locate Mexican Colonel Ugartechea, who had eluded the Texans on November 12 and slipped out of Bexar with the purpose of locating Mexican reinforcements and guiding them back to San Antonio.

On the eighteenth Fannin reported that no contact had been made with the Mexicans but that he had been informed Ugartechea had regrouped with a Mexican force in Laredo that included three hundred convicts.[13]

That same day Fannin responded in writing to Sam Houston's offer of the position of inspector general of the army. This express communiqué, written in two parts, would be the first of several issued by Fannin in which he would unabashedly promote himself for a military appointment as a field, not administrative, general in the Texan army.

In the correspondence Fannin acknowledges and thanks Houston for the offer but insists:

> I would prefer a command in the line....Having Elected one Maj Gen—Will they not also make two Brig Genls? If so, would not my claims be equal to any other? If I can get either—I would prefer it—and I respectfully request your influence for one—otherwise I will accept of the appointment you tender me, provided I can have furlough, to bring on my family, in case I am not required in the field—.[14]

Fannin, while not directly refusing an administrative position with the regular army, does specifically request a field appointment as brigadier general with Sam Houston's personal reference. In the event Houston would insist on an administrative position, Fannin suggests he would accept—on the condition he could move his family to be with him.

In a postscript to the letter, Fannin again urges Houston to organize a "Regular Army" with a place in the field for him. "I am wholly at the service of the country," he wrote Houston, "and shall not quit camp to seek office—but rather prefer the post of danger; where I may seek the enemy & beat him too, when found. . . ."

Not only was James Fannin requesting a field generalship, he was promoting this appointment by volunteering for a "post of danger" in which he could confront the Mexican army.

Other than to ignore Fannin's request, it is not known what Houston's reaction to this letter was. Another irony in the relationship between these two egotistical men was that James Fannin Jr. in the coming months would not be promoted to general but would receive that "post of danger." The true irony would lie in the fact that he would find himself in that position not because of Sam Houston, but in defiance of the commander in chief's direct orders.

When this "express" communiqué did not immediately leave Fannin's camp, he added yet another addendum dated "In Camp 4 oclk. P.M. 18th Nov 1835" in which he diplomatically agreed with Houston, stating that "With the present force—and under the present discipline, and most of the present officers, & the panic already imbibed, touching a storm, &c I must admit it [retreat from Bexar] to be the safest course. . . ."

However Fannin also took the liberty to suggest to Houston, "I must also say, that I am fully convinced that with 250 men, well chosen & properly drilled so as to rely upon each other that the place can be taken by storm, and not much loss to the party—."

One last time, he urges the organization of a Regular Army with himself in a leadership position—stating once again that he could recruit a number of U.S. Army West Point graduates to the Texan cause.

This second addendum was concluded with "Liberty & Texas—our wives & sweethearts—J W Fannin Jr."

Sam Houston, deeply embroiled in the political infighting at San Felipe and Washington-on-the-Brazos, did not respond to Fannin's plea for a position as brigadier general, his request for a furlough to return home to his wife, the offer to recruit West Point graduates, or Fannin's speculation that Bexar could still be stormed by the Texans surrounding it.

Whether Sam Houston ignored James Walker Fannin Jr. at this time because of neglect, design, or lack of time remains unknown. Fannin, however, in his frustration penned a letter to Stephen Austin.

On November 22 Austin replied with the short note:

Head Quarters before
Bexar Nov. 22, 1835

Capt. J. W. Fannin having represented to me that the abso-
lute necessity of returning home, I have granted to him an
honorable discharge and have to say that he has uniformly discharged his duty as a soldier and as an officer.

S.F. Austin
Comdr. in Chief[15]

After two months at Gonzales, Concepcion, and Bexar, James
Walker Fannin Jr. was returning home to Brazoria, Minerva, and
their two daughters. His role in the Texas Revolution was not over,
however. It was, in fact, about to begin a new phase that would
imprint his name in Texas history forever.

1   Jenkins, *PTR*, 2:300-1.
2   Ibid., 1:482.
3   Ibid., 2:336-8.
4   Barker, Eugene C., *The Life of Stephen F. Austin* (Austin: Texas
        State Historical Association, 1949), pg. 418.
5   de Bruhl, *Sword of San Jacinto*, pg. 170.
6   Jenkins, *PTR*, 2:364-5.
7   Barr, *Texans in Revolt*, pg. 34.
8   Jenkins, *PTR*, 2:396-7.
9   Ibid., 2:406.
10   Ibid., 2:429-31.
11   Brown, Gary, *Volunteers in the Texas Revolution: The New Orleans
        Greys* (Plano, Texas: Republic of Texas Press, 1999), pp. 35-6.
12   Jenkins, *PTR*, 2:429-431.
13   Ibid., 2:456-7.
14   Ibid., 2:456-7.
15   Ibid., 2:486.

Chapter Eight

Return to Brazoria

James Fannin's relationship with his wife and two daughters was another aspect of his personality that differentiated him from many of the other Texan politicians during this period.

That he wrote Stephen Austin and Sam Houston from San Antonio referring to "wives and sweethearts" and the necessity of returning home to his wife is just another suggestion that he was a devoted and loyal family man.

Nothing else in his correspondence or later reports about him suggests otherwise.

Much has been written about Sam Houston's past before he appeared in Texas—his failed marriage, his extended bouts of drunkenness, his common-law Cherokee wife, and his political scandals.

William Barret Travis also came to Texas with a questionable past and an abandoned wife. Travis' indiscretions with women— married and single—were later documented when his diary was discovered. Despite severe complications from syphilis, he continued his liaisons with various women.

That this behavior on the part of two of Texas' highest ranking leaders was considered inconsequential at the time is typical of the behavior of many of the other Texans during this period. This was, after all, the period of GTT—"Gone to Texas"—and many of those Anglo settlers and adventurers at Bexar, San Felipe, and Washington-on-the-Brazos had abandoned wives and families to seek their future in Texas.

James Walker Fannin Jr., however, was not one of those. Despite more recent scrutiny on his past—particularly his slave trading—one aspect of his life that seems to have been above reproach was his relationship with his wife and two daughters.

In the final weeks of a very volatile 1835, he tendered his request, which Austin granted, and left the disintegrating Texan army, still clustered outside Bexar, for his home and family in Brazoria.

His departure from Bexar, however, did not signal an end to his military and political ambitions. On November 31 he wrote a long, detailed letter to Governor Smith in which he called for the governor to double the anticipated size of the army and suggested that at least six months training be provided. His recommendations, although presumptuous under the circumstances, were also the result of a great deal of thought and made sense militarily. Much of what Fannin was suggesting was based upon the policies and tactics of the U.S. Army of which he had at least some background and knowledge.

Governor Smith, on the other hand, did not enjoy the position or authority that Andrew Jackson commanded over the United States soldiers stationed as close to Texas as Fort Jesup just across the Sabine River in Louisiana. As much sense as Fannin's suggestions made in the November 31 letter, they had little value to a Texan governor who was struggling to keep the disorderly Texans from abandoning the siege of Bexar completely and returning to their homes—both inside Texas and back in the United States.

Midway through the letter, Fannin gets to what he refers to as the "main object—"

> By Virtue of your Delegated powers & exegency of the case, increase the "Regular Army," to another Brigade of the like numbers with the one already ordered—As a matter of course, one Brigr. Genl. must be appointed to each Brigade—.
>
> Give to one of those officers, or some suitable Agent, the authority to nominate to the Appointing authorities most if not all of the officers . . . I have had tendered to me, for the service of Texas, several of the finest, most intelligent & accomplished young officers, now in the U States army. . . .[1]

Fannin does not make clear just who these "intelligent & accomplished young officers" are, and his correspondence with

Major Belton in Mobile had resulted in what was essentially a polite refusal to join the Texan cause.

Nevertheless, Fannin unabashedly promotes himself to Governor Smith as the ideal candidate for the proposed second brigadier general position that would be justified by recruiting duties.

The intensity of Fannin's campaign for a generalship is further underscored three days later when William Barret Travis addresses a letter to Governor Smith and the General Council in which he stated, "I approve cherfully [*sic*] the views & reasoning on the subject of the Regular Army, expressed in the Communication of Capt. J.W. Fannin jr."[2]

There was no immediate response from Governor Smith or the General Council to either Fannin or Travis. Events had taken a dangerous and irreversible turn in Bexar. The two companies of New Orleans Greys had rallied the few remaining Texan volunteers outside that city, and, using Ben Milam to "Texanize" the assault, they had stormed the city with a company of Mississippians and a small contingent from Brazoria.

The assault had gone against the prevailing advice of Austin, Houston, and even Fannin and Travis. Yet, the Texas Revolution was on the eve of becoming yet another failed filibuster effort until the Greys voted overwhelmingly to man the assault on the city—by themselves if necessary.

The result had been a brutal, five-day campaign in which the Texans were outmanned and overwhelmed by superior Mexican artillery. Using the cover of the adobe buildings in San Antonio, they had literally "tunneled" their way from the outskirts of the city into the Military Plaza where the Mexican garrison was stationed. The fighting had been, almost from the beginning, house-to-house, then room-to-room, and finally, hand-to-hand combat.

Mexican resistance had been unexpectedly fierce, and only a series of problems within the Mexican command had led to the capitulation on December 10. As part of the surrender document, General Cos agreed to retreat back across the Rio Grande towards Mexico City, and suddenly the Anglo Texans found themselves occupying a Texas free of Mexican military presence.

Anahuac, Nacogdoches, and Velasco were now firmly under Texan control, and Texan forces still occupied the crucial military outpost at Goliad. The coastal ports were now controlled by Texans, and the primary political and commercial center of Mexican Texas—San Antonio de Bexar—was now in the hands of the Texans.

But no Texan leader—James Fannin included—believed that Mexican president and commander in chief Antonio Lopez de Santa Anna would acquiesce to the Texans and allow the separation of the territory from Mexico. It was generally acknowledged that it would only be a matter of time until Santa Anna returned to reclaim Texas.

While some counseled consolidating defensive positions throughout Texas, other Texans advocated taking the fight to Santa Anna and Mexico without waiting for reprisals. Led by a group of land speculators who had lost lucrative *empresario* contracts in Coahuila and Texas, a movement was launched immediately to mount an assault on the town of Matamoros across the Rio Grande River.

But on December 10, 1835—the day of the Mexican surrender in Bexar—a proclamation was issued to the people of Texas by the General Council. In it, the Texans were urged to converge on Bexar and establish a citizen army to save Texas from a long and bloody war.

The proclamation further stated:

> Be it further resolved, that J. W. Fannin, junior, and Thomas J. Rusk be appointed, and they are hereby appointed by the General Council aforesaid, forthwith to proceed, the one upon the east side of the Trinity, the other upon the west side, for the purpose of collecting reinforcements, and have them enrolled for service. . . .
>
> . . . J. W. Fannin, jr., and Thomas J. Rusk, be and are hereby constituted agents or contractors for supplying ammunitions, provisions and other necessaries for carrying into effect these resolutions, and they or either of them are hereby vested with full powers, to purchase any and all articles necessary for said volunteers. . . .
>
> Be it further resolved, that the preceding report and resolutions be printed and circulated throughout Texas.[3]

The General Council had finally acted upon calls for a volunteer army, and now James Fannin, along with Thomas Rusk, would head the recruitment and procurement of equipment and weapons. Fannin had received his appointment of senior recruiting agent for Texas, but it had come without the coveted promotion to brigadier general. Ironically, for a military leader who was increasingly voicing his opinion in favor of a trained, professional army, he now found his commanding position was that of presiding over a volunteer army.

And his new position and authority would not elevate him above the political bickering and infighting that would become trademarks of his leadership. Back in Matagorda on December 11—the day after the proclamation—and possibly before he had even learned of his appointment, Fannin became embroiled in a controversy over impressment of private goods that would divide several Texan leaders and threaten the already fragile coalition trying to mount a concerted military effort against the powerful Mexican army.

The incident involved an American schooner, the *Hanna Elizabeth*, which had been grounded near Matagorda attempting to elude two Mexican gunboats. Challenging the Mexicans, a group of Texans from Matagorda managed to get possession of the American ship and escort it to Matagorda where the valuable supplies were plundered—allegedly under the direction of Samuel Rhoads Fisher. Since much of the material impressed ended up in private hands rather than Texan military quartermaster supply depots, the case ended up in civil court. The cargo aboard the *Hanna Elizabeth* has been likened to winning a giant lottery today.[4]

It is likely that James Fannin and Samuel Rhoads Fisher had met prior to the hostilities at Velasco and Gonzales. Matagorda in 1835 had become an important Texas port not far south of Fannin's plantation home at Brazoria. Fisher, who would later become secretary of the Texas navy during the republic era, had come to Texas from Pennsylvania in 1830 with his wife and four children. They had settled at Matagorda where he had become involved in politics and was representing Matagorda at San Felipe.

Fisher, like Fannin, was very opinionated, obstinate, and ambitious. It is not surprising the two men took a dislike to each other.

Fannin, who had been given almost unrestricted rights of impressment under the General Council's December 10 resolution establishing him as a recruiting agent, took exception to Fisher's handling of the *Hanna Elizabeth* incident.

Fisher had commanded a contingent of men from Matagorda who had christened themselves "marines" and, aided by the assistance of a Captain Hurd with another schooner, the *William Robbins*, had succeeded in docking the *Hanna Elizabeth* and appropriating the supplies.

From Matagorda, Fannin addressed a blistering letter to Governor Smith and the General Council on December 11, 1835, that accused Fisher and Hurd of what were essentially theft charges. "He (the Mexican officer)" Fannin wrote "accordingly surrendered his party; when captain Hurd and Fisher commenced having the goods landed . . . a sale was ordered, without survey or any sort of notice, even to the whole party who were out on the expedition."[5]

"Great pains being taken," Fannin continued, "to keep on board the wreck, those most likely to purchase dry goods, whilst the sale was to go on shore." Not only did Hurd and Fisher illegally confiscate the goods aboard the vessel, according to Fannin, but: "In a like manner, the vessel was sold, with all on board, without going on board and exposing the goods to the public eye. Captain Hurd appointed Fisher his agent, and between the two parties, all was claimed as a lawful prize, and brought in, and no one to receive one dollar."

Samuel Fisher was a volatile man who also would be the center of much controversy during his lifetime. That he would have ignored Fannin's letter and charges to the governor and General Council would have been unthinkable. His immediate response was an undated letter written sometime during December in which he gave his account of the incident and claims that the near capture of the *Hanna Elizabeth* was the result of cowardice on the part of the fifteen Americans and five Mexicans on board the vessel.[6] Fisher stops short of calling the American ship captured war bounty, but in correspondence dated the following January 11 (erroneously listed as "1835") and addressed "To The People of

Texas," he submits a long, detailed, and often rambling commentary and inventory of the incident in response to Fannin's charges.[7] Among the documents included were the testimonies of several of his Matagorda neighbors, dated December 17, stating they were allowed to take part in the auction of the property.

The January 11 document included a detailed list of those participating in the incident and a list of articles seized. Also included is a listing of the items sold, buyers, and amounts of sale. In this group of documents, Fisher does refer to the question of adjudication: "Whether it be a question of salvage, or whether she be a legal prize, she is, undoubtedly, the property of the salvors or captors, and as such, I present myself to you as the agent of the party interested."

Another of the documents, dated December 18, addresses the fact that he has received from fellow Matagorda neighbor and chairman of the General Council Richard Royster Royall a copy of Fannin's charges. Fannin, he charged, "has, in a most pains-taking manner, assumed to himself the duties of an inquisitor on our coast, and ferreted out through every vile and filthy channel, the base and false accusations trumped up in that letter."

Fisher then included in the correspondence a letter addressed to Fannin from Matagorda and dated January 12 in which he venomously attacked Fannin's character and reputation and essentially challenged him to seek out Fisher in response.

After refuting Fannin's basis for the charges, Fisher then attacks his character and reputation. "Has your character and condition in life so far removed you from the society of those witnesses, that you were compelled to make your charges from hearsay evidence?" he questioned. "You sought to bolster and prop up a falling reputation . . . and would direct the attention of the public and your fellow-citizens from your own breaches of humanity."

The "falling reputation" and "breaches of humanity" Fisher was referring to were Fannin's reputation as a slave trader back in Brazoria. It was a reputation that James Fannin had acquired early and never succeeded in overcoming. It was a reputation that would follow him even after death when Texas was searching among the participants of the revolution for heroes and martyrs.

But Fisher was direct in his charges: "Your African emigrants have scarce yet gained a residence in our country; their native lingo yet betrays their recent importation." Fisher also questions Fannin, "Did you expect to gull the Government and Council, and the public, by your whining affections..., when but a few months have rolled round since your last Ethiopian speculation and importation?"

Fisher further challenged how Fannin could question any other person's actions with regard to personal property in Texas when he himself had "disgraced its borders by the introduction of slaves, natives of, and immediately from, Africa?"

In conclusion, Fisher notifies Fannin that he desires no further correspondence. In an apparent challenge to defend his honor, Fisher tells Fannin he wishes "to remind you, with what you are already acquainted, that my residence is in the town of Matagorda."

Fannin may have heard about the challenge later, but he probably never saw a copy of the letter. By this time, his military career with the volunteer army was moving forward at a quickening pace.

At the time he penned his letter condemning Fisher, he had also started performing his duties as chief recruiting agent. On December 12 he wrote the governor and General Council recommending Joseph Pedelton as collector of duties for the port of Matagorda. Six days later he notified the politicians at San Felipe that he was appointing three sub-agents to raise men and arms and procure horses with the instructions that they issue certificates for all private property taken.

On December 20 Sam Houston issued orders from Washington-on-the-Brazos in which he addressed Fannin as "Colonel J.W. Fannin Jr., 1st Regiment Artillery." "You will on receipt of this proceed without delay to Matagorda," Houston wrote, "and there establish your Head Quarters for a recruiting Rendezvous you will report your arrival there to Head Quarters."[8]

Houston further issued brief instructions on the recruitment of officers and ordered Fannin to rendezvous his officers by the first of March. "Much is expected from your known skill & capability" Houston concluded.

It was in this position as a recruiter that James W. Fannin Jr. found his abilities and energies best suited for the Texan revolutionary cause. Although his dream of a mass migration of U.S. Army officers into Texas never developed, he was nevertheless able to effect the recruitment in the United States of several companies of volunteers willing to fight for the Texan cause. His most notable success came from his native Georgia.

Within days of the issuance of Sam Houston's orders to rendezvous at Matagorda, the Georgia Battalion under the command of William Ward would arrive at Velasco.

Their appearance in the Texas struggle would alter forever the direction and conduct of James Fannin's command and his place in Texas history.

1	Jenkins, *PTR*, 3:61-4.
2	Ibid., 91-3.
3	Ibid., 142-4.
4	Guthrie, *Texas Forgotten Ports*, Volume I, pg. 132.
5	Jenkins, *PTR*, 3:158-60.
6	Ibid., 3;387-8.
7	Ibid., 4:211-223.
8	Ibid., 3:272.

Chapter Nine
Arrival of the Georgia Volunteers

While Fannin, Royall, and Fisher were feuding along the Texas coast and Houston, Travis, Governor Smith, and the General Council were bickering at San Felipe and Washington-on-the-Brazos, a group of men was assembling at Macon, Georgia.

Their objective was to travel to Texas and enlist in the Texan cause. Later correspondence would indicate they had no idea of the political quagmire they were entering.

From the heart of Georgia two men, Dr. Robert Collins and William Ward, began enlisting volunteers to join the Texans. At a public meeting in Macon on November 12, 1835, Ward enlisted one hundred twenty men from the central Georgia communities of Macon and Milledgeville and the town of Columbus on the Alabama and Georgia borders. The Georgia volunteers were formed into three companies, armed with weapons from the Georgia state arsenal, and supplied in large part by the personal contributions of Collins and Ward.

After formation, the units traveled south towards New Orleans through the Georgia community of Knoxville, in Crawford County, where Joanna Troutman presented them with a unit banner. The flag was constructed of white silk with a blue single star. The flag is credited with being the basis for the "Lone Star" tradition associated with the revolution.

From Crawford County, Ward and his three companies continued south through Mobile, Alabama, to New Orleans. By the time they reached New Orleans, they had recruited additional volunteers and totaled around two hundred men. From New Orleans, they chartered four ships and, following the recent example of one company of New Orleans Greys, sailed across the gulf to the Texas port of Velasco, arriving on December 20, 1835.

Ward's Georgia Battalion entered Texas with a flag of white silk, bearing a blue five-pointed star and the inscription, "Liberty or Death." It was unfurled at Velasco on January 8, 1836, and later carried to Goliad and is claimed by some historians to be the basis for the "Lone Star" legacy in Texas. This replica is displayed today at Presidio La Bahia.

The arrival was anything but smooth, however, when one of the ships—the schooner *America*—beached on one of the treacherous sandbars at the mouth of the Brazos. As the men made a dangerous and tricky transfer into open boats to evacuate the wrecked ship, several of the Georgia Battalion broke into the liquor supplies and became roaring drunk and refused to leave until faced with forced evacuation.[1]

One of the volunteers traveling with these Georgia volunteers was a young man by the name of John Sowers Brooks. Through a series of letters to various members of his family back in Georgia, we are given a firsthand account of the Georgia Battalion after they arrived in Texas.

Ward, Brooks, and the other Georgia volunteers were met at Velasco by Fannin on December 20. Brooks' first letter home—to his father—describes what the Georgians found upon arrival at Velasco. The letter is a curious mixture of youthful naivete and optimism tempered by a realization of the complexities and treacheries of Anglo Texan politics.

"... my fate is now inseparably connected with that of Texas," he wrote his father. "From what I have learned since my arrival here, I do not consider the service extraordinarily dangerous."[2]

Brooks reports the recent victories over the Mexicans, particularly the battle for Bexar, but admits, "All is confusion—it is contemplated to reinforce us and then detach us to attack the city of Matamoras. . . ."

He reports that he has been appointed adjutant of one of the companies and requests his father have letters of reference forwarded to Sam Houston and James Fannin. "You shall never blush for your wayward boy's conduct on the field of battle," he reassured his father in conclusion.

The Georgia Battalion arrived in Velasco on December 20 and three days later officially presented themselves for service in Texas. On that date Ward, three of his captains, and several other officers addressed a resolution to Fannin. The resolution read more like a salute to the Georgia they had left behind rather than the Texas they were about to enter.

"As Georgians we hail you [Fannin] as a brother, and recur with pleasing sensations to the home of your and our nativity," the battalion recorded that day.[3] Fannin was further saluted in that "Georgia's honor and chivalry stood proudly vindicated in your person" and that "it is deeply sensible to the kind partiality which you have exhibited for the State we claim to represent."

For his part, Fannin officially responded in writing two days later, on Christmas day, in which he was the consummate politician and diplomat: "ere I forget myself a 'Georgian' or neglect her warm-hearted sons, in whatever clime we may meet."[4] The response was filled with references to Washington and Jefferson, knights of the holy cross, and the Georgians' "legitimate descent from the true stock of 1776."

The December 25 letter provides little new information about James Fannin or his thoughts during this difficult period. One brief reference near the end, however, does once again reveal the ambition and desire for fame that was characteristic of the man. "Let me exhort you to look to the past and remember the 'Brazos Guards,'... which I have had the honor and good fortune to lead to victory," Fannin exhorted the Georgia Battalion—referring to his role in the battle at Concepcion.

Fannin also addressed a letter, dated simply "December 1835" to Major James Kerr, a member of the Council, in which he urged the calling of another convention and unabashedly campaigned for promotion to brigadier general. "With respect to the military, one major-general has been elected. His command, of course, in a military point of view, would be a division—say two brigades. If two brigades, you should then appoint two brigadier-generals...."[5]

But the spirit of camaraderie between Fannin and the Georgia Battalion was not being shared by all along the Texas gulf coast. On that same date, Christmas day, Stephen Austin addressed a letter to Richard Royster Royall, a member of the executive council in San Felipe, from the hamlet of Quintana just across the mouth of the Brazos River and Velasco.

James Fannin, Richard Royall, John Wharton, and Branch Archer all had one characteristic in common with Stephen Austin: They had each accepted Austin's invitation to immigrate to his colony and settle in Texas. What they did not share in common with Austin was his dream of a unified Texas free of political parties and self-serving adventurers.

Austin had been replaced as commander of the Texan forces and appointed with John Wharton to travel to the United States as emissaries to enlist support and funding for the Texan struggle. That Christmas Day in 1835 he was at Quintana on his way to New Orleans when he wrote his old neighbor from Matagorda, Richard Royall.

In a rambling letter, Austin exhibited moments of depression, even despair, over the course of events taking place. Austin, a man known and respected throughout Texas and the United States as a diplomat, appears almost gullible and naïve in his writings to Royall.

"The affairs of Texas are more entangled than I suspected they were," he wrote.[6] "I have been deceived and treated with bad faith...What ought the owners of the soil, the old settlers of Texas, who have redeemed this country from the wilderness and made it what it is, think of men who will collect the signatures of persons on their first landing. . . ."

Austin was not referring here to the recently arrived Georgia Battalion or any of the other volunteers gathering at Velasco and Quintana. He was referring to his fellow emissary, John Wharton, whom he accused of attempting to take power for his own selfish advancement.

The letter, which Austin indicated he was posting with James Fannin, accused Wharton and the other members of the War Party of "saddling the people with an army, and a debt, and involving them in a war that will be difficult to bear." The war Austin was referring to was the move to advance on Matamoros and take the fighting into Mexico.

A Matamoros expedition was not a new idea: Houston had earlier endorsed the proposal but had now retracted his support. Now, on the eve of 1836 and after the victory at San Antonio, Wharton and other speculators—namely F.W. Johnson and James Grant—were openly demanding the military evacuate San Antonio and Goliad and march on Mexico.

Not only was this idea sheer folly, Austin felt, but it also was dangerous in that it guaranteed the alienation of the Federalist Mexicans who had supported political autonomy for Coahuila and Texas but would not participate in a declaration of independence from, or war against, their native Mexico.

Fannin, too, supported a Matamoros expedition in addition to his other pursuits of personal ambition. This does not appear to have placed him at odds with Austin, however, who concluded his letter to Royall by stating: "I beg leave to recommend my friend, Col. Fannin, to you and my friends generally as a man who is identified with the soil and interests of Texas, and as an honorable soldier."

Fannin, it appears, in his short tenure on the Mims Plantation at Brazoria had established a good rapport and reputation with Austin.

With the passing of the Christmas holiday, James Fannin resumed his recruiting duties in earnest. On December 28, from Matagorda, he wrote Captain J.W.E. Wallace, another Austin Colony settler, and ordered him to begin recruiting men without delay. Fannin also instructed him on the structuring of the companies that Wallace was ordered to create and admonished him, "Much is expected of you."[7]

And then, as 1835 drew to an end, Sam Houston issued an order to Fannin. Issued on December 30, it is not clear when Captain George Washington Poe, Houston's adjutant general, delivered it to Fannin.

The order to Fannin was very brief and to the point:

> If possible I wish you to report in person at headquarters as soon as practicable after the receipt of this order.
>
> You can detail such officer of your command as you may deem proper to succeed you during your absence from the district which has been assigned to you.
>
> Lieut Colo Neil has been ordered in command of the Post of Bejar
>
> The detail being special and at the time indispensable he will remain until further orders.[8]

Fannin, preparing to depart for Matamoros along the coast with the Georgia Battalion and other volunteers assembling at the mouth of the Brazos, refused Houston's request to report to Washington-on-the-Brazos. While Houston did write Fannin to report "if possible," Fannin's response prompted Captain Poe to file the following statement:

> [Addressed:] To Col. J.W. Fannin
> Brazoria
> Texas
> Capt. Poe
> [Endorsed:] Gen'l Houston to Fannin
> left in my hands by Fannin

The above is in the handwriting of Capt. Geo. W.
Poe—A.A. General who delivered this order to Col. Fannin by
whom it was ignored.

A.J.H.[Andrew Jackson Houston]7/2/23

Filed 13th June 1835
D.P. Richardson[9]

Despite listing a filing date of June 1835 that was obviously wrong—the report was posted in 1837—the document is significant in that it indicates Fannin did not report to Houston out of critical necessity—but, instead, out of an act of simply ignoring Houston's directive.

This affront to Houston would not be the last instance of Fannin ignoring or refusing the commander in chief's orders. On this occasion, Houston was attempting to rally all volunteers along the coast and direct them to the port of Copano—which was exactly what Fannin himself was attempting to do with the Georgia Battalion.

In another set of undated orders, also later filed on June 13, 1837, Houston ordered Fannin, the Georgia Battalion, and all other volunteers to report to Copano and begin building a permanent port there. Again, Houston was very clear in his directive: "It is ordered that the volunteers remain in posse[ss]ion of the station [meaning in command of the post] until such time as they will receive orders to advance.... Let no campaign be undertaken without orders.[10]

This directive Fannin appears not to have ignored, but more directly, chose to disobey. It appears that while Houston was counseling patience and restraint, James Fannin had finally begun to achieve his goals. The Georgia Battalion had arrived in Texas, and he now had a private army of volunteers with which to take action and create a name for himself.

While Houston sought consolidation of forces, Fannin sought to begin the campaign against Mexico. The fact that Houston and the Council had ignored his requests for a generalship seems to have been a moot point: Such a position would come quickly enough after military victories in the field.

On January 8, 1836, and in direct defiance of Houston's orders to report to Copano and build a port, Fannin published the following notice to the public in the *Telegraph and Texas Register*:

ATTENTION, VOLUNTEERS!
To the West, face: March!

An expedition to the west has been ordered by the General Council, and the Volunteers from Bexar, Goliad, Velasco and elsewhere, are ordered to rendezvous at San Patricio, between the 24th and 27th instant, and report to the officer in command. The fleet convoy will sail from Velasco, under my charge, on or about the 18th, and all who feel disposed to join it, and aid in keeping the war out of Texas, and at the same time cripple the enemy in their resources at home, are invited to enter the ranks forthwith.

J.W. Fannin, Jr.

January 8th, 1836.[11]

This directive is a direct affront to and refusal of Sam Houston's orders on several counts. Rather than rendezvousing at Copano, as Houston had ordered, Fannin calls for a convergence at the Irish colony of San Patricio, south of Goliad.

Houston had demanded that the volunteers remain in possession of the port at Copano until he issued orders to advance. Fannin in this appeal calls for volunteers to "keep the war out of Texas" and "cripple their resources at home," which was basically a call to advance on Matamoros.

Choosing to ignore Houston's orders, Fannin claims that he had received orders from the General Council and "Volunteers from Bexar, Goliad, Velasco and elsewhere." In reality, what he was referring to were not orders, but designs of James Grant and Robert Morris in Bexar, Philip Dimmitt at Goliad, and himself at Velasco.

Although it had already occurred in fact, on January 8, 1836, James Fannin published in public what Austin had already realized. The rebellion against Mexico was no longer being waged by the original Anglo settlers against a corrupt Mexican government.

It was now, officially on this date, being waged by land speculators who had incalculable wealth to be gained by Texan independence.

Talk of constitutional reform and personal liberties was now just empty rhetoric. Texas was quickly filling up with land-hungry volunteers and greedy lawyers and speculators. And James Fannin was positioned at Velasco in January of 1836 to lead the way with his Georgia Battalion.

But he miscalculated one very formidable obstacle between himself and his dream of obtaining a generalship and leading an army against Mexico: Sam Houston.

Houston had received word of the unauthorized Matamoros campaign and, incensed by Johnson's blatant confiscation of the men, armament, and supplies at Bexar and the Alamo, wrote to Governor Smith of his intentions to intercept and stop the expedition. On January 8, 1836—the same day as Fannin's call to arms—Sam Houston wrote Smith in private correspondence from Washington-on-the-Brazos:

> Dear Sir, I will set out in less than an hour for the Army. I will do all that I can. I am told that Frank Johnson and Fannin have obtained from the Military Committee orders to Proceed and reduce Matamoras. It may not be so. There was no Quroum, and the Council could not give power. I will proceed with great haste to the Army and there I can know all. I hope you will send me an Extract of Austin's letter about the New Confederacy, and what he says about the "Capitulations" of Bexar. Please write me about this.
>
> Sam Houston[12]

James Fannin, with his limited knowledge of the rough-and-tumble politics of the American South and especially Jacksonian Democratic politics, could not have foreseen how the wily Sam Houston—a product of those turbulent practices—could sabotage his plans.

As early as mid-December 1835 the General Council had attempted to dilute Houston's authority as commander in chief by ordering him out of San Felipe to Washington-on-the-Brazos. In response, Houston had initiated a counteroffensive to thwart the growing popularity of Francis Johnson and James Grant in the aftermath of the victory at Bexar.

Houston issued orders that would have placed a Matamoros campaign in the hands of one of the few men in Texas he trusted, James Bowie. He also issued a call for volunteers to rendezvous at Copano for formation under the command of Fannin.

By these means Houston expected to place an effective body of troops under Bowie and Fannin, whom he seems to have also trusted at this point, and to neutralize Grant by starting Bowie to Matamoros first. Should the feint appear promising of results, it was in Houston's mind to appear in person at the head of the army and avail himself of the glory.[13]

Houston caught up with Grant and his mercenary army at Goliad in mid-January only to find that the Scottish land speculator had also raided the considerable supplies from Dimmitt at La Bahia as he had done Neill at the Alamo earlier.

He also discovered that Bowie had remained at Goliad—unaware of Houston's order to organize a march southward. Now, Houston dispatched him to Bexar with orders to survey the Alamo with regards to destroying it and withdrawing with the considerable cannon and armament back to Gonzales.

Grant, who had by now assumed for himself the title of commander in chief, ignored Houston and departed for the small Irish community of Refugio to the south of Goliad. Houston, correctly analyzing the situation and mood of the men, was content to join the expedition and lobby against continuing past Refugio to Matamoros. At Refugio, Houston delivered a stirring address to the troops. Total and complete independence from Mexico was the only viable choice for Texas, he said, and to that end there was to be a convention in March.

Houston managed to hit upon the fears and resentments of the volunteers and satisfactorily answer them. Increasingly, the volunteer militias were vocally questioning where the Texas settlers were when the fighting was going on. More unsettling to them, they saw the governor and council as insensitive to their needs in providing desperately needed supplies and food.

But now, in Houston's final address to them, they were reassured that the governor and council had not given up on them and that the local Texans did support their efforts. Houston had also given them a clear objective: separation and independence from Mexico. And he had given them a promise of supplies. Once again they were fighting men with military objectives. Grant's promises of untold riches to be plundered south of the Rio Grande no longer seemed that enticing.

But while Houston could undo Grant's scheming at Refugio, he could not prevent the unraveling of the government he had left behind at San Felipe. On January 10 Governor Smith attempted to dissolve the Council, which in turn impeached him and named James W. Robinson as his successor. Smith, claiming that there was no quorum present and the vote was null and void, refused to give up the office, and as a result both men claimed to be governor. In the midst of this political turmoil, the issue of the Matamoros expedition continued to divide the Council—many of whom openly opposed Houston's leadership.

On January 20, 1836, Texas was fractionalized almost beyond repair. James Fannin was at Velasco preparing to sail for Copano with the Georgia Battalion, Houston was at Refugio dissuading Grant's soldiers from continuing south, Governor Smith had attempted to dissolve the Council, which had then attempted to impeach him. A disillusioned Stephen Austin was in the United States, and Neill was stationed in the indefensible Alamo mission with the pitiful nucleus of what had previously been the elite of the Texan fighting forces and no supplies.

Houston, who had his hands full trying to convince the Greys and other volunteers with Grant to abandon their campaign on Mexico, found his situation further complicated by the absence of Fannin, Ward, or the Georgia Battalion at Refugio when they arrived. That evening F.W. Johnson, Grant's partner, arrived from San Felipe and was shown into Houston's quarters. The General Council in San Felipe had deposed Governor Smith and placed Fannin in overall charge of the Matamoros expedition, giving him powers as great as those of the despot in Mexico. Houston's command had been taken from him.[14]

Deposed Governor Smith, attempting to reconcile the split in government, wrote the Council on January 12 apologizing and urging constraint. He did, however, specify his objections to the Council placing Fannin in charge of the volunteers: "If the act of your body was ratified by me, it is plain and evident, that neither the Commander-in-Chief, the Council, nor the Executive, could have any control over him."[15]

January 21, 1836, dawned as a very troubled day for Anglo Texas. Sam Houston, stripped of his command, left for the piney woods of east Texas. James Walker Fannin Jr., poised to leave the port at Velasco, discovered most of his demands had been granted. He had repeatedly requested a command position, a "post of danger," and an advance against the Mexican government and army.

On January 21 he commanded the Georgia Battalion and the volunteers awaiting him to the south, while unknown to him his "post of danger" lay in disrepair at La Bahia in Goliad and he was now officially commissioned to execute the Matamoros expedition.

He was now the military commander he had dreamed of becoming.

1   Jenkins, *PTR*, 3:295-7.
2   Ibid.
3   Ibid., 3:305-6.
4   Ibid., 3:322-3.
5   Ibid., 3:386.
6   Ibid., 3:315-7.
7   Ibid., 3:349-50.
8   Ibid., 3:372.
9   Ibid.
10 Ibid., 3:398.
11 Ibid., 3:445.
12 Ibid., 3:446.
13 James, Marquis, *The Raven, a Biography of Sam Houston* (New York City: Blue Ribbon Books, Inc., 1929), pg. 220.
14 de Bruhl, Marshall, *Sword of San Jacinto*, pg. 177.
15 Jenkins, *PTR*, 3:499.

Chapter Ten
Advance to Refugio

On December 20 Sam Houston ordered Fannin to advance to Matagorda to establish his recruiting post. In another directive he had ordered Fannin, the Georgia Battalion, and all other volunteers to report to Copano and begin building a permanent port there.

In 1836 the port at Copano was literally the door to the interior of Texas. For Santa Anna, loss of the use of the port would require an extended overland march across desolate territory to reach the centers of Mexican Texas: San Antonio de Bexar and Goliad. For Sam Houston, any supply and reinforcement of the Texan army from the United States would require possession and control of the port.

El Copano had served as probably the first Texas port for nearly a century when the Texas Revolution broke out. Historians generally agree that Copano Bay had been used as a place to offload supplies destined for La Bahia and Bexar as early as 1750.[1]

By the time Stephen Austin had started his colony further north at the mouth of the Brazos River, the port at Copano had already been established as the supply point for Spanish missions at Refugio and Goliad. After Austin's Colony had been established, Irish immigrants entered Texas through Copano and colonized the communities of San Patricio and Refugio.

The Texas coastline slopes southwest from the mouth of the Sabine River at the Louisiana border. Along the coast, there is a series of islands and peninsulas that form a protective barrier for the natural coastline. It was through Aransas Pass that ships in 1836 accessed Copano Bay and the port of Copano.

Because the port had become the entrance point for so many American immigrants, the Mexican government had established a military garrison and customshouse as early as 1833.

Sam Houston recognized the port's strategic importance when, in several dispatches, he ordered James Fannin and others to secure and develop the landing for Texan use. All that remained of the Mexican custom's office in 1836 was a single, one-story building that had been used as a warehouse.

Thus, toward the end of January in 1836, while Sam Houston was struggling to subvert Grant's Matamoros expedition at Refugio, James Fannin was preparing his Georgia Battalion and other volunteers at Velasco.

On January 12, 1836, he made an ambitious contract with Joseph Mims at his plantation in Brazoria. The contract recites that Mims owned three thousand acres of land on the San Bernard; that he had eight Negroes, men and boys, sixty head of cattle, two yoke of oxen and carts and yokes, four work mules and two horses, five plows and gear, three hundred bushels of corn and eighty head of hogs. All these lands and chattels he put into a farming partnership with Fannin at a valuation of $25,000. Fannin put in twenty-three African Negroes, to wit, twelve men, seven women, and four boys, valued at $17,250. He bound himself to pay Mims the difference of $7,750 in five equal installments. "But should the tranquillity of the country authorize it, said Fannin is at liberty to pay the whole of said debt in negroes at a fair valuation."[2]

Whether Fannin or Mims were aware of it at the time it was signed, the contract effectively ended James Fannin's short tenure as a Texas businessman in Austin's Colony. He would now be, for the rest of his life, the soldier he had always aspired to be.

General Cos, who had been sent back to Mexico overland after his humiliating surrender concluding the battle for Bexar, had arrived at Copano with four hundred men and supplies the previous autumn. Now, Fannin was preparing to depart for the port with his Georgia Battalion and other volunteers he had collected at Velasco.

Although Fannin did record some correspondence with Texan leaders at San Felipe during this period, it is through the letters of one of the members of the Georgia Battalion that we get a first-hand account of the events taking place around Velasco.

In a letter to his father dated January 18, John Sowers Brooks describes the countryside around the mouth of the Brazos as "some of the richest and prettiest land in the world."[3] This is in direct contrast to the harsh characterizations of Velasco by Burr Duvall and other later volunteers, but Brooks writes in glowing terms of the land and natural resources.

Two days later, another letter to his father describes the political situation as he interpreted events going on around him: "The 'Georgia Battalion of Permanent Volunteers,' to which I am attached in the capacity of Adjutant will embark tomorrow morning (the 21st) on some vessels lying in the mouth of the Brazos and proceed to Copano lower down the coast for the purpose of forming a junction with 6 or 700 other troops and then taking up the line of march for the invasion of Mexico."[4]

Brooks, who as newly appointed adjutant of the battalion may have had access to Fannin's confidences, reported that either Houston or Fannin would lead the attack on Matamoros. The goal of the expedition, according to the young volunteer, was not the occupation of Mexico itself but to secure a base of operations from which to "carry the war out of Texas" while giving "employment to the Volunteers."

Brooks then launches a very detailed analysis of the political situation in Texas including the feuding parties and the issue of independence and sovereignty as opposed to federal union with Mexico. He informs his father that they had just learned of the overthrow of Governor Smith by the Council.

In a series of postscripts, he offers two additional pieces of significant information. Brooks, who was himself a veteran of the United States Marine Corps, wrote, "There is but one other professional soldier in the Battallion, besides myself, Sergeant Major Chadwick, from West Point." This statement is important because it shows that Fannin's call for a cadre of West Point or at least U.S. Army officers had not succeeded. While the volunteers were, in fact, beginning to arrive in Texas to support the cause, they were not the professionally trained soldiers Fannin had sought.

Another postscript states that "... our next object will be the City of Tampico where there is attack upon that place by Gen. Mexia and the result. All the Americans who were taken were shot...". Because of this statement, it is certain that James Fannin and the volunteers accompanying him were aware of Santa Anna's proclaimed policy of executing armed pirates and mercenaries entering Texas—as they themselves were doing at that very exact time.

In addition to preparing passage to Copano, Fannin continued his campaign for a position as brigadier general with the new governor and the divided Council. From Velasco on January 21 he wrote "His Excellency James W. Robinson, Governor" and the General Council that he was prepared to sail for Copano that evening on the schooners *Columbus* and *Flora*. He announced that he had about two hundred fifty men at Velasco and was planning to stop over at Matagorda and collect another one hundred volunteers calling themselves the Alabama Red Rovers.[5]

In a major miscalculation, he announced that he would be met at Copano with the necessary men and carts to transport the provisions and supplies to Refugio.

Fannin also candidly addresses the political feuding going on among Texan leaders and his role in commanding with Sam Houston. "With regard to any anticipated difficulties with the general-in-chief, you need have no sort of apprehensions; I shall never make any myself." While this statement may in itself seem conciliatory, it has an underlying threat directed to Houston and his command strategies.

Besides suggesting that any future difficulties between himself and Houston would be the commander in chief's doing, Fannin also issues the succinct warning: "... should general Houston be ready and willing to take command, and march direct ahead, and execute your orders, and the volunteers are, willing to submit to it, or a reasonable part, of them, I shall not say nay, but will do all in my power to produce harmony and concert of action, and will go forward in any, capacity."

While this statement may also seem conciliatory, it too has an underlying threat: If the volunteer soldiers do not follow Houston's leadership, he is willing to take command. Fannin also acknowledges that the expedition itself is one cause of complaint designed to displace Houston as commander. "But rest assured of one thing," he writes the acting governor and Council, "I will go where you have sent me, and will do what you have ordered me, if possible."

In a situation of political turmoil and challenge to Sam Houston's generalship, it appears that James Fannin is, once again, making himself available as Houston's replacement.

In this long and often rambling correspondence, Fannin once more advises the leaders in San Felipe of his military assessment of the situation along the coast and the makeup of the Texan armed forces: regular and volunteer.

He also directly attacks ex-governor Smith and accuses him of fostering further dissent and even conspiratorial motives, suggesting that Santa Anna himself might be using the turmoil among Anglo leaders to "accomplish the downfall of the government, which certainly would be finished if 'His Excellency' should go by the board."

He also laments what he interprets as Smith's criticism of the volunteers at Bexar who had ignored his orders and launched an assault on the city the previous December.

According to Fannin, this letter from Smith to undermine Robinson's authority and sway the volunteers was addressed to William Ward, the commander of the Georgia Battalion.

Ward, it appears, was unwilling to get involved in the Fannin-Robinson/Smith-Houston dispute at this time. Noting that Ward was "at present reluctant to give a copy, or I should forward it to you for use," Fannin also pointed out that "It will be remembered that he [Ward] is a stranger to Governor Smith, having just arrived in the country."

Although the situation in San Felipe was still entangled and confused with the result that nobody—executive or Council—seemed to be in charge, James Walker Fannin Jr. made absolutely clear with this letter that he felt Texas' and his own personal fortunes lay with acting governor Robinson.

The following day the volunteers began boarding the ships. One, the *Columbus,* had been used two months earlier to transport Captain Robert Morris' company of New Orleans Greys from that city to Velasco. It was now employed to transport the Georgia Battalion, and Fannin also issued the following directive to Captain Appleton of the schooner *Flora*:

Velasco 22nd. January 1836

Sir You will forthwith place your vessel in sailing orders and take on board Captns. Tickners and Guerreas companies and such baggage & provisions as may be, to guard by them, and hold yourself subject to my orders—to proceed from this port to that of the Aransas and up to Copano—
Given under my hand & Seal &c. &c.

J.W. Fanning Jr. Seal
Col Comt
Agt. Provl Govt. Texas.[6]

Fannin's reference to "Captn. Tickner" was in fact Captain Isaac Ticknor of Montgomery, Alabama, who had arrived with his company of Alabama Greys only a few days before Colonel Fannin sailed.[7] "Captn. Guerreas" referred to Captain Luis Guerra's Tampico Company,[8] who were veterans of Mexia's Tampico expedition and experienced Mexican artillerymen. Fannin himself sailed on the *Invincible*.

On January 28 Fannin reported that the ships had sailed to Aransas Pass—the mouth of Copano Bay—but were stranded due to wind and the treacherous sandbar. [9]

The letter, addressed to Robinson and the General Council, also announces that General Mexia had informed him that Santa Anna had arrived in Matamoros. Fannin recommends the politicians in San Felipe issue a call for a general convergence of Texan forces at San Antonio and Goliad or else Santa Anna's advance would require massive retreating and possibly disastrous defeats.

He concluded the letter by promising Robinson and the Council to report again once he had reached Copano or Refugio.

The next recorded correspondence from Fannin is a series of receipts issued in his name and dated February 1, 1836—indicating he had arrived at the port of Copano by that date. In those memorandums, Fannin acknowledges receipt from Captain Appleton of the *Flora* of food provisions and seventy gallons of brandy, which made up one-third of the expenses.[10] On February 3 he also issued a voucher payable to Captain Appleton for $470 for transporting troops from Quintana to Copano.[11]

Upon his arrival at Copano, Fannin was running far behind schedule. Sam Houston had been puzzled to find that he and the Georgia Battalion had not arrived at Refugio when he addressed Grant's volunteers on January 21. On January 30 F.W. Johnson wrote the General Council from San Patricio, "I am still without any intimation of the movements of Col. Fanning, and quite at a loss to account for the want of due information on this head—"[12]

On February 2, while Fannin was consolidating his men and supplies at Copano, Houston's adjutant general George Poe was stationed at Columbia. On that date he wrote Houston in Nacogdoches: ". . . There is a report here that you have been super-seded in the Command of the Army by Johnson & Fanning—if so please let us know what is the state of the case—I speak in behalf of several officers here who *do not* nor *will not* know any other General than Sam Houston. . . ."[13] Poe also admonished Houston: "But beware of Fanning—he is I think aiming at the highest command."

While Fannin had anticipated he would have men and wagons awaiting him at Copano the following week, it was noted that Fannin's command was scouring the countryside for carts to move supplies toward Refugio.[14]

Fannin confirmed this on February 4 when he wrote Robinson and the General Council, "I have the honor to inform you, that I have succeeded in desenbarking my men, and have marched them up to the mission of Refugio, a distance of fifteen miles—I have not yet succeeded in getting Carts and Teams, to transport our baggage lc—tho, I hope to have them tomorrow—or the next day—."[15]

Fannin also notifies the acting governor and Council that John-son is awaiting him some fifty miles away at San Patricio and that together they will "take up the line of march for Rio Grande."

Despite reports that the Mexican army was organizing at Matamoros, Fannin still harbored the belief that a quick strike would end the war. "Matamoras is poorly supplied with troops—

our friends [the Federalists] are in power—I have reason to believe, that if a quick movement is made, not a shot will be fired," he prophesied.

And so, on February 4, 1836, James Fannin finally arrived at Refugio to find that much of his dream had been fulfilled. He was now, in Houston's absence, the commander in chief of Texan forces, and although still not a brigadier general, he was in control of the majority of Anglo volunteer soldiers occupying Texas. And with the General Council's encouragement, he was finally in charge of the infamous Matamoros Expedition.

Although Houston still addressed his official communications to Governor Smith and the garrison at Bexar also sided with Smith, the volunteers under Fannin and Johnson corresponded mainly with the Council.[16]

Although Sam Houston had succeeded in stopping Grant's expedition to Matamoros, the Scotsman had continued south anyway with a skeleton army of about seventy men where he was awaiting Fannin's arrival. But Houston himself was now in east Texas on furlough.

The command of James Walker Fannin Jr. had just begun.

1   An excellent history of the Texas coastline and historical ports can be found in a three-volume set by Keith Guthrie titled *Texas Forgotten Ports* (Austin: Eakin Press). Volume I outlines the histories of the mid-Gulf ports including Aransas Bay and El Copano.

2   Wharton, *Remember Goliad*, pp. 26-7.

3   Jenkins, *PTR*, 4:55-57.

4   Ibid., 4;82-85.

5   Ibid., 4;103-6.

6   Ibid., 4;114.

7   Davenport, Harbert, "The Men of Goliad," *The Southwestern Historical Quarterly*, Vol. XLVIII, No. 1, July 1939, pg. 15.

8   O'Connor, Kathryn Stoner, *The Presidio La Bahia del Espiritu Santo de Zuniga 1721 to 1846* (Austin: Von Boeckmann-Jones Co., 1966), pg. 117.

9   Jenkins, *PTR*, 4:165-6.

10   Ibid., 4:232 and 4:233.

11   Ibid., 4:247.

12   Ibid., 4:197-9.

13   Ibid., 4:241.

14   Guthrie, *Texas Forgotten Ports,* Volume II, pg. 16.

15   Jenkins, *PTR*, 4:255-7.

16   Smith, Ruth Cumby, "James W. Fannin, Jr., in the Texas Revolution," *The Southwestern Historical Quarterly*, Vol. XXIII, No. 3, January 1920, pg. 178.

Chapter Eleven

Retreat to Goliad

James Fannin was still in the process of transporting supplies and materials from Copano when, on February 7, he received a dispatch that would ultimately impact the effectiveness of his leadership and alter his field strategy in ways that would doom his command in the eyes of most subsequent Texas historians.

He had arrived at Copano after issuing a call to arms and announcing a rendezvous at Refugio with the stated goal of taking the war into Mexico. He had arrived at Refugio with a clear mandate and direct—although disputed—leadership over the greatest assembly of volunteers in Mexican Texas.

On February 7, 1836, he was poised to organize those men and advance south to Matamoros. But it was also on this day that a courier brought him an urgent message from Major Robert Morris at San Patricio.

Morris, a former New Orleans Grey commander and veteran of the battle of Bexar, had ignored Houston's arguments and continued on with Grant and Johnson. Unknown to Fannin, the men had divided their small force and Morris had remained behind at San Patricio.

The urgent message, based upon information given Morris by Guadalupe Victoria alcalde Placido Benavides, gave Fannin his first idea of the Mexican opposition he was facing.

Matamoros, according to Morris and Benavides, now garrisoned a force of over one thousand Mexican soldiers including three hundred experienced, veteran cavalrymen from the interior of Mexico. More reinforcements were expected, and the Mexican staff at the highest level was preparing a massive invasion to reclaim Texas.

"One thousand men are already on the Rio Frio," Morris wrote, plus "one thousand more on the march near the Rio Grande destined for some point of Texas."[1]

Many Texans had felt that General Cos' surrender and evacuation from Bexar had signaled an end to Mexican determination to maintain control over the Anglo settlers. Northern Mexico, after all, had been free of all Mexican soldiers once Cos had retreated with his army south of the Rio Grande.

Other Texans, including Austin and Houston, had warned that Santa Anna would return—probably in the spring of 1836—but the warnings had been either unheeded or acknowledged with only a token effort to prepare defenses.

While commander in chief, Houston had recommended a withdrawal from Bexar and Goliad to Gonzales, but Bowie and Neill were determined to hold on to the flimsy Alamo fortress in Bexar and had chosen instead to fortify rather than retreat.

Morris' report was particularly important not only because it verified the predictions of a massive invasion by Santa Anna but also specified where the Mexican campaign would be directed.

"It is believed that an attack is intended on Goliad and Bejar simultaneously," Morris continued in his letter. He qualified his information by naming Benavides as his source. "This information he (Benavides) received from the first alcalde of Matamoras. He has been within 20 leagues of the town and corresponded with him."

Morris further relayed Benavides' recommendations based upon this information: "Don Placido deems it of the utmost importance that troops be sent to Bejar as well as others retained in the direction and also assures me that Santa Anna wishes to draw the troops of Texas out to Matamoros in hopes to throw a strong force in their rear while he makes his attack on the upper part of the Colonies."

Santa Anna had sworn to "Take Texas or lose Mexico," Fannin was informed.

Fannin, at Refugio only three days, had no way of knowing if Morris' report was accurate. Benavides was a highly respected and loyal *Tejano*, and the information he was reporting was only a verification of what others—including Houston—had prophesied.

Still, Anglo Texas was rife with rumors and false reports. Without the advantage of a second opinion or means of verification, Fannin had no way of knowing the paramount importance contained in the information provided him that day in Morris' letter.

Readily apparent, however, were several points that Fannin considered with regards to his own command. First, not only was Santa Anna responding, but he was doing so with massive numbers. Secondly, he was advocating a simultaneous attack on both Bexar and Goliad, meaning that he would be dispatching at least two armies across the Rio Grande. A third and very critical point that was not lost on Fannin was the prediction that Santa Anna wanted to "draw the troops of Texas out to Matamoros in hopes to throw a strong force in their rear while he makes his attack on the upper part of the Colonies."

Seventy-two hours earlier, James Fannin had been commanding a growing number of American volunteers intent on marching to Matamoros and extending the war into Mexico by occupying that sparsely garrisoned town.

Now, with Morris' letter, all that had changed. Houston had been right: The Matamoros expedition was a dangerous and foolish campaign. Grant and Johnson might have dreams of recovering lost wealth in Coahuilla through pursuing the campaign, but the information in Morris' letter indicated to him that it was not in his—or Texas'—best interest to continue with the expedition.

Morris reported that Grant and thirty men had not been accounted for in the past two days. He added a postscript to his letter in which he claimed the Mexican high command was extorting the soldiers and subjugating the women in their effort to drive the Mexican army into Texas. "His soldiers have assassinated many of the most influential citizens, and the wives and daughters are prostituted—the whole country is given up to the troops to induce them forward."

Not only was James Fannin confronted with a massive Mexican army, but now it was reported he was faced with a brutal despot who intended to drive the Anglo revolutionaries completely out of Texas. "Santa Anna has sworn to Take Texas or lose Mexico," Morris had written.

This message was written by Robert Morris on February 6 and delivered to Fannin on the seventh. Fannin's response was to issue two directives: He dispatched a group of Greys to Morris' aid at San Patricio and also wrote a long, detailed letter to Acting Governor Robinson and the General Council in which he relayed Morris' information and his own recommendation.

"Not the least doubt should any longer be entertained, by any friend of Texas, of the design of Santa Anna to overrun the country, and expel or exterminate every white man within its borders," he wrote the politicians.[2]

Fannin's letter to the provisional government was written the same day he had received Morris' dispatch. In many ways it was, as he claimed, a forwarding of the alarming report. In other ways, however, it reflected how the news affected Fannin as a field commander. At times his tone almost appears to border on hysteria.

While Morris had postscripted his letter with the reference to the Mexican abuse of their own people—especially the subjugation of women—Fannin opens his letter to the Acting Governor and Council by paraphrasing Morris' charges. Fannin, however, suggested that the real intent of the Mexicans was the subjugation of Anglo women.

"Can it be possible that they—that any American—can so far forget the honor of their mothers, wives, and daughters, as not to fly to their rifles, and march to meet the Tyrant and avenge the insults and wrongs inflicted on his own country-women on the Rio Grande? What can be expected for the *Fair daughters* of chaste *white women*, when their own country-women are prostituted by a licensed soldiery, as an inducement to push forward into the Colonies, where they may find *fairer game*?" Fannin asked the politicians.

That Fannin should use racial fears as a mobilization technique was not new—certainly for an American southerner from Georgia. Even in Texas in 1836, the fear of racial conflict or insurrection was constantly on the minds of the white settlers.

While slavery was certainly prevalent in Texas during this period, it was not as institutionalized as in the American South. Fannin, after all, had risked criminal prosecution for the importation of African slaves into Brazoria just before the conflict.

Nevertheless, the Anglo Texans had quickly learned that the threat of racial violence was an effective mobilizer when all else failed. Apprehensive Texas leaders had charged Santa Anna and the Mexicans with fomenting a black rebellion in the summer of 1835. The greatest uncertainty centered on slaves along the Brazos who in October reportedly made an attempt to rise as part of an elaborate scheme to seize the land.[3] James Fannin and Joseph Mims, significantly, were heavily involved in plantation and slave affairs along the Brazos during this very period.

On February 7, 1836, James Fannin—in frustration at the lack of support by Anglo Texans for the military campaign—lashed out in the one way he felt would be effective in mobilizing support: He alleged a racial affront to "fair daughters of chaste white women" and Anglo "fairer game" by advancing Mexican soldiers.

That Fannin would resort to inflaming racial fears at this time certainly was not unusual. Only days earlier Sam Houston had resorted to the same tactic in his argument that the volunteers should abandon Grant's march on Matamoros: "Nor will the vigor of the descendants of the sturdy north ever mix with the phlegmatic attitude of the indolent Mexicans, no matter how long we may live among them."[4]

Much of the reason for Fannin's frantic call for support stemmed from growing frustration over the absence of support from established Anglo settlers in Texas. While the majority of white settlers who had emigrated to Texas before 1835 probably supported rebellion directed at reestablishing guarantees under the Constitution of 1824, very few appeared to support outright independence from Mexico.

In February of 1836 the rebellion had been taken over by outsiders who quickly abandoned all rhetoric of civil liberties and now openly advocated independence from Mexico.

Fannin, by virtue of his less than two years in Texas, was technically one of the "older" immigrants in the higher echelons of the provisional Texas government. That he should complain of the lack of support from established settlers is somewhat ironic given that he was himself one of the more "established" Texans.

"I doubt if twenty-five citizens of Texas can be mustered in the ranks—nay, I am informed, whilst writing the above, that there is not half that number;—does not this fact bespeak an indifference, and criminal apathy, truly alarming?" Fannin wrote Robinson. "Do the citizens of Texas reflect for a moment, that these men, many of whom have served since November last have not received the *cent's wages*, and are now nearly naked, and many of them barefooted, or what is tantamount to it?"

Already in these earliest days of his command, Fannin was aware of the critical shortages his men were faced with. Many of his volunteers had traveled to Texas without resupply. Those New Orleans Greys who had come to Texas with Captain Thomas Breece had walked from Alexandria, Louisiana, to Bexar while the other Greys had walked from Velasco to San Antonio. Some volunteers— the Greys and Mississippi volunteers in particular—had fought in the battle for Bexar and were literally clothed in rags by the time they had arrived at Refugio.

"Could they hear the just complaints and taunting remarks in regard to the absence of the old settlers and owners of the soil?" Fannin admonished Robinson and the General Council.

The tone of Fannin's letter makes it apparent that for Fannin the war with Mexico had suddenly—with Morris' letter—become very real.

"At the same time . . . appraise all our friends in the United States of our true situation, that a sufficient inducement may be held out to draw them to our standard, in this hour of trial," Fannin pled. Referring to his situation as "this hour of trial" suggests that he may finally have realized not only was the threat of warfare imminent but that he might be in serious trouble.

"Evince your determination to live free or perish in the ditch," he wrote. In reality, however, it was he and his men—not the politicians in San Felipe—who would ultimately be given the choice to live free or perish in the ditches.

Fannin continued his letter with detailed recommendation for the future conduct of the military operations including the establishment of supply depots and a reserve force on the Colorado River.

Prior to arriving at Refugio, James Fannin had been a high profile proponent of the Matamoros expedition. Within hours of receiving Morris' letter, however, he had suddenly abandoned all talk of aggression and become very defensive-oriented in his approach to the coming fighting. There can be no question that Robert Morris changed the strategy of James Fannin and his conduct of future military operations in south Texas with his letter from San Patricio.

Fannin also acknowledged his vulnerability in that "It is useless to controvert the fact that our true strength and geographical situation are well known to Santa Anna." This suggests he was aware that the Mexicans were closely following his every move—a situation that would only become more apparent in the coming weeks.

The letter to Robinson was written at 10:00 P.M. the night of February 7 but not posted immediately. At 7:00 A.M. on the eighth he added a postscript in which he acknowledged that a retreat might be necessary.

He had also dispatched Captain William Cooke and a contingent of Greys to Morris' aid at Refugio. "I have sent forward a reinforcement to San Patricio, to bring off the artillery and order a concentration of the troops at Goliad, and shall make such disposition of my forces as to sustain Bexar and that post. . . ." he informed the Council.

At the conclusion of this extended postscript, Fannin—an officer in the regular army—makes what appears to be a contradictory statement to Robinson. "Spare us, in God's name, from elections in camp; organize at home, and march forward in order, and good may result from it." Fannin, who had been campaigning for a regular, established officer corps deplored the volunteer practice of electing officers and voting on strategy.

He was himself, however, an appointed officer commanding an army comprised entirely of volunteer soldiers. His next paragraph ironically informs Robinson, "I have barely time to say that an election was holden on yesterday for Colonel and Lieutenant Colonel, and that myself and Major Ward received nearly a unanimous vote."

Mexican informants were not the only problem Fannin had to deal with at Refugio. While at that abandoned Irish community, he stayed in the home of Irish colonizer Ira Westover, who had remained loyal to the Texan cause. He had also, however, remained loyal to Sam Houston.

On February 7, the same date as Morris' letter and Fannin's response to Robinson, Westover also wrote Sam Houston:

> . . . .Colonel Fannin is at my house and has been a number of days endeavoring to obtain an organisation of the Army which is not likely to take place, last evening a meeting of the Officers took place and an Election was to have taken place to day. . . .*Colonels* Johnson & Grant are at San Patricio with about fifty men they left immediately after you left this place. Colonel Fannin says the whole number of troops at this and San Patricio is about 400 men, the newly created officer called an Agent for the expedition to Matamoras has correct views as to the organsation of the troops if he has the command there shall be no independent volunteers recognized by him. . . .[5]

Westover's letter appears to be at least marginally supportive of Fannin in principle, but it also verifies that Houston's influence had remained at Refugio even after his departure.

Fannin had announced his intention to "order a concentration of troops at Goliad." F.W. Johnson, however, did not agree with that strategy since it signaled a rejection of his—and Grant's—independent expedition against Matamoros.

From San Patricio, he wrote letters to Fannin and Robinson on February 9. "If a force of 3-400 men is sent agst Matamoras, Vital Fernandez, who commands with 800 Tamaulipas troops, will immediately join you—And the whole of the frontier Towns will immediately follow—"[6] he baited Fannin. "Fear nothing for Bexar or Goliad or any point of Texas if an attack is made on Matemoras. . . .[T]he true policy is to unite all your forces here, leaving small garrisons in Bexar & Goliad & proceed without delay into the interior. . . ."

Even in the face of overwhelming evidence that the Mexican army was concentrating massive and formidable numbers on the banks of the Rio Grande, Johnson continued to mock the enemy: "Felisola is an old woman—& Santa Ana will not retire unless the Wigwam is in serious uproar."

To Acting Governor Robinson, he dispatched two separate letters that day. "The field is ample & splendid—but all do not see it—a short time will I hope to serve to open the eyes of every lover of his Country & then it will be seen what freemen can achieve when divested of prejudice & open to a conviction of their own real power—"[7] he admonished Robinson. In a second letter, Johnson attempted to undermine Fannin's report to the Council. "To prevent any undue alarm from an express forwarded to you by Col. Fanning. . . ."[8]

At Refugio, Fannin continued to consolidate his forces and supplies for a retreat to Goliad. The political maneuvering at San Felipe continued without gaining any consensus or agreement.

Amos Pollard, a medical doctor who had joined the Texans at Gonzales and traveled to Bexar, was now chief surgeon for the forces remaining in the Alamo compound. From his hospital on February 13, he wrote deposed Governor Smith complaining of no supplies. "We are threatened with a large invading army," he reported and, "I wish General Houston was now here on the frontier to help us crush at once both our external and internal enemies."[9]

Pollard's letter indicates that, in Bexar, the Anglo volunteers were also—as in Goliad—finally aware of the impending attacks planned against them. Pollard also shows, once again, the split in Texan politics at this period: Factions were divided between Governor Smith and Sam Houston and Governor Robinson and James Fannin. Pollard's February 13 message also revealed another aspect of this split. "Some method should be devised to neutralize Fannin's influence," he concluded in a postscript to Smith. Smith, no doubt, agreed.

Governor Robinson, on the other hand, continued his support of Fannin in a letter also dated the thirteenth. This support, however, suggested that Robinson had finally washed his hands of Grant and Johnson and was now accepting the advice of Fannin.

"You will occupy such points as you may in your opinion deem most advantageous it is desirable to maintain the Mission of Refugio. . . .Fortify & defend Goliad and Baxer if any opportunity fairly offers, give the enemy battle as he advances, but do not hazard much until you are reinforced [as] a defeat of your command would prove our ruin—all former orders given by my predecessor, Gen. Houston or myself, are so far countermanded as to render it compatible to now obey any orders you may deem Expedient—," he dispatched Fannin.

James Walker Fannin Jr., on paper at least, had finally been given the executive order he needed to take command of the army at Refugio and follow those orders he "deemed Expedient." In other words, Fannin now had the acting governor's permission in writing to refuse all previous commands issued by Sam Houston or Governor Smith.

Then, almost as an afterthought, Robinson penned a second letter to Fannin that same date. This correspondence informs him that Robinson did not anticipate an attack on Bexar or Goliad but that "he [Santa Anna] will endeavor to throw reinforcements in to Matamoras is more than probable—Therefore you will always Keep in view the original objects of the campaign against the latter place, and dash upon it as soon as it is prudent to do so in your opinion."[10]

Fannin was now faced with two sets of orders from Robinson: "Fortify and defend Goliad" in one letter and to "keep in view the . . . campaign against [Matamoros] and dash upon it as soon as it is prudent to do so" in a second correspondence.

This confusing set of orders issued on the thirteenth turned out in the end to be insignificant points.

James Fannin had withdrawn to Goliad the day before they were written.

---

1   Jenkins, *PTR*, 4:274-6.

2   Ibid., 4:279-283.

3   Smallwood, James M., "Slave Insurrections," *New Handbook of Texas in Six Volumes* (Austin: The Texas State Historical Association, 1996).

4   Charlotte Churchill's 1968 translation of Ehrenberg's diary *With Milam and Fannin* does not mention this incident, but a 1993 translation by Dr. Peter Mollenhauer does describe it. His translation can be found in the 1997 book by Natalie Ornish, *Ehrenberg: Goliad Survivor, Old West Explorer* (Dallas: Texas Heritage Press, 1997), pg. 184.

5   Jenkins, *PTR*, 4:284.

6   Ibid., 4:293-4.
7   Ibid., 4:294-5.
8   Ibid., 4:295.
9   Ibid., 4:324-5.
10   Ibid., 4:326.

Section III

The Reluctant Leader

Chapter Twelve
Command Staff

James Fannin had arrived at Copano to find an advance party of five former New Orleans Greys camping in the single dilapidated building on the coastline. After offloading equipment and supplies, at least three days were spent transporting them to the mission at Refugio.

What Fannin inherited at Refugio was a Texan army that was divided with regards to the Mexican Centralist/Federalist question and the choice of independence or confederation with Coahuila under the Constitution of 1824. There is evidence that the men were also divided over loyalties.

Sam Houston had succeeded in more than just stopping Grant and Johnson's independent expedition against Matamoros: He had also succeeded in sowing the seeds of dissension toward the continuation of the campaign under any future leader including James Fannin.

Of the Texan troops over which Fannin assumed control when he arrived in south Texas, the New Orleans Greys and some Mississippi volunteers were the only soldiers with combat experience. The Greys had carried the brunt of the nearly week long fighting at Bexar the previous December—having fought house-to-house until reaching the Military Plaza and the final furious firefight at the priest's house.

But with Houston's departure for Nacogdoches, many of the Greys had become disillusioned with the southern expedition. After the victory at Bexar, the Greys had joined Grant's campaign but only after leaving behind a considerable number of their men—some wounded—with Neill in the Alamo.

Now, with the Matamoros expedition collapsing, the Greys were demanding to return to San Antonio to rejoin the Greys remaining there, who were now under the command of Travis. When Fannin arrived at Refugio, he found the Greys had left the other soldiers and were camping across the river and two miles away at a Mexican plantation.[1]

On February 7 Fannin received Major Robert Morris' letter from San Patricio. Within a few hours of San Patricio, Morris had written, were over one thousand Mexican soldiers marching northward.

Fannin's immediate response was to send Captain William Gordon Cooke and the remaining Greys to Morris' aid, and in an incredible forced march that totaled forty-eight miles in one day, the Greys reached the tiny Irish hamlet of San Patricio Hibernia.[2] Fannin, in turn, relocated his army at Goliad where he began reinforcing the old Spanish fort.

Morris' report of the Mexican patrols turned out to be a false alarm, but he, Grant, and Johnson refused to abandon their independent raid on Mexico and continued south on February 9.

Cooke returned to Goliad on the twelfth and left the service of the volunteers to join the regular army at Washington-on-the-Brazos. The Greys, now under the command of Samuel Pettus, remained at San Patricio but returned to Goliad on the eighteenth with the stated intention of resupplying and continuing on to Bexar to reinforce Travis and the Texans there—including the remaining New Orleans Greys.

Fannin was able to abort their plans only through refusing to resupply them and in doing so, managed to avert the first of many crises involving threats by his men to desert or furlough rather than serve under his command.

While Morris' letter with its suggestion of imminent Mexican army arrival had been a harbinger of bad news, other reports also began coming in to Goliad that were discouraging.

A few days after Morris' letter, Fannin learned that the *Tamaulipas*, in attempting to sail from the mouth of the Brazos with Captain Turner's two companies and the Texan army's stock of powder, shoes, clothing, and ordnance supplies, had been cast away on the Brazos bar. The *Emeline* was also lost, in Matagorda Bay, with her cargo of flour and corn. The other provision schooner, *Caroline*, discharged her cargo February 14, at Cox's Point.[3]

As a result, Captain Turner's men and the critically needed supplies never reached Goliad. Other bad news arrived when it was learned that reinforcements and supplies aboard the *Mattawamkeag* had been seized by British authorities in the Bahamas and charged with piracy. Although the men were later released, they never reached Fannin or Goliad.

Although the New Orleans Greys and some Mississippians were Fannin's only combat veterans, he did assemble a formidable military force of Anglo Texans—and some Mexican Federalists—at Goliad and the old La Bahia presidio there in February.

In 1939 Harbert Davenport published his classic study "The Men of Goliad" in *The Southwestern Historical Quarterly*.[4] Some sixty years after its publication, his article remains the most comprehensive and definitive study of Fannin's command. The following is a summarized version of Davenport's listing of Fannin's units:

Leader	Unit	History
Francis Thornton	Infantry	Consisted of survivors of the Tampico Campaign
Ira J. Westover	Artillery	Recruited from Irish colonists around Goliad and reinforced by Mexican survivors of Mexia's Tampico expedition
B. F. Saunders	Volunteer	Volunteers recruited at Matagorda
John Chenweth	Volunteer	Mostly veterans of the battle for Bexar who had been assigned to occupy Copano after the fighting
William Cooke	San Antonio Greys	New Orleans Greys veterans of the battle for Bexar
David N. Burke	Mobile Greys	Organized in Mobile during November 1835 and enlarged with New Orleans Greys previously of Breece's command
Benjamin Lawrence	Mustangs (cavalry)	Originally recruited in Tennessee and enlarged with cavalry from the Louisville Volunteers

Leader	Unit	History
H.R.A. Wigginton	Volunteers	Unmounted portion of the Louisville Volunteers enlarged with members of other divided groups
Thomas Pearson	Artillery	A small company that had landed at Paso Cavallo the previous November and transported the eighteen-pounder to Bexar
Thomas Lewellen	Volunteers	Combination of veterans of the Bexar fighting and reenlisted after the victory there; left Refugio for San Patricio with Grant and Johnson
Peyton S. Wyatt	Volunteers	Recruited at Huntsville, Alabama, and Paducah, Kentucky, in November/December 1835
Amon King	"Light Company"	Unit attached to Capt. Wyatt's volunteers
Wm. Wadsworth	1st Co., Ga. Battalion	Enlisted at Columbus, Georgia, in November 1835 under the direction of William Ward and Dr. Robert Collins
Uriah J. Bullock	2nd Co., Ga. Battalion	Enlisted at Macon, Georgia, by William Ward
James C. Winn	3rd Co., Ga. Battalion	Also recruited at Macon, Georgia, and enlarged by Mississippi volunteers after arriving in Texas
Isaac Ticknor	Ala. Greys	Recruited from Montgomery, Alabama
Burr H. Duval	Kentucky Mustangs	Enlisted at Bardstown, Kentucky, in early December
Jack Shackelford	Alabama Red Rovers	Volunteers from Courtland and Tuscumbia, Alabama, and enlarged with additions after arriving in Texas

Leader	Unit	History
John C. Grace	Volunteers	Recruited in Tennessee and Mississippi and joined Capt. Shackelford's Red Rovers after arrival at Goliad
Samuel Sprague	Volunteers	Dispatched by the General Council from San Felipe
Hugh Fraser	Refugio Militia	Used as couriers and to oversee evacuation of Irish colonists

At Refugio Fannin was joined on his march to Goliad by Ticknor's company of about forty men from Alabama, and his troops now numbered about two hundred fifty. At Goliad he found a few regulars, and there, too, he was joined by Shackelford and other volunteers, mainly from Alabama, Kentucky, and Tennessee. Fannin, on February 28, declared that his garrison consisted of about four hundred twenty men.[5]

Fannin retreated from Refugio to Goliad on February 12, and from that date until March 19 he spent most of his time and energies reinforcing the old abandoned Spanish fort.

His decision to relocate to Goliad would ultimately prove to be a tragic mistake—or, at least, one of a series of tragic mistakes. But there were also sound, legitimate reasons for the move.

Fannin had initially been ordered by Houston to proceed to Copano and rendezvous there until further orders. General Cos had already demonstrated the strategic importance of Copano. The Mexican general had arrived in Texas from Matamoros at Copano Landing and traveled overland through Goliad to Bexar. After the siege of Bexar had begun and the Texans had occupied Goliad, his line of supplies from Copano had been severed. During a relatively short siege situation with no supplies, he had been forced to wait for Mexican reinforcements traveling overland from the interior of Mexico.

In the end, the lack of provisions and supplies had played as important a part in his surrender as had the dogged attack of the Texans. This fact was not lost on most Texan leaders including Sam

Houston, who issued the orders to Fannin to occupy and reinforce the port.

But Houston had also advised that tents would be necessary at Copano or Refugio, and those tents had not been sent. Fannin had assumed command over an army that was not only ragged but without shelter. Goliad, with its Spanish presidio, offered at least the framework from which to build a defensive position including protection from the elements.

The logistical problem with Goliad, however, was its geographical distance from Copano and Matagorda Bay. But it was also during this period that Fannin learned American insurance underwriters, particularly in New Orleans, would no longer insure cargoes bound for Copano.

This development diminished greatly the strategic importance of Copano since the ships would not be entering Matagorda Bay any longer but, instead, would be landing supplies and men further north at Cavallo Pass and the port at Lavaca.

With the closing of Copano as a base of entry, the fort at Goliad also lost strategic importance. But with the Matamoros expedition stalled, or abandoned, due to Mexican military buildup along the Rio Grande, movement to the south from Refugio was out of the question.

Goliad was the only logical destination for Fannin to rendezvous his four hundred twenty men unless he chose to follow Sam Houston's previous orders and retreat to Gonzales. But James Fannin in February of 1836 was the commander in chief—not Sam Houston—and he had written orders countermanding Houston's previous directives. He was to proceed as he "deemed Expedient," and his decision was to retreat from Refugio to Goliad and begin repairing the Spanish fort into a defensive position.

Before leaving Refugio, he had dispatched Captain Cooke and the Greys to aid Morris at San Patricio and had assigned a guard squad at Copano. He left Amon King and his small "light company" as a reserve force to serve as scouts at Refugio.

While repairing and modifying the fortress at La Bahia would consume most of his time for the coming weeks, one of Fannin's initial moves after arriving at Goliad was to establish his command staff and structure.

When Morris had refused to return with the Greys, William Cooke traveled to Goliad on the twelfth, immediately discharged the army, and left with some Mexican prisoners for San Felipe. The Greys returned to Refugio under the command of Samuel Pettus and remained there until they also retreated to Goliad on the eighteenth, demanding resupply so they could continue on to Bexar.

Fannin had reported to Robinson that elections had been held on February 7 and that he had been elected colonel and William Ward lieutenant colonel "without debate." This would be the basis of his reorganization of his command.

The Georgia Volunteers, however, insisted upon choosing a major, and Dr. Warren J. Mitchell, of Columbus, Georgia, was elected to that post.[6]

Initially, command staff organization was developed around the companies of the Georgia Battalion. When Captain Pettus led the Greys back to Goliad on the eighteenth, however, Fannin refused to issue them supplies to return to Bexar. While this assured the Greys would remain within his command at Goliad, it also created a significant number of angry volunteers, who would maintain a bitter and divisive influence on his command at Goliad.

The arrival of the Greys also created a need for Fannin to divide his command, organizationally, into two battalions. The first battalion continued to be organized around Ward's Georgia volunteers and to be known as the Georgia Battalion. The second battalion, named the Lafayette Battalion, was developed around the nucleus of the other volunteer groups that had formed at Goliad in late February.

The Grey's arrival back at Goliad also created this need for reorganization because it also signaled a dramatic reduction in numbers. Several popular leaders had left Fannin's service by this time, and their departures had resulted in many of their men also leaving the service of Texas.

William Cooke, in particular, had been an extremely popular leader of the New Orleans—renamed the "San Antonio"—Greys. After his departure, many of his men had discharged or furloughed to return to the United States.

On February 23 Fannin indicated he had furloughed or discharged fifteen volunteers with partial payment including New

Orleans Grey Francis Leonard, a Louisiana native who had enlisted with Morris and traveled to Texas through Velasco. Fannin's entry was recorded:

> Recd 23d Feby 1836—Fort Defiance from J W Fannin Jr Agt Provl. Govt of Texas the sum of Twenty Dollars in part payment for services rendered as a Volunteer in the N.O. Greys, Capt Cook's Company—and regularly credited in my discharge—
> $20   F.G. Leonard[7]

Other volunteer units were experiencing a departure of dissatisfied volunteers as well. When Sam Houston had departed Refugio on January 21 he had also taken Captains Lawrence and Wigginton to serve as army recruiters in the United States—causing many of the men under their commands to also withdraw from the service.[8]

Captain Peyton S. Wyatt of Huntsville, Alabama, had recruited two companies of men at Huntsville and Paducah, Kentucky, the previous November and had arrived in Nacogdoches the following month with sixty-seven men and muskets borrowed from the State of Alabama.[9]

Grant, after raiding the provisions—including Amos Pollard's medical supplies—at Bexar had marched to Goliad with his "Federal Army" and had demanded of Dimmitt that he also give up the considerable store of supplies and munitions that had been captured at La Bahia.

Dimmitt had initially refused, and there had been a period of extreme tensions in which the two Texan groups nearly went to war themselves. Finally, Grant's army prevailed and Captain Peyton Wyatt replaced Dimmitt as commander of the Goliad garrison. After Sam Houston's speech convinced most of Grant's men, including Wyatt's Kentucky and Alabama volunteers, to abandon the Matamoros campaign, Grant left anyway with his much-reduced force. Houston temporarily left Wyatt in command but later transferred him to Refugio.[10]

At Copano, however, Wyatt and his men were so disillusioned with the events surrounding the Matamoros campaign that Wyatt personally paid for their return to the states. Chartering one of the ships that had transported Fannin and the Georgia Battalion to Copano, Wyatt and his men returned to the United States.[11]

Thus Fannin, with a dwindling army, reorganized into two battalions. The Georgia Battalion was commanded by fellow Georgian Lieutenant Colonel William Ward, while an artillery officer in the regular army, Pennsylvanian Benjamin C. Wallace, was promoted to major and given command of the Lafayette Battalion.

The battalions were then organized with assignments as to surgeons, adjutants, and quartermasters. For his own command staff, Fannin selected John Sowers Brooks—the young Georgian who had traveled with Ward's group to Texas as adjutant. Shortly afterward, Brooks resigned his position as adjutant to become Fannin's personal aide. During the period of fortification of La Bahia, he would be the chief artillery engineer. With eleven months service in the United States Marine Corps, he had at least some knowledge of military tactics—something Fannin desperately needed.

After Brooks resigned to become Fannin's aide, Joseph M. Chadwick, who was also an engineer, became adjutant general. Like Fannin, Chadwick had attended West Point briefly and dropped out early. He had been sergeant major in the Georgia Battalion at Velasco and was closely associated with both Ward and James Fannin.

New Orleans Grey Nathaniel Brister was appointed regimental adjutant. This may have been in an attempt to placate the rebellious Greys since Brister was well established with that unit. A Virginian, he had come to Texas through Velasco with Morris' unit of the Greys and had served as first sergeant during the battle for Bexar.

While the Georgia Battalion was organized around the four companies Ward had brought to Velasco, the Lafayette Battalion developed around several groups of volunteers and included several mergers of splintered groups.

The Greys were assigned to the Lafayette Battalion in two units. The San Antonio Greys, under Pettus' command, were actually the remnants of Robert Morris' original New Orleans Greys. The other unit of New Orleans Greys—Thomas Breece's unit—was assigned to Captain David N. Burke's Mobile Greys. The other Lafayette Battalion units were Westover's regulars, consisting mainly of Irish colonists; Captain Burr H. Duval's Kentucky Mustangs; the Alabama Greys, commanded by Captain Benjamin F. Bradford (who had taken Peyton Wyatt's place); the Kentucky Volunteers, commanded by Amon King; and Captain Jack Shackelford's Alabama Red Rovers.[12]

And so as February of 1836 drew to a close, James Fannin found himself in charge of the largest volunteer army at that time in Texas. Santa Anna, however, was poised just across the Rio Grande to sweep into Texas and initiate two major campaigns against the Anglo Texans—one of which would be directed against him at his La Bahia fortress in Goliad.

---

1   Ehrenberg, Herman, *With Milam and Fannin* translated by Charlotte Churchill (Austin: The Pemberton Press, 1968), pg. 130.

2   Brown, *Volunteers in the Texas Revolution—The New Orleans Greys*, pg. 160.

3   Davenport, "The Men of Goliad," pg. 10.

4   Ibid., pp. 12-16.

5   Smith, "James W. Fannin, Jr., in the Texas Revolution," pg. 188.

6   Davenport, pg. 16.

7   *Lamar Papers*, Mirebeau B., Texas State Library, Vol. 5, pg. 92.

8   Davenport, pg. 17.

9   Ibid., pg. 15.

10   O'Connor, *The Presidio La Bahia del Espiritu Santo de Zuniga 1721 to 1846*, pg. 116.

11   Davenport, pg. 17.

12   O'Connor, pg. 117.

Chapter Thirteen

The Georgia Units

O f the various volunteer units in and around Goliad, James Fannin identified most closely with the Georgia Battalion. The correspondence between Ward and Fannin the previous Christmas established that both parties shared a special "Georgia" connection.

Much remains unknown about the Georgia volunteers because, as with so many other units, the original muster rolls were destroyed. In the case of Ward's battalion, the muster rolls are assumed to have been destroyed during the burning of San Felipe.

Initial mobilization and enlistment began with a public meeting in Macon, Georgia, on November 12, 1835. Thirty-two men signed up for service that night, and over three thousand dollars were subscribed to pay their costs.[1]

Because of official American "neutrality" in the Mexican/Texan conflict, the units were not allowed to organize on American soil, which is why they had waited until after their arrival at Refugio to form companies.

In reality, however, the companies were formed before the men ever left Georgia. With William Ward as commander, the approximately one hundred twenty men were formed into three units loosely based upon enrollment at Macon, Milledgeville, and Columbus, Georgia.

The Columbus Volunteers were led by Captain W. A. O. Wadsworth; Captain Uriah Irwin Bullock commanded the Macon Volunteers; and Captain James C. Winn led his company named the "Georgia Riflemen."

The men of the Georgia Battalion represented a cross section of frontier Georgia in 1835. Many of the recruits were in their "early teens" while a few other volunteers had had at least limited militia and army experience.

William Ward, one of the first landowners in Macon, was a slaveholder and an ardent supporter of Nullification. Court records reveal that he was sometimes sued for assault and battery and that he was probably in financial straits when he set out for Texas. An Alabama newspaper called him as "brave and dauntless a man as is known in Georgia," probably because of a well-publicized brawl in a Milledgeville tavern in November 1833, during which he was shot and nearly killed by mistake while trying to stop the infamous gambler Henry Byrom from wrecking the place.[2]

Bullock, captain of the Macon volunteers, was described as a "lovable, magnetic, and impractical man, who was brave and civic minded, but visionary."[3] After arrival at Velasco, he was afflicted with measles and, unable to sail with his men, later traveled overland to Copano.

At Velasco he was sick and financially broke, prompting Fannin to write this letter of reference for him: "My friend, Captain Bullock, is too unwell with measles to go by water, and proceeds by land to Copen [Copano]. He has spent several hundred dollars in bringing to our aid his company and is now without resources. I am nearly so, and must ask you to advance him from twenty to fifty dollars, and I will repay you when I get back, and greatly oblige."[4]

When he returned to Georgia after the revolution, Bullock was deeply in debt and the subject of litigation over his finances, but still managed to be elected and to serve in the Georgia Senate for one term.

James Rufus Munson, a seventeen-year-old first corporal, was described as "tall for his age, slender built, very dark complexion, with black hair and eyes. He was very erect, of bold and independent carriage, and had no mark or blemish of any kind. He was truthful, honorable, bold and gallant, and a great favorite with his comrades."[5] Corporal Munson, unlike Captain Bullock, did not live to return to Georgia.

Others, like Thomas S. Freeman, Samuel T. Brown (Ward's nephew), and George Vigal, later obtained land grants for homesteading in Texas. Another, Private Isaac Aldredge, left a wife and three children in Georgia to fight for Texas and obtain land so his family could immigrate. Aldredge, who had some military experience, did not live through the revolution, and fraudulent speculators later claimed his land until the eve of the Civil War when one of his daughters succeeded in suing and obtaining the land based upon his service with the Georgia Battalion.

William Ward departed with approximately one hundred twenty men. At Knoxville, they were presented with the Lone Star flag by Joanna Troutman before continuing on to Columbus where they added more volunteers. Additional men were also enlisted at Mobile and at New Orleans. By the time they sailed, their original number had almost doubled.

One of those non-Georgians enlisting and joining the battalion was Virginian John Sowers Brooks. Despite his relatively young age of twenty-one years, he had worked as a newspaperman with the *Staunton Spectator* in Virginia and had served in the United States Marine Corps for nearly a year. His impassioned—and unanswered—letters home to members of his family give us a virtual diary of his thoughts and impressions about the events surrounding James Fannin and the campaign at Goliad in 1836.

The *Macon Telegraph* ran an article on January 21, 1836, announcing: "On Sunday, December 20, four schooners, the *Pennsylvania*, *Camancho*, *America*, and *Santiago* arrived in Velasco, having on board 220 volunteers in the cause of liberty, from the State of Georgia."[6]

After landing on December 20, Ward and the Georgia Volunteers presented themselves formally to James Fannin on the twenty-third. Fannin formally responded by welcoming them to Texas on Christmas Day of 1835, and the next month they began preparations to sail to Copano. They arrived at Refugio on February 14 and at that time elected officers and officially organized into three companies (they would later add a fourth).

It has been claimed that the Georgia Battalion was the only unit in the Texas Revolution that furnished its own arms and ammunition, doing so with the help of the arsenal of the state of Georgia.[7] Other units, however, also benefited from the donation of rifles upon organizing.

The New Orleans Greys, upon enlisting at Bank's Arcade in November of 1835, were promised that the first fifty volunteers would be issued new rifles at the expense of Texan alcalde Adolphus Sterne. There were nearly one hundred thirty recruits that night, however, and the arcade had, on the second floor, an armory belonging to a group known as the Washington Guards. Probably some of the additional weaponry issued that night came from that armory.[8]

On November 8, 1835, a company of Alabama volunteers under the command of Captain Peyton S. Wyatt left Huntsville for Texas "equipped with fifty first-class muskets borrowed by Wyatt from the state of Alabama."[9]

The donation of the Georgia rifles, however, caused some later friction between Texas and Georgia. In 1855 Georgia made a claim to Texas for compensation for the arms and equipment belonging to the state of Georgia that were captured by the Mexicans at Goliad.[10]

In August of 1856 the Texas Legislature approved an appropriation of up to three thousand dollars to settle the claim. The two state governments agreed to use the money to create a "Georgia Battalion Memorial" to be located at Goliad. No monument has been constructed at Goliad or La Bahia, and the claim and stated intentions of both states have gone unfulfilled.

The only known monument to any members of the Georgia Battalion located in the state of Georgia is at Lawrenceville, just east of Atlanta. There, a monument is dedicated to Captain James Winn and Sergeant Anthony Bates that recites:

> This monument is erected by their friends to the memory of Captain James Winn and Sergeant Anthony Bates, volunteers of this village, who were taken in honorable combat at Goliad, Texas, and shot by the order of the Mexican Commander, March 27, 1836.[11]

Inside Texas, no monument existed, however, until the city of Albany, Texas, erected a Georgia Battalion memorial fountain in 1976.[12]

---

1   Scarborough, Jewel Davis, "The Georgia Battalion in the Texas Revolution: A Critical Study," *The Southwest Historical Quarterly*, Vol. 63, April 1960, pg. 512. This article includes an excellent

in-depth study of the men comprising the Georgia Battalion, their travels to Texas and later to Goliad, and the litigation between Georgia and Texas after the revolution.

2   Davis, Robert S. Jr., "Goliad and The Georgia Battalion, Georgia Participation in the Texas Revolution 1835-1836," *The Journal of Southwest Georgia History*, Vol. IV, Fall 1986, pp. 26-7.

3   Ibid., pg. 519.

4   Brazoria County (Texas) Clerk's Office, Angleton, Texas, Letters of Credit, Letter Number 29.

5   Scarborough, pg. 521.

6   Ibid., pg. 513.

7   Ibid., pg. 511 and Roell, Craig, "Georgia Battalion," *The New Handbook of Texas.*

8   Brown, *Volunteers in the Texas Revolution: The New Orleans Greys*, pg. 11.

9   Elliott, Claude, "Alabama and the Texas Revolution," *The Southwestern Historical Quarterly*, Vol. L, No. 3, January 1947, pg. 321.

10   Scarborough, pp. 515-519.

11   Ibid., pg. 519.

12   Roell, Craig, "Georgia Battalion," *The New Handbook of Texas.*

Chapter Fourteen

The Greys

Several units inside Texas in 1836 were using the name "Greys" or "Grays," but the first and premier unit to enter Texas using that name was a unit consisting of two companies formed in New Orleans.

The result of a recruiting meeting formed by Nacogdoches alcalde Adolphus Sterne and New Orleans entrepreneur William Christy, the Greys enrolled approximately one hundred thirty volunteers on the evening of November 13, 1835.

Unlike the units formed in Georgia and Alabama, the Greys units were not local. The rosters for the two units included men from eighteen states as well as members from England, Ireland, Germany, Wales, Scotland, Upper Canada, and Nova Scotia.[1] Thus the Greys were neither "New Orlean" nor "Louisianian" nor even completely American. They were, for all practical purposes, a multinational mercenary unit.

Like the Georgian volunteers, the Greys represented a cross-spectrum of young men clamoring for a fight in Mexico. By the time the Greys were united with Fannin at Refugio, they had become the most combat-experienced soldiers in the Texas Revolution, and several of their leaders had already become prominent in Texas politics.

Robert C. Morris of New Orleans had at least some military experience prior to coming to Texas. Inside Texas, he had been elected captain of one of the units and during the fighting at Bexar had been promoted to major upon Ben Milam's death. Joining Grant and Johnson in leading the Greys south after the battle for Bexar, Morris had discharged the Greys and joined the independent army in its determined march toward Matamoros.

It was Morris who dispatched the urgent letter to Fannin from San Patricio, warning of the impending massive Mexican assault on Goliad and Bexar, that had convinced Fannin to retreat to Goliad and fortify.

William Gordon Cooke was a druggist from Virginia who had found the revolution in Texas more exciting than the life of a pharmacist in New Orleans. During the fighting at Bexar, he had been promoted to captain to replace Morris and had led his men in the desperate—almost suicidal—assault on the priest's house adjoining the Military Plaza on the final day of the fighting. Entrenched in a "death trap" literally yards away from General Cos' best soldiers, Cooke and his men had escaped execution only when the Mexican general opted to surrender. It was Cooke who accepted the surrender of the white flag and helped negotiate Cos' evacuation from Texas.

Like Morris, Cooke had accompanied Grant to Goliad and Refugio, but unlike the other Greys commander, he had been swayed by Houston's speech and abandoned the expedition. His association with James Fannin was very limited: Fannin dispatched Cooke and the Greys to San Patricio to reinforce Morris' unit, but Cooke later discharged the Greys and became closely associated with Sam Houston. Back at Goliad, Fannin discharged him and sent him to San Felipe in charge of some Mexican prisoners.

Robert Mussleman had served with the U.S. Army in the Seminole wars in Florida, and Englishman John Cook was an experienced artilleryman with service as a British marine. Michael Cronican had apprenticed as a newspaperman in Massachusetts and was a skilled printer. Stephen Dennison, an Englishman, was a painter and glasscutter by trade.

There were at least two medical doctors with the Greys: William Howell had been a doctor in New York and Albert Moses Levy, born in the Netherlands but a naturalized citizen and graduate of medical school at the University of Pennsylvania, was a surgeon. At least one of the Greys, William Hunter, had training and experience as a lawyer.

Francis Johnson had been born in Virginia and educated in Tennessee as a surveyor. At age thirty-two he was one of the older Greys, but before reporting to New Orleans he had worked as a grocer, miller, constable, miner, and militiaman as well as a surveyor. Thomas Saltus Lubbock, at age seventeen, was working in a New Orleans cotton warehouse when he enlisted. Herman Ehrenberg, thought to be as young as sixteen, was a German who had studied writing and engineering at the University of Jena. Robert B. Moore, at age fifty-five, was the oldest Grey and had remained behind in Bexar where he was the eldest of the Alamo defenders there.

Julian Harby came from Charleston, South Carolina, where his father was credited with introducing and establishing Reform Judaism in Charleston and the United States. Thomas William Ward, an Irishman who would later be seriously wounded at Bexar, had immigrated to Quebec and then to New Orleans where he was studying engineering and architecture.

With these backgrounds, the Greys represented the most diverse and international force inside Texas. Within days of their formation at Bank's Arcade, one group left on the schooner *Columbus* and arrived at Velasco three days later. After organizing and electing Robert Morris as their commander, they went by steamer up the Brazos to Columbia. From there they marched through Victoria to Goliad where they attempted to appropriate horses from the Mexicans there. The result was less than successful since the Mexicans donated unbroken wild mustangs, and the Greys continued marching toward San Antonio, arriving at Bexar in the latter part of November.

The other unit of the Greys also left New Orleans by boat but traveled up the Mississippi and Red Rivers to Alexandria then marched overland to Nachitoches. Electing Thomas Breece as their commander, they continued following the ancient El Camino Real and force-marched to the Sabine and crossed at Gaines Ferry and continued on to San Augustine and Nacogdoches.

At Nacogdoches they camped at the home of Adolphus Sterne, who donated horses—these were broken—and the company then continued on through Bastrop to join Morris' company at Bexar just before the decision to storm the city.

Just prior to the assault on the city, the Greys had participated in the siege by practicing as artillerymen. During the attack, the Greys formed one of the two columns entering Bexar and for five days fought house-to-house, room-to-room, and, often, hand-to-hand with the Mexicans. It was under Morris, and later Cooke, that the Greys spearheaded the drive on Military Plaza that forced the Mexican surrender.

After the victory at Bexar, some of the Greys had furloughed to New Orleans for medical treatment—they had sustained heavy casualties but only one death—while others discharged. When Grant led his independent army south, many of the Greys joined, looking for additional fighting at Matamoros. A significant number of the Greys remained at San Antonio and the Alamo, however, and were reorganized into Blazeby's Infantry unit.

The Greys who journeyed south with Grant were reorganized into a unit under Captain William Cooke and renamed the "San Antonio" Greys. Most of Cooke's men were former members of Morris' unit. A number of Greys who had served under Breece also joined the Matamoros expedition and were merged with Burke's Mobile Greys.

Except for Robert Morris and two or three other members, the Greys had heeded Sam Houston's call to abandon Grant and his independent army. Remaining at Refugio under the command of Cooke, several including Ehrenberg had served as the advance party greeting James Fannin when he arrived at Copano.

Fannin and the Greys almost never got along. The Greys were the sort of volunteer soldiers that Fannin both disdained and needed: undisciplined combat veterans who were unafraid to fight. Their relationship would be strained from the very beginning at Refugio and at times would become almost direct rebellion against his command.[2]

The fact that members of the Greys—some wounded from the Bexar fighting—had remained behind in San Antonio and the Alamo further increased the strain between those members at Goliad and James Fannin. After returning to Goliad from Refugio, they had demanded supplies and equipment to continue on to Bexar only to be refused by Fannin. This in turn only exacerbated the antagonism between the commander and the Greys and would be a point of contention throughout the Goliad campaign.

After the revolution, those few Greys who survived would go on to become some of Texas' finest leaders. Cooke, Ward, and

Hunter would hold high political posts in the Republic of Texas while other former Greys would serve in the Mexican border wars as military and Texas Rangers. At least two would serve as Confederate officers in the Civil War.

But the New Orleans Greys, as a unit, would be decimated as a military unit at the Alamo and in the events at Goliad. Those who had journeyed south, however, and ended up under the command of James Fannin exemplified the best and most experienced soldiers Texas could muster in 1836. Before the revolution would end, members of the Greys would have served at Bexar, the Alamo, San Patricio, Agua Dulce, Refugio, Coleto, and Goliad. At least five would somehow find their way to San Jacinto and participate in the battle there.

By the time James Fannin had assumed leadership over those Greys at Goliad, they had served in various assignments as marines, infantry, cavalry, and artillerymen. He desperately needed the Greys: They were literally his universal soldiers at La Bahia.

I   Brown, Gary, *Volunteers in the Texas Revolution: The New Orleans Greys*, pg. 16.

2   Herman Ehrenberg's diary *With Milam and Fannin* gives several instances of the Greys openly defying Fannin or threatening to act against his will and orders.

Chapter Fifteen

Alabama Red Rovers

Alabama's contributions in money and manpower to the Texas Revolution were also substantial. The most readily recognizable were the Alabama Red Rovers—probably because of their distinctive red clothing, their prominence in the fighting at Coleto, and the diary of Captain (and medical doctor) Jack Shackelford.

The Red Rovers, however, were not the only—or even the first—Alabama volunteers to travel to Texas in 1835-1836. As in other cities such as New Orleans and Montgomery and in smaller towns throughout Georgia, Mississippi, and Kentucky, mass rallies were held after the events at Gonzales in October of 1835.

One of those meetings on October 17, 1835, at the Shakespeare Theater in Mobile, Alabama, led to the subscription of fifteen hundred dollars and several volunteers for service. That meeting would also result in an Alabama resident being sent as a courier to Texas and personal immortality. A copy of the proceedings of the meeting was prepared so that James B. Bonham, who attended the session, could send it to Texas.[1]

Bonham, a lawyer from South Carolina, was practicing law in Alabama at the time. Thought to be a distant relative or boyhood acquaintance of William Barrett Travis, Bonham served in the Texas revolution as a confidant of Sam Houston, a courier for Travis, and finally as an Alamo martyr.

On October 31 another rally was held at Huntsville, Alabama, that resulted in the formation of a company of Alabama volunteers under the command of Colonel Peyton S. Wyatt.

Although a small unit—about twenty men—they were outfitted with rifles borrowed from the state of Alabama and left Huntsville November 8. Following an overland route along the Red

River and Nachitoches, Wyatt's volunteers then entered Texas and journeyed to Nacogdoches—probably following the route of Breece's company of New Orleans Greys.

By the time Wyatt arrived at Nacogdoches early in December 1835, his number had increased to about seventy, including a company of light infantrymen under the command of Captain Amon B. King of Kentucky, the two groups forming a battalion under the command of Captain Wyatt.[2]

From Nacogdoches, Wyatt and his battalion arrived at Washington-on-the-Brazos late in December, just missing the combat action during the battle for Bexar. In January they were dispatched to Goliad to relieve the garrison there and assumed control of the presidio during the tense days in which Grant was demanding the Goliad supplies for his Matamoros campaign.

On January 22 Wyatt and his men rendezvoused at Refugio with the other Texan volunteers, and many of his men—probably because of the political maneuvering they were experiencing—became discouraged. Wyatt was among those disillusioned and personally paid for his men to return to the States. Chartering one of the ships that had transported Fannin and the Georgia Battalion to Copano, Wyatt and his men returned to the United States.[3] Twelve of his men sailed from Copano with him, six others were granted furloughs, and another six were transferred to Fannin's voluntary artillery force.[4]

About a month after Wyatt and the Huntsville Company departed Alabama for Texas, on November 30, another company was created at Montgomery. From the state of Georgia, William Ward was marching his Georgia Battalion across Alabama towards Texas—recruiting and campaigning for the Texan cause. At one of those meetings in Montgomery, their efforts resulted in the organization of fifteen Alabama volunteers under the command of Captain Isaac Ticknor. Although sometimes referred to as the Alabama "Blues," Ticknor's company is officially listed as the Alabama Greys.

While the volunteer units were being sent off by rousing, cheering crowds at Macon and Columbus, such may not have been the case for Captain Isaac Ticknor and his men from Montgomery, Alabama.

According to one source, Isaac Ticknor was "the ruling spirit among the sporting gentry" in Montgomery, who caused peaceable citizens a lot of trouble and at one time was arrested with John Tittle for disturbing the peace. Additionally, "The next happy riddance to the community of this dangerous class occurred when about forty of them left in Captain Ticknor's Company to aid the struggling Texas Colonists in 1836."[5]

Ticknor's Alabama Greys were mustered into the Texas army on January 19. The unit was always associated with Ward's Georgia Battalion—probably because of the recruiting circumstances—and assigned to that battalion and sailed with it to Copano on January 24. The unit is often referred to as the "fourth" company of the Georgia Battalion and—although comprised of Alabama natives—it is remembered as part of Ward's Georgia Battalion.

If Ticknor and his men had caused the "peaceable" citizens of Montgomery a great deal of trouble, they also did so for the Mexicans in 1836. The unit's short history would be decorated with considerable tragedy not associated with combat. According to the Texas General Land Office Index to Military Rolls, three of Ticknor's men—J.H. Elmore, William Jacques, and J. Wilson—drowned at Velasco. Two would be lost and abandoned at Galveston Island including Munroe McLean, while John McIntosh would die of tuberculosis at Refugio. Another, James M. Robinson, would be accidentally shot at Goliad.

Other Alabama volunteers were organized in November in the communities of Courtland and Tuscumbia. These men, under the command of Captain Jack Shackelford, would be known as the Alabama Red Rovers. The term "Red Rovers" was attributed to their distinctive red uniforms. Some sources have suggested that only their pants were dyed red while others claim that their entire uniforms were crimson.

The Red Rovers initially numbered about fifty-five men and were armed with muskets borrowed from the state arsenal.[6] They departed Courtland on December 12 and arrived at New Orleans on January 1, 1836. After being inspected by Stephen F. Austin and Adolphus Sterne at New Orleans, the company arrived at Matagorda Bay on January 19. The men remained at Dimitt's

Landing until accepted for Texas service on February 3.[8] They joined Fannin at Goliad about February 15.

During their short unit history in south Texas, the Alabama Red Rovers would serve in several campaigns and fight with distinction at the Battle of Coleto. Like the New Orleans Greys, they displayed an intense dislike for James Fannin and his command style.

The October 17, 1835 rally at the Shakespeare Theater in Mobile had succeeded in raising funds and volunteer pledges and inserting James Bonham into Texas politics. Those volunteer pledges were later realized in the form of another Alabama unit created by Bonham, A.C. Horton, and Samuel P. St. John, which, through a combination of delays, failed to arrive at the Texan camp at San Antonio until three days after the surrender of Cos.[9] Commanded by Captain David N. Burke, the unit was known as the Mobile Greys.

Arriving at Copano and traveling to San Felipe on November 30, they were ordered to San Antonio but—missing the fighting there—then went south to Goliad where they were mustered into service under Fannin on February 12.

On Christmas Day, Burke joined several other leaders of Texan volunteer companies in protest against being placed under the same regulations as the regular army of Texas.[10] A few days later the Mobile Greys joined Grant and Johnson on their independent Matamoros campaign. When Grant refused to abandon his expedition, Burke and the Mobile Greys were placed under James Fannin's command.

At Goliad, Burke's command was enlarged by adding the remaining members of Breece's New Orleans Greys. By February 29 (1836 being a leap year), Burke, however, was absent from his command and was listed as being on furlough at that date and had "since died." Other records, however, indicate that Burke was ordered to attend the convention at Washington-on-the-Brazos. While there, on March 29, Sam Houston reported to William Christy in New Orleans that he had dispatched Burke to New Orleans and Mobile to recruit more volunteers.

Instead, Secretary of the Navy Robert Potter sent Burke to Galveston, where he took charge of the brig *Pocket*. After the battle of San Jacinto, Burke rejoined the army and arrived at Houston's headquarters on the *Yellow Stone*.[11]

The Alabama Red Rovers, Wyatt's Huntsville Company, Ticknor's Alabama Greys, and Burke's Mobile Greys accounted for between one hundred sixty-five and one hundred seventy-seven Alabama volunteers in Fannin's command at one time or another during the early period of his Goliad campaign.[12]

A.C. Horton, who had been instrumental in the October 17 rally at the Shakespeare Theater in Mobile, was no stranger to Texas or its politics. He had traveled to Texas in the spring of 1835—well before the Gonzales incident—and settled at Austin's Colony near Fannin's plantation at Brazoria. While in Texas he became an ardent advocate of the revolution.

Much of the fifteen hundred dollars subscribed that night was done so by Horton, who also outfitted most of the Mobile Greys at his own expense. At Matagorda, he organized a company of cavalry volunteers in February and enlisted in Fannin's command in March. By U.S. or Mexican army standards, Horton's small unit did not even resemble a true cavalry unit, but they were the basis for Fannin's only scouting capability around Goliad.

While Horton was a native of Alabama, his cavalry unit is not recognized as an Alabama unit. The limited service Horton and his horse soldiers were able to give Fannin was, however, crucial, and it is often overlooked that Horton was responsible for procuring and delivering the limited number of oxen available to Fannin at La Bahia.

1 Elliott, Claude, "Alabama and the Texas Revolution," pp. 315-6.

2 Ibid., pg. 321.

3 Davenport, Harbert, "The Men of Goliad," pg. 17.

4 Elliott, pg. 322.

5 Quoted from the *Alabama Historical Quarterly*, XIX, by Scarborough, Jewell Davis, "The Georgia Battalion in the Texas Revolution: A Critical Study," pg. 528.

6 Elliott, pg. 323.

8 Huson, Hobart, "Red Rovers," *The New Handbook of Texas*.

9 Davenport, pg. 14.

10 Cutrer, Thomas W., "Burke, David N.," *The New Handbook of Texas*.

11 Ibid., and Elliott, pg. 323. Both sources are quoting Harbert Davenport, *Notes from an Unfinished Study of Fannin and His Men* (MS, Harbert Davenport Collection, Texas State Library, Austin; Barker Texas History Center, University of Texas at Austin).

12 Elliott, pg. 323.

Chapter Sixteen

Kentucky Mustangs

It was not a hard freeze, but three or four inches of snow covered the ground on the late November 1835 morning when a small group of men from Bardstown, Kentucky, departed for Texas. Like so many other volunteer units being formed throughout the American South that fall and winter, the unit was destined for the conflict in the northern province of Mexico.

This particular group had formed in the home of William Pope Duval, who had been the first territorial governor of Florida before settling in Bardstown southeast of Louisville.

That autumn, the eldest Duval son, Burr, recruited and organized a small group of volunteers. At the last moment, in late November when the unit was departing, his twenty-year-old brother John Crittendon Duval joined. Both Duval brothers were well educated—having attended the St. Joseph's College in Bardstown. Burr did not survive the revolution, but John managed to escape the Mexicans and later wrote his account titled *Early Days in Texas, or, the Adventures of Jack Dobell*.[1]

Although several historians have dismissed some of his writings as "fanciful" or exaggerated remembrances of the revolution, the fact that the younger John C. was educated and literate gives us a sort of diary with which to study his Kentucky unit.

Young John Duval does not provide many specific dates, but instead, lists general time frames. He reported that in "late November of 1835" he left Bardstown with his brother and their small company marching in the snow. The first day, he reported, they had marched twenty miles north to the small Salt River. On the second day, they marched into Louisville and stayed at the well-known Galt House Hotel.

On the third day of their trip they boarded a steamer traveling down the Mississippi River for New Orleans. The next day they left the winter climate behind and entered the land of the "Spanish moss" and five days out of Bardstown reached the coast and New Orleans.

Duval doesn't state if provisions had been made prior to their arrival in New Orleans, but they were able to immediately book passage on a sailing ship and left the next evening. After being towed overnight to the mouth of the Mississippi, they were set loose through the Southwest Pass bound for the Texas coast.

Enduring one bout of stormy weather, the journey otherwise went smoothly for seven days until they arrived at the Velasco and Quintana communities at the mouth of the Brazos River where they were held up another two days because of wind and tides.

They landed at Quintana and joined other volunteer groups. Because he does not list specific dates, it cannot be verified, but the Kentucky volunteers probably arrived just before Ward and his Georgia Battalion. Duval does not mention the Georgians or even James Fannin, who was at Velasco across the mouth of the river to meet his fellow Georgia natives.

At Quintana, being outside the jurisdiction of U.S. "neutrality laws," the group enlisted in the Texas volunteer army—choosing to serve "for the duration" rather than twelve-month enlistment. When the company reported to the provisional government, the elder Duval requested that they be mustered as mounted rangers.[2]

For a brief period they served aboard the Texas navy ship *Invincible*, patrolling the coastal waters searching for the Mexican warship *Bravo*. They returned to Quintana after a few days and then reboarded the *Invincible* for transport to Copano.

Sailing overnight, they arrived at Aransas Pass in the morning and camped several days on Matagorda Island before taking a small boat to Copano. Once on the Texas mainland, they marched through Refugio to Goliad and joined James Fannin's command.

Fannin combined Duval's Kentucky Riflemen with Benjamin L. Lawrence's Tennessee volunteers and made Burr Duval the commander while at Goliad.

It was while the Kentucky volunteers were garrisoned at Goliad that they received their unit citation, the "Mustangs." John Duval later wrote,

> Not long after our arrival at Goliad the soubiquet of Mustangs or Wild Horses was acquired by our company from the following incident: M—., our second lieutenant [J.Q. Merrifield], was a man of great physical powers, but withal one of the most peaceful and most genial men when not under the influence of liquor. But occasionally he would bet on a "spree" and then he was as wild as a "March hare" and perfectly uncontrollable. The Mexicans seemed to know him and to fear him, also, and when he was on one of his "benders" they would retreat into their houses as soon as they saw him and shut their doors. This proceeding, of course, was calculated to irritate M—., and he would forthwith kick the door from its hinges. On a certain occasion he battered down the doors of half a dozen houses in one street, and from that time the Mexicans called him the "Mustang," and finally the name was applied to the company.[3]

While Duval's Mustangs were the most prominent of the Kentucky volunteers, they were not the only native sons from that state serving in Fannin's command at Goliad.

Captain James Tarleton traveled to Texas with his company of Louisville Volunteers. This company was recruited as the cavalry unit of the Johnson and Grant army. At Goliad under Fannin, the mounted portion of the Louisville Volunteers were merged with Captain Benjamin L. Lawrence's Tennessee volunteers and also named the "Mustangs." The unmounted members of the Louisville Volunteers were then combined with Captain H.R.A. Wigginton's Company.[4]

Amon Butler King had wandered much of his young life until he settled in Kentucky and had become town marshal of Paducah. When Captain Peyton Wyatt passed through Paducah with his Huntsville Company in October of 1835, King and about eighteen other men from the community joined. Either before leaving

Paducah or while on the way to Texas he decided to organize a Kentucky company and formed the Paducah Volunteers.[5]

King and his men then accompanied Wyatt to Texas through Nacogdoches to Washington-on-the-Brazos on December 25. From there, they traveled with Wyatt southward to Refugio and Goliad.

1   Duval, John C., *Early Days in Texas, or, the Adventures of Jack Dobell*, 1892; reprint (Lincoln: University of Nebraska Press, 1986).

2   Roell, Craig H., "Duval, Burr H.," *The New Handbook of Texas*.

3   Duval, pp. 42-3.

4   Davenport, Harbart, "The Men of Goliad," pg. 14.

5   Huson, Hobart and Roell, Craig H., "King, Amon Butler," *The New Handbook of Texas*.

Section IV

The Final Quest for Honor

Chapter Seventeen

Refugio and La Bahia

James Walker Fannin Jr. withdrew from Refugio to Goliad and began consolidating his men and fortifications around mid-February of 1836. All around his position at La Bahia, events began churning out of control at a dizzying speed almost immediately.

At Bexar, James Clinton Neill was maintaining a skeleton garrison in the city and at the Alamo mission and had been writing letters to the Council complaining about Grant's plundering of the supplies and men. He was also shoring up the defenses of the Alamo compound when James Bowie arrived on January 17 with Sam Houston's discretionary orders to remove the artillery, destroy the compound, and retreat to Gonzales.

Neill had inherited an enviable inventory of cannon, although much of it needed mounting. In his haste to depart for Matamoros, Grant had not appropriated the ordnance, and after his arrival, Bowie agreed with Neill that the Alamo compound was defensible against a Mexican advance.

By mid-February, the time that Fannin consolidated at Goliad, Neill left the Alamo to attend to family problems and left William B. Travis in temporary command, assuring the men that he would return.

Travis, a regular army officer, immediately encountered resistance from the volunteers under his command and developed a very hostile working relationship with Bowie—who was now showing signs of serious illness while drinking heavily night and day.

The volunteers, refusing to submit to an officer they hadn't chosen, demanded an election, and Travis acquiesced. As a result, the regulars chose him as commander while the volunteers unanimously chose Bowie to lead them. The Alamo then had two commanders who could hardly communicate with each other.

In east Texas, Sam Houston was still on furlough and negotiating a treaty with the Cherokees that would insure they would remain outside the fighting and not side with Santa Anna nor mount a war on the Anglo settlers in the far, isolated areas of the Texas Anglo settlements.

At San Felipe, the governor's office continued to be claimed by the deposed Henry Smith and acting leader Robinson. The Council also continued to remain deadlocked. In December of 1835 a call for a convention had been made over the veto of Governor Smith and elections called for in February.

Upon leaving his post at Refugio, Sam Houston had also announced his candidacy for the convention and was later elected. At Velasco, Copano, Refugio, and other areas around Anglo Texas, elections were also conducted and delegates chosen. The convention met on March 1, 1836, at Washington-on-the-Brazos, and delegates, including Sam Houston, were finally assembled. The convention's actions would have profound effects on all Anglo Texans but particularly on James Walker Fannin Jr., the "acting commander in chief" at Goliad.

The major issue dividing the Anglo settlers and the newly arrived volunteers generally involved the restoration of 1824 civil liberties as opposed to a complete separation from Mexican governmental control. On March 2 the convention settled the issue and set the course for the remaining conflict: The Declaration of Independence was adopted, and members began signing it on March 3.

The convention also began establishing a temporary government and named David G. Burnet as interim president. More significantly, two days after the declaration of independence from Mexico, the convention reappointed Sam Houston major general of the army with instructions to organize the secessionist military forces.

James Fannin, who had assumed the position as commander from the divided council upon Houston's departure to east Texas, now found himself back under the command of a man with whom he had previously publicly disagreed and, on one occasion at least, disobeyed.

To the south, James Grant, F.W. Johnson, and Robert Morris were continuing their independent advance on Matamoros—no longer a part of the Texan forces Fannin was commanding at Goliad. Morris, in particular, had taken great pains to separate from the Texans, choosing, instead, to accept a military commission in the Mexican Federalist army.

Johnson and Grant had departed Refugio after Houston's speech and took a small force of sixty to one hundred men to San Patricio. Needing horses for their advance south to Matamoros, the two men split up their forces. Grant searched to the south for more horses while Johnson camped at the abandoned Irish colony of San Patricio with those horses they had already obtained.

Johnson in turn divided his men between an outlying ranch and the empty town and was surprised by General José de Urrea in the early morning hours of February 27. Between the two locations, at least twenty Texans were killed and thirty taken prisoner. Johnson and four of his men managed to escape and return to Goliad where they rejoined Fannin.

Grant and Robert Morris, who had been on a horse roundup as far south as the Rio Grande, were attempting to rejoin Johnson at San Patricio when they camped on Agua Dulce Creek. There, on March 2, Urrea's cavalry surprised and attacked them, killing Morris, Grant, and twelve other Texans.

James Grant, the speculator who had suspiciously manipulated an extensive and potentially lucrative land deal from the Coahuila and Texas legislature only to see it slip from his control with Santa Anna's occupation of that federal capital, was particularly hated by the Mexican authorities.

There are several accounts of his death: He was trampled under the hoofs of the wild horses he was herding; he was viciously set upon with swords; or he was tied to the hoofs of a wild mustang and dashed to death on the prairie. But it is for certain that his Mexican captors were aware of his political treachery and land grabbing prior to the revolution, and his death was particularly revengeful.

The men captured at Agua Dulce and those prisoners from San Patricio were imprisoned at Matamoros, making them, ironically, the only men in Grant's expedition to actually reach their destination.

And so James Fannin, in mid-February at Goliad, was still considered by many to be the commander in chief of the army, but even he could realize he was in the midst of a political and military revolution that was clearly out of control and drifting toward disaster.

Faced with an enormous Mexican military force not far to his south, Fannin found himself commanding with orders from Sam Houston—which he had chosen to ignore—and at least two sets of contradicting orders from Acting Governor Robinson—that he at least chose to recognize. He had been variously ordered to withdraw and to occupy and fortify his position.

Even worse, he was in charge of a significant army that resented his leadership and resisted his command.

This was in some ways a direct response by the volunteers to his indecisive leadership style. Even in the earliest days of his command, indecision was a criticism leveled at him by his field force—officers and volunteers alike.

He had arrived at Copano after publicly announcing his intention to "take the war into Mexico" and—after receiving Morris' letter—abandoned his attack strategy and immediately withdrew into a defensive mode. After campaigning relentlessly and shamelessly for command and military rank, he achieved it only to publicly question his ability and desire to lead.

The seeds of destruction and catastrophe had been sown all around his tiny fortress at La Bahia by mid-February of 1836, and James Fannin did little to stop their development.

As early as February 14 he began addressing correspondence to Governor Robinson and the General Council at San Felipe from Goliad. On the sixteenth he wrote the governor and council advising them again of his intelligence gathering around Goliad and the fact that General Urrea was expected to advance on his position.

Once more he listed needs and tactics for the politicians, who had little or no means to implement them. "Stir up the people, but do not allow them to come into camp unless *organized*. I never wish to see an election in camp where I am responsible in any manner,¹" he admonished them, obviously ignoring that he had himself been elected with William Ward by that same method.

"If General Houston does not return to duty on the expiration of his furlough, and it meets your approbation, I shall make head quarters at Bexar, and take with me such of the force as can be spared," he continued.

The council did not approbate: The command headquarters at Bexar was already full. With three commanders—Colonel Neill, Colonel Travis, and Colonel Bowie—and another, Colonel David Crockett, on the way, Bexar already had too many colonels.

"Bexar and Guadalupe, and Colorado, I think will be the posts of danger and honour," he prophesied in his letter. He had previously asked Houston for such a post and now, at Goliad with Urrea's army nearby, he indicated to the council that he felt he could be better utilized elsewhere.

"No aid be expected from Mexicans," he continued. "Nothing certain from Johnson & Co. The Artillery is on the way up here. Nothing from Colonel Wharton & co." The artillery in question involved the pieces being retrieved from Refugio by the contingent of Greys who had been sent to Morris' aid earlier.

The next day, the seventeenth, Fannin addressed another letter to Robinson again reiterating that it was the "design of Santa Anna to overrun the country and overrun or exterminate every white man within its borders."² And once more he spelled out his aversion to elections in camp.

He seemed to have become obsessed with preventing dissention within military camps. The reason for this at this particular time may have been that his own camp control and disciplinary problems were approaching a crisis stage. No less an ally than fellow Georgian William Ward had become entangled in the politics of Fannin's command.

Ward, it appears, had visited Governor Smith shortly after arriving in Texas, and the two men had become friends. In the following days, Smith had confided in Ward through letters and dispatches—one of which had been delivered to Ward by James Fannin.

Given the fact that Fannin had publicly distanced himself from Smith in favor of Robinson, Ward's friendship and sharing of confidences with Smith after his deposition as governor would not have set well with Fannin.

Fannin identified very closely with the Georgia Battalion, and although he was its commander, the fact remained that William Ward was the unit's lieutenant colonel and the man who had raised and escorted the group to Texas. The men looked to Ward, not Fannin, as their true field commander.

The letter in question that Fannin had delivered from Smith to Ward evidently contained some common concerns the two men had regarding the political turmoil going on inside Texas. Ward had shown the letter to Fannin who, after Smith had been deposed, quoted excerpts in correspondence to Smith's considerable number of political enemies at San Felipe and Washington-on-the-Brazos.

As a result, Ward had received an official request to turn the letter over or furnish a copy to the committee at San Felipe. In a long and detailed response dated February 20 from Goliad, William Ward reveals himself to be a man of resolve and principle—and a leader unafraid to take a moral stand.

His letter suggests he has already become disgusted with the political bickering and turmoil in which his commander in chief, James Fannin, was involved and the colonel's attempt to involve Ward.

". . . .you call upon me to furnish you with the copy of a letter, written by the said Smith to me some time during the past month, extracts from which have been furnished you by Col. J.W. Fannin, Jr.,[3]" Ward wrote the committee. "I feel myself compelled to decline compliance with your request, and a sense of self-respect and courtesy to your body prompts me to explain to you frankly the reasons which prompt me to adopt this course," he continued.

Ward explains the background of his friendship with Smith and the exchange of views that were based upon the expectation of confidentiality. ". . . .in yielding it [the letter] to the possession of his enemies, would I not act the part of a traitorous and faithless friend?" he pointed out. Then Ward assails the betrayal of his own confidences with James Fannin:

> Col. Fannin was himself the bearer of the letter from
> Gov. Smith to me. . . .I submitted the paper to his inspec-
> tion. He made several applications to me for the purpose
> of obtaining a copy and the liberty of using the privilege
> with which I had confidentially intrusted him, to all of
> which I gave an unqualified and prompt denial. Judge of my
> surprise and astonishment then, when your letter
> informed me that, with an abandonment of delicacy and
> decorum that I thought appertained to a character with
> which Col. Fannin acknowledge no affinity, he had used me
> and my confidence to feed the flame of discontent and
> hatred against the Governor, in which it seems he is ambi-
> tions to act a conspicuous part.

Ward further accuses Fannin of misquoting and "perverting" the general sense and meaning of the letter. "In the character of an informer, he should give a false coloring to a document," Ward further denounced Fannin.

This letter is significant for what it indicates about Ward, about Fannin, and the relationship between the two highest leaders in the Goliad command during February of 1836.

Not only did Fannin have a nearly continuous rebellion on the part of many of his volunteer army—particularly the Greys—but he also had managed to alienate his closest ally and second in command. Whether due to careless miscalculations or blind ambition, James Fannin throughout the short Texas revolution alienated many of the people with whom he relied upon for his own personal success.

Nevertheless, he continued to fortify his defenses at La Bahia in Goliad. The old Spanish presidio, although abandoned several times during its history and in need of repairs, remained the most formidable fort in Mexican Texas.

Heavy stone walls three feet thick and ten feet high surrounded the three-and-one-half-acre quadrangle. Under the direction of Adjutant General Joseph M. Chadwick, a military and topographical engineer trained at West Point, the walls were refortified and strengthened.

Unlike the Alamo mission compound in Bexar, this presidio was designed as a fortress and had a sally port, or main gate, located on

Our Lady of Loreto Chapel at La Bahia

La Bahia walls and grounds

The ancient Spanish presidio, La Bahia, played a pivotal role in James Fannin's command in South Texas. It was here he headquartered his army, dispatched the ill-fated rescue mission to the Alamo, divided his army to assist Irish refugees nearby, and finally evacuated in a move that led to the Battle of Coleto.

In this small courtyard inside the Presidio La Bahia, James Fannin was executed after the massacre of his men on Palm Sunday, 1836.

the south side. Chadwick and John Sowers Brooks supervised the rebuilding of the main gate and the construction of a smaller gate on the north wall.

The presidio had been built on the highest area of the rolling hills in the area but near the bank of the San Antonio River. To assure access to water during a prolonged siege situation, the smaller gate on the north wall became known as the "water gate." From this gate, a trench was dug to the river and covered so as to provide a protected avenue of access to the river water.

The inside quadrangle was developed as a parade ground. Along the west wall were the officer's barracks, and on the south wall, east of the sally port, were additional buildings constructed along the stone wall. On the west side of the sally port was a stone building used as a jail, or calaboose.

Bastions were located on each corner and were of sufficient size to accommodate artillery pieces. The northwest bastion, in particular, was important since it provided artillery access to the north of the town and overlooked the San Antonio River.

Along the north wall was constructed the chapel, named Our Lady of Loreto. The chapel had a bell tower that provided an excellent lookout post commanding the countryside in all directions. Designed for use by Spanish presidio soldiers and their families, the chapel was tiny by mission standards, eighty-five feet long and about thirty feet wide with a small alcove on one side. Toward the top of the high, arched ceiling were three octagonal windows.

Under the direction of Chadwick and Brook, Fannin ordered these defenses shored up with stone and dirt. Inside the courtyard, a trench was constructed around the perimeter—the dirt being used to reinforce the walls. A new blockhouse was built and existing ones improved.

Artillery was strategically placed in the bastions and the volunteer units were assigned positions inside the quadrangle. "This will all be completed, and nine pieces of Artillery mounted by the Ides of March," Fannin wrote Robinson on February 21.[4]

By this date, Fannin was acutely aware of the Mexican spies surrounding him. He had previously warned not to trust the Mexicans around Goliad, but by the time he had occupied and started rebuilding the old fort, the Mexicans in Goliad had abandoned the town.

Today the community of Goliad is situated some two miles away from the presidio, but in 1836 the community was located directly surrounding the fort itself. By the time Fannin and his army arrived, most of the local Mexicans had retreated to the safety of nearby ranches. However a few had remained, and at least one local cantina continued to operate for the soldiers.

As described by historian Harbert Davenport:

> It may be remarked, in passing, that Colonel Fannin and other Texans underestimated the importance of these Mexicans of Goliad, and the resentment in their hearts due to having had to leave their homes. Unlike the Mexican citizenry of San Patricio and Victoria, who came, for the most part, of good *ranchero* stock, the *Badenos*, as they called the people of Goliad, were descendants of the presidial soldiers stationed at La Bahia through the years, and were not too highly regarded by their countrymen, or by anyone else. They were indolent and none too honest, but they were expert horsemen—among the world's best—knew every acre of the Goliad region and for a hundred miles around, and, contrary to the prevalent belief of the Texans, were anything but cowardly when convinced of the advantages of being brave. Their leader, Carlos de la Garza, had dignity and force of character, and courage and intelligence, as well. They had abandoned Goliad at his bidding, and it was to his *rancho* on the San Antonio that they had gone. He and his men were "everywhere" after General Urrea came.[5]

One response by Fannin to this problem of local spies was to arrest an "old Priest" and thirteen soldiers preparatory to sending them to the seat of government.[6]

"*This man* [Padre Valdez] *of God* is the blackest of old villains—a murderer, adulterer.&c., and his influence is almost unbounded" Fannin continued in his February 21 letter to Robinson.

The priest and his nephew were eventually the only prisoners to be dispatched to Washington-on-the-Brazos. William Gordon Cooke, who had left the Greys behind at Refugio, took the two prisoners with him when he traveled north to join Sam Houston's staff as assistant inspector general.

In a postscript to his February 21 letter, Fannin made the poignant comment that "In relieving guard yesterday, the corporal marched off *bare-footed*. Many of the men are so near *naked*, that only certain parts of their body are covered."

The letter also had one additional comment that, although seemingly insignificant, would suggest Fannin was having second thoughts about his command.

"I hope you will soon release me from the army, at least as an officer," he wrote Robinson. Interspersed into the dialogue about the arrest of the old priest, this single sentence seems almost to have been inserted by mistake. No further mention of the issue is made in this letter, however the next day Fannin addressed another letter to Robinson in which he made clear he no longer wanted to command the forces at Goliad.

At this time Sam Houston had not been reinstated as commander in chief, however many in Texas still considered Henry Smith the legitimate governor and Sam Houston as the military leader. That, and the fact that both Grant and Johnson were calling themselves commanders in chief of their forces, meant that Texas had at least four aspirants to the top position. It was through Acting Governor Robinson's influence that Fannin had actually assumed control over the largest army in the field—that at Goliad and La Bahia.

The day after describing the fortifications at La Bahia and announcing the arrest of the old priest, February 22, Fannin wrote another long letter to James W. Robinson. This time, however, he addressed at length his personal doubts about his leadership role at Goliad.

> I am critically situated. General Houston is absent on furlough, and neither myself nor army have received any orders as to who should assume the command. It is my right; and, in many respects, I have done so, where I was convinced the public weal [sic] required it. I know that

many men of influence view me with an envious eye, and either desire my station, or my disgrace.[7]

While Fannin is adamant about his right to the command and his ability to assume it, it is also obvious by this time that he was unhappy with his position as commander and anxious to be relieved of his duties. Much of this disillusionment appears to be directed at the volunteer army over which he was struggling daily to exercise control.

"I did not seek, in any manner, the one I hold" he informed Governor Robinson on February 22, ". . . and if I am qualified to command an Army, *I have not found it out.* I well know I am a better company officer than most men now in Texas, and might do with Regulars &c., for a Regiment."

Fannin also included in this letter, as he had so many times previously, his recommendations for the direction of the war effort in Texas and the organization of the army by the council. In a passage that makes obvious his intent to withdraw from his position as commander he referred Robinson to some of his officers. "Will you allow me to call your attention to some young men, the best qualified men I have ever seen in Texas, Captains Wm. G. Cook, and N.R. Brister, both of the New Orleans Greys—John S. Brooks, and Joseph M. Chadwell, who have each served the 24th of December, as Adjutant and Sergeant-Major. . . ."

He then approached the topic of his furlough by telling Robinson, "After near eighteen months absence, nothing but dire necessity can keep me from my wife and children."

Then, on February 25, came the catastrophic confirmation that a second Mexican army had driven deep into Texas towards San Antonio de Bexar—a force led by president and general Antonio Lopez de Santa Anna himself.

As Fannin, Chadwick, and Brooks oversaw the fortification efforts during the twenty-fifth, a messenger arrived from Bexar with a short communiqué from Colonels William Barret Travis and James Bowie.

It was a day that would change everything—virtually everything Anglo in Texas—from that date on. The message was short and to the point. But the words it contained changed forever the course of Texas history:

[To J.W. Fannin Jr.]   [23Feb 1836]

.... We have removed all our men into the Alamo, where
we will make such resistance as is due to our honour, and that
of the country, until we can get assistance from you, which we
expect you to forward immediately. In this extremity, we hope
you will send us all the men you can spare promptly. We have
one hundred and forty-six men, who are determined *never to
retreat*. We have but little provisions, but enough to serve us
till you and your men arrive. We deem it unnecessary to repeat
to a brave officer, who knows his duty, that we call on him for
assistance. . . .

[W. Barret Travis]
[James Bowie][8]

The news was electrifying throughout the garrison at Goliad
and La Bahia and throughout Anglo Texas. Fannin planned to leave
the next day with three hundred twenty volunteers and four pieces
of artillery.

1   Jenkins, *PTR*, 4;350-1.
2   Ibid., 4:371.
3   Ibid., 4:388-391.
4   Ibid., 4:391-2.
5   Davenport, "The Men of Goliad," pg. 12.
6   Smith, Ruth Cumby, *James W. Fannin, Jr., in the Texas Revolution*,
    pg. 195.
7   Jenkins, *PTR*, 4:398-401.
8   Ibid., 4:419.

Chapter Eighteen

Fannin's "Ides of March"

Fannin had announced that he would have the fort at La Bahia fortified by the "Ides of March" in his February 21 letter to Robinson. Always dramatic, Fannin doesn't indicate if he was referring simply to a calendar date or alluding to some sinister prophecy. As the month of March developed, however, it became clear that he was in fact a player in complicated, complex, and very dangerous schemes by the politicians in San Felipe and Washington-on-the-Brazos.

While the month of March during 1836 would prove to be a series of daily crises, Fannin's problems during this period actually began during the final days of February when he attempted to respond to Travis' and Bowie's call for aid.

One element of Fannin's legacy has been that of indecision under pressure. What is often overlooked, however, is that Fannin also never refused a call for aid. He had responded immediately—and divided his own force—by dispatching Captain Cooke and the Greys to Morris' aid at San Patricio. In the coming weeks, he would again split his troops when Irish colonists around Goliad requested aid in evacuating.

And on February 25, as he stood at La Bahia reading the plea from the Alamo, he reacted immediately. There was no indecision—no hesitation.

The decision to march to the aid of the Alamo was met with a great deal of enthusiasm by Fannin's volunteers. The New Orleans Greys, who had nearly revolted when denied horses and supplies to rejoin their comrades at San Antonio earlier, were overjoyed.

"Elated by this decision, we packed our things, left the fort, and made camp on the other side of the river, taking it for granted that next day we should be on our way to the scene of our first triumphs," Herman Ehrenberg later recalled.[1]

The other volunteers, many of whom had found life boring and tedious at La Bahia, were anxious to finally have the chance of a fight with the Mexicans.

Fannin left Captain Westover and his men in charge of the presidio and headed north to Bexar and the Alamo. While still within sight of the fort, Fannin attempted to cross the San Antonio River only to have one wagon—some reports claim as many as three—break down. The volunteers camped out overnight in freezing rain on the other side of the river, separated from their supplies and ammunition.

In a scene that resembles a burlesque tragedy, the relief campaign quickly unraveled. It was discovered that they had no provisions. "Not a particle of bread stuff, except a small portion of rice, and no beef, and not a head of cattle, except the oxen drawing the wagon."[2] To make matters worse, the inexperienced wagoners had allowed the oxen to graze unfettered overnight. The animals had wandered off, leaving the army with no way to transport any supplies or food on the trip to San Antonio.

After a council of war—that democratic vote-taking that Fannin so despised among the volunteer army—it was decided to return to the fort and continue to fortify the defenses there. "This morning whilst here I received a note from the officer commanding the volunteers requesting, in the name of the officers of his command, a Council of War, on the subject of the expedition to Bexar, which, of course, was granted," Fannin wrote Robinson on the twenty-sixth.[3] He later wrote to Captains Desauque and Chenworth "...a council of war was unanimously demanded of me by the Volunteer officers and granted of course it was resolved to...return and complete the Fortification and await our doom until relieved whipped or we conquer."[4]

It would appear in these letters that Fannin was at least partially attempting to shift the responsibility for the decision to retreat back to Goliad to the "unanimous" vote of the volunteer officers.

Ehrenberg claimed that Fannin had other motives:

Fannin, however, would neither retreat nor march to the aid of San Antonio, preferring to await the onset of the enemy behind the fortifications he had erected in Goliad. There, at least, he was the undisputed leader, whereas if he returned to the main army he would have to give up his supremacy. With the hope of changing his selfish resolution, we reminded him constantly of the probable fate of our brothers-in-arms if we turned a deaf ear to their appeal. But our efforts were in vain, and vain also were our entreaties imploring him to abandon Goliad. He stuck to Goliad—though to be sure he did not adhere to his course without a struggle. His contradictory orders revealed to us the conflict between his ambition and his generosity. . . .[5]

Ehrenberg, it should be remembered, penned these words years later while safely residing in the halls of German university academia. Fannin, at La Bahia, had no such luxury, plus his responsibility as a commander to make decisions and act—something Ehrenberg himself would later prove unable to do—required him to make crucial decisions. He did so. He decided to attempt a rescue mission. When the mission failed, he ordered the army back to La Bahia. Ehrenberg was incorrect in his assessment that Fannin "would neither retreat nor march to the aid of San Antonio."

Ehrenberg was also wrong in his assertion that Fannin preferred to remain at Goliad where he was the undisputed leader and not required to give up his supremacy. Fannin's own letters to the top officials in Texas government clearly prove that he wished to relinquish his command and was eager to accept the authority of Houston as commander in chief.

Ehrenberg also later reported, "The only explanation offered to us for this sudden overthrow of our new hopes was that most of the volunteers in our group were against the march to San Antonio and preferred to stay in Goliad. How Fannin obtained this information was a mystery to us, since he did not even give his troops a chance to express their opinion about the unexpected reversal of his plans."

In this complaint Ehrenberg may have had a valid point. Fannin never specifically indicated who was included in his "council of war," only that the decision was "unanimous." The New

Orleans Greys, including Ehrenberg, were openly hostile to Fannin's leadership so they may not have been included in the "council" when the final decision was made.

One of those officers who did attend the session, however, was John Sowers Brooks, a Georgia Battalion member who was by this time Fannin's aide-de-camp. "Yet everyone saw the impropriety, if not the impossibility of our proceeding under existing circumstances. . ." he later wrote his mother.[6]

And so, in the freezing rain, the New Orleans Greys, Georgia Battalion, and other Texan volunteers retreated once again to the fortress at Goliad. One hundred miles away, the cannon had started pounding the walls of the Alamo compound at San Antonio, but the Texans at Goliad could not have known this.

Equally ominous in the silence of the south Texas plains was the fact that General Urrea's Mexican army had finally arrived and was advancing on Johnson and his men at San Patricio. Recruited from the villages of Jalapa, Cordoba, and Orizaba, many of the Tres Villas Battalion soldiers were of Indian descent.[7]

Most of them were from the tropics and had never felt such a winter's blast. Six of them froze to death. But they managed to surprise Colonel Johnson, who occupied the town with forty men.[8]

After making a successful trip to the Rio Grande to capture wild horses, Johnson, Morris, and Grant had returned to San Patricio where Johnson stabled the horses on a nearby ranch. He then bivouacked in the abandoned colony with a small force while Grant and Morris left to obtain more horses.

During the night of the twenty-sixth, in the midst of the brutal "blue norther," General Jose de Urrea surrounded the ranch and captured the horses and eight Texans while killing four men.

In San Patricio, Captain Pearson and eight Texans were camping in the public square while Johnson and the rest were billeting in abandoned houses. At 3:00 o'clock on the morning of the twenty-seventh the Texans were awakened by gunfire, followed by a cease-fire in which the Mexicans offered Johnson's men a free pardon if they would surrender. They ignored the offer and continued to fight throughout the night until daylight when they surrendered in order to obtain aid for their wounded.

In the midst of the initial firefight, Johnson and four others did escape to return to Goliad. In San Patricio, eight Texans were killed, including two Mexicans loyal to the rebel's cause, thirteen were taken prisoner, and six, including Johnson, escaped. Morris and Grant, on another horse-gathering trip during the attack, maintained their position twenty-six miles to the south near Agua Dulce Creek.

Back in Goliad, Johnson's arrival and his story of the defeat of Texan forces at San Patricio confirmed reports that General Urrea was in their immediate vicinity. Within days, more bad news arrived at the presidio.

Five of Morris' and Grant's men appeared at the gate of the fort to announce that Urrea's soldiers had surprised them at Agua Dulce Creek and destroyed their force. Morris was killed early in the encounter. A total of twelve Texans were killed, four were captured, and six had escaped. Dr. James Grant was captured in the ambush and, while a prisoner, murdered.

The news of these disasters was a harbinger of events already unfolding around the countryside surrounding James Fannin and his command. On February 28 he wrote a short letter to his partner at Brazoria, Joseph Mims, that indicated he had finally accepted the danger posed by the oncoming Mexican forces and had become even more disillusioned by his role in the conflict.

"I will never give up the ship, while there is a pea in the ditch. If I am whipped, it will be well done—and you may never expect to see me,"[9] he warned Mims. "Look to our property—save it for my family, whatever may be my fate," he continued, "... But I must now play a bold game—I will go the whole hog. If I am lost, be the censure on the right head, and may my wife & children and children's children curse the sluggards for ever. I am too mad, and too much to do—any thing but fight."

Concluding his letter on an ominous note, he told Mims: "Hoping for the best, being prepared for the worst, I am in a devil of a bad humor."

Still, he insisted on maintaining his position at Goliad and on March 1 notified the governor and Council of Johnson's return with the news of the destruction of the force at San Patricio.

"I am now pretty well prepared to make battle," he notified them. "I have nearly completed my fortifications, and have enough beef for twenty days. . . . I am resolved to await your orders, let the consequence be what it may."[10]

Fannin also reiterated his complaint that he and the volunteers were shouldering the burden of the revolution while the Anglo settlers seemed content to remain at home and leave the fighting against the Mexicans to the American volunteers.

This grievance against the settlers was a restatement of an indictment Fannin had written Robinson three days earlier, on February 28, when he stated " . . . but should the worst happen—on whose head should the burthen [sic] of censure fall—not on the heads of those brave men who have left their homes in the United States to aid us in our struggle for Liberty—but on those whose all is in Texas & who notwithstanding the repeated calls have remained at home without raising a finger to keep the Enemy from their thresholds. . . ."[11]

Fannin's complaint about the lack of support by the established settlers, especially of those volunteers who had marched across Texas to arrive at Goliad, probably reflected the general feeling around the courtyard at La Bahia.

Initially, the Anglo settlers had held rousing welcomes for the incoming volunteers. Breece's company of New Orleans Greys had been toasted and banqueted at San Augustine, Nacogdoches, Bastrop, and every other Anglo community on the way to San Antonio. The other company of Greys—Morris' unit—had met the same reception at Columbia and Victoria as they crossed the prairies to San Antonio.

Adolphus Sterne, the Nacogdoches alcalde who had so graciously welcomed the Greys at his home in a "feast of liberty," also traveled to New Orleans to personally greet the Alabama Red Rovers and assure them of their support inside Texas before they sailed to Matagorda Bay.

Wyatt's Alabama volunteers had entered Texas at Nacogdoches to cheering settlers before working their way down to Goliad.

But by March of 1836 the settlers were conspicuously absent from the ranks of the soldiers at Goliad and, to the north, inside the Alamo compound. That these volunteers—mostly American southerners—should resent this apparent abandonment of support would seem to be justified. Harbert Davenport, however, presents a sound argument for what appeared to be indifference on the part of the settlers.

". . . Austin's 'old settlers'; those whose families were in Texas, and who owned and tilled the soil had been told, and had believed, since the previous autumn, that Cos' defeat meant the end of the war," Davenport wrote in 1939.[12] They had shared their homes, food, and even animals with the incoming volunteers but their job in 1836, he continued, was to plant corn, which required their wagons, teams, and tools. This also required their presence in the fields.

". . . if Texas did not grow corn, Texan families, as well as the Texan soldiers, would surely go hungry before the end of the year. War was a pleasurable excitement, but one to be enjoyed after the crops had been gathered in the fall. Meantime, the Texans and their families had to eat," he continued.

Davenport also pointed out that in the point of view of the "Old Settlers": ". . . feeding the army was, first of all, the duty of the government, they were right; and that the government did not so feed them, Colonel Fannin, as much as any other individual, was to blame. His letters were all directed to 'Acting Governor' Robinson, and the discredited remnant of the Council, which was too lacking in character and credit and had become too impotent and feeble to so much as hire a courier, much less find wagons, teams, provisions, and the military transport or supplies."

And so, ironically, while Fannin bemoaned the lack of support from the settlers, they in turn pointed to the corruption and indecision from the divided Texan government that was trying to exert authority over them all.

Part of this indifference toward the government and Fannin's army may also have been directed toward the objectives of the conflict with Mexico as the settlers saw it in March of 1836. In the previous seven months, there had been attempts by Mexican authorities to tighten the Centralist controls over the colonists followed by some minor clashes.

Then had come the siege of San Antonio de Bexar. The small band of Gonzales settlers who followed the Mexicans from

Gonzales back to San Antonio had quickly grown into a small army. Once the siege had begun, however, the settlers almost immediately returned home to their fields and crops. The remaining Texan "army" in San Antonio had very quickly become a mercenary force of American volunteers centered mostly on Mississippi volunteers and the New Orleans Greys.

The settlers were not represented in the siege army during the final days before the assault and were therefore noticeably absent during the five-day battle for San Antonio.

Grant and Johnson's Matamoros expedition from San Antonio had further alienated the established Texan settlers. To the Anglo farmers, discussion and argument of the restoration of certain liberties were relevant, while Grant and his mercenary force that marched to "take the war to Mexico" meant nothing to them. In fact, the settlers were noticeably indifferent to Grant's campaign to reclaim his lost land and riches in Coahuila. They certainly didn't feel an obligation to feed and supply a "private army" that didn't represent their interests.

Also, the warmness between the settlers and incoming volunteers had, in many instances, been destroyed by the conduct of some of the Americans crossing the Sabine late in 1835. Incidents of drunkenness and vandalism by the volunteers had severely damaged the support from the settlers.

So while Fannin complained bitterly of the lack of support from the Texans in 1836, he also commanded at Goliad many of those same volunteers who had antagonized the very people they were purporting to represent. And, significantly, he was also commanding the core basis of the army that had left with Grant on the Matamoros expedition two months earlier.

James Fannin and his army at Goliad were in many ways an "army of occupation" in the eyes of the Anglo setters as well as Santa Anna's, and the Texans felt little or no obligation to support him. And he, in turn, felt betrayed.

In his letter, he again attempted to shed his role as commander: "I cannot, in a military point of view, be considered now as *acting* commander in chief, as I have never received orders to that effect, nor has the army."

He again stressed his desire to take a furlough—which he claimed had been approved—beginning in April.

"I am desirous to be erased from the list of officers, or expectants of office, and have leave to bring off my brave foreign volunteers, in the best manner I may be able," he concluded.

And thus, by the beginning of March it appears that Fannin had not only made obvious his desire to leave his command, but to remove the Georgia Battalion and personally rejoin his family.

Much had occurred since his entry into the Texan fight at Gonzales the previous October. But now, in his fortress-turned-prison, all blind ambition from those early days was gone. Gone, also, was the incessant demand to the politicians at San Felipe that he be awarded a brigadier generalship.

In March of 1836 the Texas "Revolution" had all but unraveled. The political affairs of Texas were even more divided and confused. Fannin's command was disputed by many inside and outside his army. Houston was again the commander in chief, and Travis and Bowie were now trapped inside the Alamo compound awaiting the reinforcements from Goliad that Fannin could not deliver.

Now, as he sat in the half-frozen mud and slush inside La Bahía, all James Walker Fannin Jr. wanted was to go home to his family.

By this time, however, his role in the unfolding tragedies surrounding Goliad and La Bahía had already been established by events outside his control. Although by March 1 he had completed most of the fortifications at La Bahía and had "enough beef for twenty days," the volunteers under his command were in fact in dire need of clothing, ammunition, and other critical supplies.

Fannin had notified Robinson that he had supplies at Matagorda—Cox's Point and Dimitt's Landing—on February 28 and that he was attempting to transport them to Goliad. They had not arrived.

If the situation at Goliad was perilous, the conditions at the Alamo compound had become catastrophic. On February 23 Travis had expressed his announcement that they were besieged in the Alamo to Fannin with the plea for aid: a communiqué that Fannin had received on the twenty-fifth. Between those dates, on February 24, Travis also wrote another short letter: One that would cement forever his place in Texas history. It is one of the most quoted of all documents of Texas history:

Commandancy of the Alamo
Bejar, Feby. 24, 1836

To the People of Texas & All Americans in the World

Fellow citizens & compatriots

    I am besieged, by a thousand or more of the Mexicans under Santa Anna I have sustained a continual Bombardment & cannonade for 24 hours & have not lost a man The enemy has demanded a surrender at discretion, otherwise, the garrison are to be put to the sword, if the fort is taken I have answered the demand with a cannon shot, & our flag still waves proudly from the walls I shall never surrender or retreat. Then, I call on you in the name of Liberty, of patriotism & everything dear to the American character, to come to our aid, with all dispatch The enemy is receiving reinforcements daily & will no doubt increase to three or four thousand in four or five days. If this call is neglected, I am determined to sustain myself as long as possible & die like a soldier who never forgets what is due to his own honor & that of his country VICTORY OR DEATH.

William Barret Travis,
Lt. Col. comdt.

P.S. The Lord is on our side. When the enemy appeared in sight we had not three bushels of corn. We have since found in deserted houses 80 or 90 bushels and got into the walls 20 or 30 head of Beeves.

In later years William Barret Travis would be assailed for aspects of his personal life and background, but so long as this letter exists, he will always remain a hero and martyr of the Texas Revolution.

The letter also assured that James Walker Fannin Jr. would always have a secondary position and role in the history unfolding in Texas in the spring of 1836. Travis' appeal, as copies of it made their way to newspapers in the United States and Europe, focused attention not on Goliad, or even Texas, but squarely upon the tiny Franciscan mission and compound to the northeast of San Antonio de Bexar.

In many ways, this remains true today.

By March 3, however, the call had gone largely unheeded. In the early morning hours of March 1, thirty-two volunteer reinforcements—men from the Gonzales Ranging Company of Mounted Volunteers—had responded. But they had been the only response to Travis' emotional appeal.

And it was on this date, March 3, that Travis penned another urgent message to the president of the convention. "Colonel Fannin is said to be on the march to this place with reinforcements, but I fear it is not true, as I have *repeatedly* sent to him for aid without receiving any. Colonel Bonham, my special messenger, arrived at La Bahia fourteen days ago, with a request for aid, and on the arrival of the enemy in Bexar, ten days ago, I sent an express to Colonel F., which arrived at Goliad on the next day, urging him to send us reinforcements; none have yet arrived."[13]

Travis obviously was unaware of the aborted rescue mission Fannin had launched on the twenty-sixth. Continuing to hope for Fannin's arrival, he was also unaware that, one hundred miles to the south, Fannin and his men were again busily fortifying the old Spanish presidio.

Fannin, who had asked for furlough and relief from his command, was also awaiting orders from San Felipe or Washington-on-the-Brazos. Those orders were issued on March 6 by Acting Governor Robinson but did absolutely nothing to clarify Fannin's position or instruct him. "In accordance with our official duty & our oaths we have to say & instruct you to use your own discretion to remain where you are or to retreet as you may think best for the safety of the brave Volunteers Under your command . . . unless you shall be instructed otherwise by Genl. Houston who has been by this new convention confirmed & appointed commander in chief of the Army of Texas Militia & volunteers; as well as regulars,"[15] Robinson ambiguously wrote Fannin.

While this letter at first appearance would seem to relieve Fannin of responsibility by reestablishing Sam Houston as commander in chief, in fact the correspondence only made Fannin's position at Goliad even more precarious.

The volunteers under his command, spoiling for a fight with the Mexicans since their arrival in Texas, had initially resisted his efforts to rebuild the fort at La Bahia. Mainly due to the efforts of Brooks and Chadwick, they had finally been coerced into refortifying only to have Fannin announce they would be withdrawing to San Antonio on the twenty-sixth of February. When that mission failed and they had returned to La Bahia, there had been additional fortification done, and now the men wanted to make their stand and fight the Mexicans.

Fannin correctly foresaw that any order by him to withdraw after all this would be met with open hostility if not insubordination. Sam Houston, on the other hand, was now again the commander in chief, and any order to withdraw issued by him would be Fannin's duty to obey.

Robinson and the council had done Fannin no justice by issuing permission to remain at Goliad or retreat "at discretion." His actions were now dictated not by what he felt as a military leader but what he felt he could coerce his men into agreeing to. His dislike and distrust of "democratic" volunteer armies had proven to be accurate assessments of the weaknesses of such organization.

Sam Houston, however, did have a plan for Fannin and the volunteers at Goliad. On March 8, Houston sent an express communiqué to Fannin ordering him to withdraw to Gonzales at once. The next day, Houston wrote Burleson, requesting him to unite with Colonel Neill and recommend a route by which Fannin could join the main force at Gonzales. Fannin received Houston's order on March 12 and was preparing to comply the next day when his command at Goliad, which had been tenuous at best for weeks, began to completely fall apart.

> Sir: You will, as soon as practicable after the receipt of this order, fall back upon Guadalupe Victoria, with your command, and such artillery as can be brought with

expedition. The remainder will be sunk in the river. You will take the necessary measures for the defence of Victoria, and forward one third the number of your effective men to this point, and remain in command until further orders.

Every facility is to be afforded to women and children who may be desirous of leaving that place. Previous to abandoning Goliad, you will take the necessary measures to blow up that fortress; and do so before leaving its vicinity. The immediate advance of the enemy may be confidently expected, as well as a rise of water. Prompt movements are therefore highly important.[16]

At this time Fannin and the Texans also learned the fate of Colonels Travis and Bowie and the Alamo defenders at San Antonio. On March 13 Houston wrote James Collinsworth, Chairman of the Military Committee: "On seeing the various communications of Colonel Fannin at this point, I would not rely on any co-operation from him. . . .I fear La Bahia [Goliad] is in siege."[17]

That same day Houston penned another letter to Colonel H. Raguet at Nacogdoches in which he stated, "Colonel Fannin should have relieved our Brave men in the Alamo. He had 430 men with artillery under his command, and had taken up the line of march with a full knowledge of the situation of those in the alamo, and owing to the breaking down of a waggon abandoned the march, returned to Goliad and left our Spartans to their fate!"[18]

Houston also advises Raguet, "The conduct of the General Council and that of their 'Agent,' [referring to Fannin] has already cost us the lives of more than 230 brave men."

Fannin had observed in several letters earlier that he was aware that Mexicans, resentful of the Texan occupation of Goliad and La Bahia, controlled the countryside. To the south, the McMullen McGloin colony had been founded in 1828 by John McMullen and James McGloin—making it a Texan colony nearly as old and established as Austin's colony in Brazoria.

The McMullen-McGloin colony had been heavily recruited with Irish immigrants, who had initially settled at Refugio, just south of Goliad. By 1831 other Irish colonists established a town on the east bank of the Nueces, which they called San Patricio de Hibernia,

Spanish for Saint Patrick. In some ways, they had adjusted to Mexican citizenship and life in south Texas much easier than the Anglo settlers in Austin's colony and the settlements to the north. One reason given for this has been the religious relationship established with the Mexican government based upon their Catholic beliefs.

With the development of violent conflict between the Mexican authorities and the Anglo colonists, many of the Irish around Refugio and San Patricio had evacuated south across the Rio Grande to await the outcome of the hostilities. Some, however, had remained behind and had sworn loyalty to the Texan cause—including independence from Mexico.

With the massive Irish evacuation, those families remaining behind were at the mercy of the Indians and Mexican army and understandably concerned for their safety. One of those Irish families was that of Lewis Ayers, who lived near Refugio with his wife and seven children.

On March 3 Ayers had arrived at Goliad with David Moses, who informed Fannin of Grant's defeat at Agua Dulce. Ayers requested that Fannin dispatch some soldiers to help evacuate his family as well as that of a Mrs. Hill and her children, who were staying at the nearby Lopez ranch.

Fannin, however, due to the critical shortage of clothing and supplies, had already sent all his carts and oxen to Lavaca to pick up the long-awaited goods that had finally arrived there. There was nothing he could do until the carts and oxen returned to Goliad, which occurred on March 10. The next day Fannin ignored every warning he had previously received—including Sam Houston's—and once more divided his force by sending Amon King and about thirty men with all the carts and oxen that had returned from Lavaca to evacuate Ayers and any other colonists at Refugio. He also on that date sent another group to the ranch of Carlos de la Garza, who was considered to be in charge of the Mexican spy network operating throughout south Texas.

King's mission was particularly shortsighted on Fannin's part, since King was sent directly into Urrea's known path with enough men to attract attention but too few to repel attack by the Mexican army. A better choice might have been to send Hugh McDonald Frazer and the Refugio militia, since they would have been aiding evacuation of their fellow colonists. Regardless, historians generally agree that sending King to Refugio was the initial significant misjudgment that ended in catastrophe for Fannin's command.[19]

But Fannin, who ironically has been historically criticized as lacking decisiveness, again reacted with dispatch and urgency once he had the ability to aid the colonists at Refugio. As in his aborted attempt to reinforce Travis at the Alamo, he responded as soon as possible to both requests for aid.

Houston's letter ordering Fannin to withdraw to Gonzales and join Neill arrived the day after King had left for Refugio. The fact that they now had provisions from Lavaca could not have compensated for the emotions Fannin must have been feeling as he read that dispatch. At last he had direct orders to abandon La Bahia and depart Goliad. Helplessly, he realized he had no carts or oxen with which to perform such an evacuation: Ayers and King had taken the entire army's transportation facilities to Refugio.

All he could do at this point was to sit and wait at Goliad until King returned with the colonists and, more importantly, with the animals and carts.

King arrived at Refugio late in the evening of the eleventh to find most of the families in the mission; others, including Ayers' wife and children, were at the nearby Lopez ranch. The next day King and his men proceeded to the ranch where they also arrested some Mexicans for looting the abandoned colonist's homes. While at the Lopez ranch King learned that there were additional looters south of the ranch, and he then further divided the Texan forces by leaving a rear guard with the families and taking about twenty men to make further arrests. This was in direct violation of Fannin's orders to assist with the evacuation and return to La Bahia quickly.

Before Captain King had joined with Major Ward to come to Texas, he had been the town marshal of Paducah, Kentucky. At this point, the captain's viewpoint seems to have reverted from that of a military officer on escort duty to that of an enforcer of the law. Whatever his motives may have been, he deviated from his orders—to assist the colonists and provide them with protection en route to a safer location.[20]

King and his men were ambushed before they reached the lower ranch, but they made their way back to the Lopez ranch and loaded the colonists and their possessions and departed for the abandoned mission at Refugio. The Mexican rancheros followed the Texans and again attacked. King and his men were able to fend off the attackers until all the colonists and Texans were safely inside the old mission.

The Mexicans quickly surrounded the church, but that evening a young Irish boy managed to escape to Goliad and inform Fannin of the disaster at Refugio. Fannin's response was once again quick and decisive, and once more, his response went against all the advice he had been given. He dispatched Colonel Ward and one hundred twenty men of the Georgia Battalion to the aid of King.

More so than ever before, the Texan forces, already pitifully depleted, were divided and spread across a hostile land completely controlled by Urrea's Mexican army and his civilian spies.

Ward arrived at the old mission that afternoon and quickly drove off the Mexicans, but instead of joining King and returning to Goliad, both commanders chose to continue the harassment of the local Mexicans and split their command that evening. Ward remained at the old mission while King traveled to the nearby Lopez ranch.

King's men were obviously entering a trap as they approached the plantation, and after a fierce firefight they were driven back to the mission for cover. Meanwhile Ward's men were already pinned down inside the old structure, and both he and King effectively used their men to hold off the Mexicans until, later in the day, they ran short of ammunition and powder. Holding off the Mexicans until after dark, the Texans managed to escape but again split forces.

King's men were quickly captured and returned to Refugio, while Ward's men successfully eluded the Mexicans by traveling to the southeast along Copano Road. In the midst of the fighting and escapes, Fannin's wagons—so critical for an evacuation from Goliad—were lost to the Mexicans.

Meanwhile, General Urrea and his army inched ever closer to Goliad and La Bahia, while Fannin and the Texans there could only sit and await King and Ward's return with the carts.

Other problems were plaguing Fannin's command during these days. After the Texan declaration of independence at Washington-on-the-Brazos on March 2, the Mexican artillerymen serving in Captain Luis Guerra's Tampico company found themselves now fighting against their native Mexico. Survivors of the Tampico catastrophe under General Mexia, they had joined Fannin to fight for the Mexican Federalist cause of a return to the Constitution of 1824. With the Texan declaration of independence, however, they were no longer fighting as Mexican Federalists but as Texans.

Given the option of resigning, they chose to do so, and on March 11 James Fannin wrote General Mexia a letter complimenting the Mexican veterans for their bravery and service: "I am pleased to say of him [Guerra] and his men, that since they have been under my command, each and every one has done his duty—and owing to his and their peculiar situation, and political aspect of this newborn nation, so widely different from what it was when they entered its service, I have this day given them an Honorable discharge, with permission and passport to proceed to N. Orleans &c."[21]

While Fannin observed the proper protocol under the circumstances, the departure of Guerrea's men resulted in his having to reorganize his artillery corps under the Polish engineers and begin training from scratch some of the Texans to serve on the cannon.

On the sixteenth they received word that King's men had been captured and summarily executed in Refugio, while Ward and his soldiers had escaped but their fate was unknown.

On March 17 Fannin received word that King himself was dead. Now, finally, he made the decision to destroy Fort Defiance and follow orders to retreat to the north.

Fannin's noncompliance with Houston's order to withdraw during the period of March 14 through 19 resulted in his allowing General Urrea to establish Mexican troops around Goliad and reduce the odds of a successful Texan retreat. This is a common criticism of Fannin and rightfully so. What is often overlooked, however, is the environment in which Fannin was attempting to make—or delay—his command decisions.

His dispatch of King with the carts was a poor decision, but it was made *before* he had received Houston's orders to retreat.

When he did receive the orders, the carts were already gone but expected back within a day. That King decided to ignore his orders to return directly to Goliad is not Fannin's responsibility.

His further dividing of the Texan forces by sending Ward and one hundred twenty members of the Georgia Battalion was another tactical blunder. But at the time he had few options. He desperately needed the carts and animals back at Goliad, and King's small force had proven to be vulnerable in the open fields around Refugio. His options were to send another small, under-staffed group out or to risk a larger, better equipped army dispatched in rescue. This second option he chose with two goals: rescue of Texan colonists and his own men, and return of his trans-portation facilities.

That he waited until the nineteenth to actually begin his with-drawal was incidental. Prior to that date he had no means to effectively evacuate; on that date he had no choice other than to ineffectively attempt to make that evacuation under the worst of circumstances.

And now, on the seventeenth of March, with notification that King and his men were dead and Ward was scattered around the countryside in escape, Fannin had run out of options. He ordered the fort destroyed and the evacuation organized.

1	Ehrenberg, *With Milam and Fannin*, pg. 154.
2	Wharton, Clarence, *Remember Goliad* (Glorieta, New Mexico: The Rio Grande Press, Inc., 1931), reprinted 1968, pg. 39.
3	Jenkins, *PRT*, 4:443-4.
4	Ibid., 4:477-8.
5	Ehrenberg, pp. 153-4.
6	Jenkins, 4:485-8.
7	Hardin, *Texian Iliad*, pg. 95.
8	Wharton, pg. 39.
9	Jenkins, 4:454.
10	Ibid., 4:400-1.
11	Ibid., 4:455-6.
12	Davenport, "Men of Goliad," pg. 20.
13	Jenkins, 4:502-4.
14	Ibid., 5:10-1.
15	Ibid., 5:51-3.

16 Ibid., 5:69-70.
17 Ibid., 5:71-2.
18 Davenport, Harbert and Craig Roell, "Goliad Campaign of 1836," *The New Handbook of Texas.*
19 Pruett, Jakie L., and Everett B. Cole Sr., *Goliad Massacre* (Austin: Eakin Press, 1985), pg. 53.
20 Jenkins, *PTR*, 5:47-48.

Chapter Nineteen

Letters Home—Fannin's Men Speak

While James Fannin's letters to various Texan leaders in 1836 give us a glimpse into his thinking—at least as stated publicly— they only give us an account of garrison life from a commander's point of view.

Fortunately, other letters were posted from La Bahia and Goliad during this period, usually through McKinney, Williams and Company at Velasco and directed to the U.S. postal system in New Orleans.

While some of these letters from Fannin's men did make it out of Texas and into the hands of the family members to whom they were addressed, it appears that very few, if any, letters were delivered from New Orleans to Goliad during the early months of 1836. Correspondence did take place between individuals in Nacogdoches and Louisiana and Velasco and New Orleans, but the outposts such as San Antonio and Goliad appear to have been restricted to courier communiqués.

Fannin's aide-de-camp, Captain John Sowers Brooks, sent numerous letters home to Georgia throughout this period. A common complaint, usually in a postscript, was that he was receiving no mail in return.

Brooks was born in Staunton, Virginia, on January 31, 1814, and had worked in the office of the *Staunton Spectator* and served in the United States Marine Corps eleven months before leaving New York for Texas on November 5, 1835. After arriving at Velasco on December 20, 1835, he became adjutant of the Georgia Battalion and traveled to Goliad in that capacity. By February 1836 he had resigned as adjutant to become Fannin's aide-de-camp. At La Bahia, he served as chief engineer and had charge of ammunition and artillery.

His direction and creativity in rebuilding the old Spanish presidio had been invaluable. He created a protective lunette around the sally port on the south wall that allowed positioning of a cannon to protect the opening. Using weapons that had been stored in the fort when Collinsworth had attacked and occupied it, Brooks created an "infernal machine" consisting of sixty-eight muskets, which could all be fired with a single match; an early nineteenth-century version of the machine gun fire.[1]

But for all his responsibility as an aide-de-camp, engineer, and architect, Brooks remained a twenty-two-year-old boy far from home and definitely in harm's way.

His letters, when viewed collectively, comprise a soldier's diary that poignantly describes the trials and hardships Fannin and his men were suffering at La Bahia during these dark days.

On February 25 he wrote his sister, Mary Ann Brooks, notifying her of the Mexican army's arrival at San Antonio and the planned attempt to reinforce Travis and the Texans there. He also reflected Fannin's bitterness at the lack of local support: "The only troops in the field at this time are volunteers from the United States, and they probably do not exceed 800, and perhaps but one third of them are near the scene of action,"[2] he wrote her. He also describes his role as aide-de-camp and his duties in the refortification, which he reports had been "arduous in the extreme."

"By the way, I have not heard from home either by letter or otherwise since I left New York. Why have you not written?" he asks her.

With a young soldier's desire to reassure his sister while emphasizing his youthful ardor, he admonishes her: "I would ask you to look upon my situation in its proper light, and to indulge in no unnecessary fears. I am a soldier both morally and physically. Death is one of the changes of the game I play and if it falls to my lot, I shall not murmur, and you should not regret. . . . We shall probably be attacked by the Mexicans on our way to Bexar, and if I should die, my services will entitle me to 1800 or more acres of land which will be valuable."

Later that night he also wrote a letter to his father in which he reflected the same information but added:

> But my dear Father, I frankly confess that without the interposition of Providence, we can not rationally anticipate any other result to our Quixotic expedition than total defeat. . . . We are almost naked and without provisions and very little ammunition. We are undisciplined in a great measure. . . . We have a few pieces but no experienced artillerists and but a few rounds of fixed ammunition, and perhaps less of loose power and balls. . . . We can not therefore, calculate very sanguinely upon victory.[3]

As in his letter to his sister, Brooks alludes to the possibility he might be killed in the coming days. To his father and his sister he explained that he owed a "Mr. Hagarty" a small sum of money he had earlier borrowed and wanted to be sure his debt would be paid in the event of his death. Again, he detailed his entitlement to eighteen hundred acres of land that could be used to settle his debt with Mr. Hagarty.

In a postscript typical of young men on their own for the first time, Brooks asks his father, "Direct your letters to the care of J.W. Fannin, Jr., Army of Texas, pay the postage to New Orleans. I have no money. I should like to have . . . send me some money if possible. I am very much in want of it, I assure you. The government has obtained a loan and will soon pay us off—when I can pay you."

On March 2 he wrote his mother, describing the situation at the Alamo and explaining the circumstances that had caused Fannin's men to abandon the relief expedition. Again, the tone of the letter is ominous: "The war is to be one of extermination. Each party seems to understand that no quarters are to be given or asked."[4]

"We are hard at work, day and night, picketing, ditching, and mounting cannon, &c. We are hourly in expectation of an attack. . . . There are about 450 men here," he informed her.

The remainder of this letter describes the fortification efforts, and Brooks states that they had received information from San Antonio that the Alamo defenders had repulsed two Mexican attacks. "Probably Davy Crokett 'grinned' them off," he informed her.

The conclusion and postscripts to this letter to his mother, however, reveal a very young man homesick and in dire circumstances. "Write me soon," he begs her, "I have not heard from home for four months." One postscript informs her, "We are all nearly naked—and there are but few of us who have a pair of shoes. We have nothing but fresh beef without salt—no bread for several days."

Brooks' homesickness appears to have been growing more severe daily. On March 4 he writes his sister again and scolds her in an overly dramatic but painful passage that indicates he is suffering deep depression:

> I have often—feared is certain—that you had forgotten your poor, wayward brother. Why is it so? Why have you not written? War, it is true, "opens a vein that bleeds Nations to death," but why should it invade the sanctity of social connection? Why should it dissolve fraternal bonds or sunder domestic ties? Is it necessary that we should be morally, as well as physically separated? That the associations of infancy, the remembrances of child hood, the anticipations of youth, and the common pleasures, hopes, and fears of better and happier days, should be forgotten and we pursue our weary and desolate track through life, as if neither had existed? Is it necessary because we are separated, because the billows of the Atlantic, or the Pillars of the Allegheny are between us, that all the ties which bound us, in other days should be severed? I trust not. Why then do you not avail yourself of that medium of communication, which language proffers? Have I rendered myself unworthy of your affection?[5]

Brooks then reviews the indiscretions of his young life and laments his past mistakes, referring at one point to a lost love. "I know my course, since I left home, has been erratic in the extreme. . . . If you can recall the events of the last few years, you must; if you can not, you may then perhaps censure me for that reckless indifference. . . ." he tells her. "It is true that I have passed unimproved many opportunities of acquiring the good opinion of my fellow men, but why was it so? Because early misfortunes have broken and seared a heart, perhaps too sensitive. . . ."

Brooks then lapses again into the gloomy predictions of his future as a soldier:

> I am a soldier of fortune; and all the premonitions of my child hood early told me that I should be one. My profession, perhaps for life, be it short or long will be that of arms. . . . If I fall, let me fall—It is one of the chances of the game I play—a casualty to which every soldier is liable. My prayer has been, since my earliest recollection, to die on the field of battle. . . .

His dark and ominous prophesying continues:

> We are resolved to die, to a man, under the walls we have thrown up, rather than surrender to a horde of merciless savages, who have declared their determination to adhere to none of the rules of civilized war fare, but to murder all Americans indiscriminately. . . . This on the part of the enemy, is to be a war of extermination, not directed solely against the armed soldiers in the field, but against the peaceful citizen, the helpless female, and the defenceless infant. They show no quarter; we do not require it; and, indeed, both parties seem to have tacitly contracted, that it shall neither be asked nor given.

This passage is particularly significant in that Brooks, only two weeks before the surrender at Coleto, appears to be aware of Santa Anna's proclaimed policy concerning armed rebels in Mexico.

On March 9 he continues his pessimistic outlook in a letter to a friend in New York: "We suffer much, and as soon as Bexar falls we will be surrounded by 6000 infernal Mexicans. But we are resolved to die under the walls rather than surrender. . . . We are in a critical situation, I will die like a soldier."[6]

The next day he again writes his father—one of his very last letters from La Bahia. This letter differs from previous correspondence in that there are no gloomy predictions for the future or youthful boasts of "fighting to the death." Instead Brooks in considerable detail reviews all the information about the events taking place in Texas since his arrival that he has previously included in his earlier letters to his family.[7] It has the tone of a self-written obituary.

Brooks was obviously not alone in his dark and gloomy assessment of the events surrounding La Bahia and Goliad. Another young soldier with Shackelford's Alabama Red Rovers, Joseph G. Ferguson, also wrote his brother on March 2: "Our commander is Col. Fannin and I am sorry to say the majority of the soldiers don't like him for what cause I don't know whether it is because they think he has not the interest of the country at heart or that he wishes to become great without taking the proper steps to attain greatness."[8]

Like Brooks, Ferguson also complains of the lack of provisions—especially food other than unsalted beef. He then reveals his dissatisfaction with what he has found in Texas: "Tho with all these advantages it is no country for me. My dislike to the country is a want of society & government both of which will hardly be realized shortly for it is filled up with people who are for their own emolument to the exclusion of others and when that is the case you may judge of things as you see proper."

"My time service will be out the 11th of April," he informs his brother, "and unless things shall change for the better, if I should live, you will see me as soon as I can get to where you live....Yes Jack, though I am surrounded by wickedest of men yet I still try to serve the Lord."

From this passage, it appears that concerns about surviving the campaign alive were common throughout Fannin's command in March of 1836.

Capt. Burr H. Duval of the Kentucky Mustangs also reflected Fannin's unpopularity in a March 9 letter to his father in Tallahassee, Florida: "As I anticipated, much dissention prevails among the Volunteers, Col. Fannin, now in command (Genl. Houston being absent), is unpopular—and nothing but the certainty of hard fighting, and that shortly, could have kept us together so long—."[9]

And so, on March 17, when Fannin made the decision to destroy Fort Defiance and follow Sam Houston's orders to retreat to the north, the La Bahia garrison was rife with suffering, discontent, and depression. The Texan army there consisted of ill-supplied and hungry young mercenaries—most without combat experience—led by a reluctant commander who just wanted to return home to his family.

The ragged, tattered group of men who departed through the sally port for Victoria on the morning of March 19 hardly looked like an army. General Urrea's spies—who were maintaining constant surveillance of the Texans—must have so informed the Mexican general, who was nearby to the south.

1   O'Connor, *The Presidio La Bahia del Espiritu Santo de Zuniga 1721 to 1846*, pg. 124.
2   Jenkins, *PTR*, 4:424-6.
3   Ibid., 4:426-7.
4   Ibid., 4:485-8.
5   Ibid., 4:507-11.
6   Ibid., 5:30-2.
7   Ibid., 5: 37-9.
8   Ibid., 4:488-9.
9   Ibid., 5:33-5.

Chapter Twenty

Battle of Coleto

At the same time Fannin received notification that King and his men were dead and Ward's force was attempting to escape across the south Texas countryside, he also received word from Colonel Horton that a force of some fifteen hundred Mexican soldiers under the command of Colonel Morales was uniting with Urrea's army just south of Goliad at the Refugio mission.

This news, plus the fact that Horton had been successful in obtaining some carts and oxen from Victoria, led Fannin to call for another council of war in which it was determined the withdrawal would begin on the next morning—the eighteenth.

Fannin had already ordered much of the ordnance, including many of the cannon, either spiked or buried inside the courtyard of the fort. In the midst of planning the evacuation for the eighteenth, word came that Mexican forces were detected nearby, so Fannin ordered the buried cannon dug up and remounted to be made operational.

As the morning of the planned departure dawned, carts were loaded and oxen hitched and yoked when Mexican cavalry were in fact discovered in the vicinity of the fort. Fannin, who for all practical purposes had no real cavalry force, dispatched Horton and several of his horsemen to drive away the Mexicans. At first it appeared the tactic had succeeded as the Mexicans withdrew with Horton and his men in chase.

They had been drawn into a trap. A short distance from the presidio, a larger Mexican force was waiting, and for the remainder of the day Horton and the Mexican cavalry maintained cautious clashes outside the walls of La Bahia. These exercises provided great entertainment for the Texans perched atop the walls of the fort but resulted in no definitive victory for either side.

What it did accomplish, however, was to delay Fannin's retreat yet another day while Urrea continued to advance more and more of his soldiers toward Goliad. At the end of the day, the Texans' few horses were physically exhausted—unfit to begin a strategic withdrawal.

Even more disastrous, however, was the discovery that in the midst of all the shooting and sparring between Horton's men and the Mexicans, the oxen had been left yoked and harnessed to the carts in the hot sun all day without food or water. As the afternoon sun began to set, it was obvious a withdrawal from La Bahia would be impossible on the eighteenth.

Fannin has been severely criticized for this oversight and with some justification. In a command of over four hundred men, however, he should have been able to rely on his company commanders to delegate animal care duties to their men. While it is true that the Texans included very few, if any, trained military teamsters, it is also true that most of the men came from the American South where the care of horses, mules, and oxen were instilled from childhood.

That the animals on the eighteenth were abused and mistreated and rendered unable to execute the withdrawal was a catastrophic and monumental military blunder, but the acting "commander in chief" should hardly have been held responsible for the negligence of his company commanders throughout the entire day.

It should be remembered, too, that many of these men—as ill fed and poorly equipped as they were—still were looking for a fight with the Mexicans. They had, after all, against their wishes spent nearly six weeks fortifying this very presidio for just such a battle. That they spent the day atop the massive stone walls cheering the Texans on horseback throughout the clashes indicates they still felt no fear towards the Mexican army and were in no hurry to depart what they still considered an impregnable fortress.

Fannin, a regular army officer in charge of volunteers, never had the necessary authority or ability to dictate distasteful orders to his men. And it was made clear that many of them found the concept of retrograde movement—retreat—distasteful.

Fannin's ability to dictate orders became even more difficult that evening. He ordered the cannon buried before they departed Goliad; then he instructed the men to dig up the guns and dig a trench around the fort. As instructed by Houston, he had destroyed everything in and about the fort that he could not take with him. Everything that would burn was fired—what grain and food he could not carry in the carts was piled up in the chapel of the fort and set on fire. Marks of this fire are still to be seen in the front end of Our Lady of Loreto Chapel. Walls of the fortification were torn down and all houses outside the walls were burned or otherwise destroyed.[1]

The morning of March 19 began with perfect weather in which to make a strategic withdrawal. There was a heavy, encompassing fog completely hiding the San Antonio River and extending up the fifty-foot slope to the north wall of the presidio.

Typical of a volunteer army, the men that morning chose to prepare for their withdrawal as they wished. Fully aware that Urrea's spies were following their every move, they wasted the cover of fog while they leisurely prepared and ate breakfast. Eating, packing supplies, and spiking cannon took up so much of the morning that by the time they actually did depart, much of the element of surprise and the cover of fog had disappeared.

Incredibly, they burned the dried meat of nearly seven hundred steers against one of the walls of the chapel, creating a smoke column that could be seen for miles. It was as if they were taunting Urrea's soldiers to try and stop their retreat. An even more incredible development was the fact that in the bustle and confusion of packing, nobody thought to load any food for the trip.

The carts, which Horton and his men had brought from Victoria, were severely overloaded with guns and ammunition, and the oxen, which were still hungry and unruly from the previous day, were harnessed to them. Fannin chose nine pieces of brass field artillery and these, too, were hitched to the beasts.

In midmorning, the Texans departed the fort and traveled toward the fording point on the river, with the Alabama Red Rovers leading the column and the Kentucky Mustangs serving as the rear detachment. In between, a total of nearly two hundred fifty soldiers including the combat-tested New Orleans Greys left La Bahia and Goliad that morning.

As always, Fannin was critically short of horses and cavalry, but he posted Horton's mounted men at the head of the column as they began their march north toward the community of Victoria that morning.

As in the previous aborted mission to relieve the garrison in the Alamo, problems developed immediately with the wagons. Just outside the fort, about a half-mile south where the army crossed the lower ford of the San Antonio River, the artillery became bogged down. Shackelford reported that the Red Rovers had to help pull the cannon up the bank once they had crossed the river.

Ehrenberg later wrote that the Texans almost immediately began discarding supplies, then the carts themselves, in an effort to hurry up the pace of the march. But Shackelford, who was leading the column, later wrote that this stage of the evacuation "moved briskly and in good order for about six miles."

After eight or nine miles, the oxen were becoming increasingly unruly and difficult to handle—to the point of refusing to continue—so Fannin made the decision to stop and rest the animals.

Much has also been written in criticism of Fannin for making this decision not to continue onto the nearby timber along Coleto Creek—a distance of less than four miles. But if the animals were refusing to budge, he had few options other than abandoning his supplies and cannon. It should be remembered, too, that the oxen had been appropriated from Mexican families in Victoria and had been trained to respond to Spanish commands and the teamster methods used by Mexican carters and were now being driven by inexperienced English-speaking volunteer soldiers.

Fannin—and his company captains—had to have known that the Mexicans were in the vicinity and following their movement. Still, Horton had not reported any movement or activity at the time the halt was ordered.

After about an hour's rest, the column started up again, but another overloaded cart broke down and the column had to halt once more while the supplies were loaded to a different vehicle. During this time, Fannin dispatched a four-man guard to watch for Urrea's soldiers.

Given the fact that Fannin knew a massive Mexican army was close behind him and almost certainly in pursuit, it is odd that he waited until this time to post a rear-guard. No doubt, the lack of horses played a part in the decision, but Fannin managed to find four available horses at this time and sent them out with an untrained teenage boy and three of his friends as scouts.

Once the army had started moving again—reports vary from two to four miles—the Texans began noticing troubling signs initially from the west then from two other directions.

Captain Shackelford, at the front of the column, later recalled that the first Mexican cavalry were observed about two miles to the west. Another report submitted later by Dr. Barnard claimed two companies of cavalry and one infantry company were seen advancing in the rear of their column. Yet another soldier, John C. Duval, would later write that two mounted Mexicans had been observed to the right in the timber, on the eastern flank, during the rest break but that after resuming their march, the Texans saw a line of cavalry on the left.

Given the different locations for the sightings of the first Mexican soldiers, it is impossible to determine where in Fannin's column the enemy was first sighted. It would appear from the later reports of these three officers, however, that at nearly simultaneous times, the Texans discovered Mexican cavalry or soldiers in every direction except to the front of their column.

Urrea, it seems, had Fannin and the Texans nearly surrounded by the time the first alerts were issued along the column in the prairie. That the Mexican army could effectively surround the column while avoiding detection can be explained, in part, by the fact that Fannin was woefully short of horsemen to use as scouts. Horton, with his small nucleus of mounted soldiers, was properly scouting the path to the front of the column and was therefore unable to maintain surveillance on the sides or to the rear of the column.

One aspect of this situation that often is overlooked is the role of the rear guard. The teenaged boy assigned to the guard was Herman Ehrenberg, a New Orleans Grey, who would later become one of Fannin's most vehement critics. Ehrenberg wrote years later in Germany that the four-man unit had been trailing Fannin and the volunteers from a distance of approximately two miles and had noticed a single rider. According to Ehrenberg, the guard party had stopped to again graze their horses when they noticed "a long black streak."[2] John Duval would later use an almost identical expression, a "long dark line on the left" in describing the first detection from within the column itself.[3]

Once the Mexican presence had been verified, Fannin ordered a six-pound cannon deployed and three shots were fired. While these shots achieved no purpose other than to warn the Mexicans, it also apparently warned Fannin's own rear guard.

Ehrenberg claimed the rear guard immediately mounted and started racing toward their comrades after the "dark streak" was determined to be the enemy and does not mention the three rounds fired by the main column. Eight days later, however, Dr. Barnard would accuse the rear guard of sleeping and allowing the Mexicans to surround the column. "It appears that four horsemen had been left in the rear and that they, instead of keeping a look-out, had, under a false sense of security, laid down, and were only aroused by the close approach of the Mexicans."[4]

Another explanation might be that the cannon shots had awakened them. The rear guard party rushed back to the main column—a distance of approximately two miles—only to find the Mexican army was quickly surrounding the Texans. In this moment of crisis, three of the party continued riding to the north towards Victoria while only Ehrenberg rejoined his comrades.

For that action, Ehrenberg deserves credit, and his courage cannot be questioned. But the fact remains that Ehrenberg later wrote what was basically a character assassination of Fannin based in large part on his actions on this grassy plain called Coleto. If, as Barnard charged and others suggested, Ehrenberg was guilty of sleeping on the rear guard as Urrea's soldiers advanced, then the young German was himself guilty of a wartime charge that could have warranted the death penalty.

After the revolution, Ehrenberg never returned to Texas nor did he maintain any known contact with other Greys or volunteers who served at Coleto that day. Ehrenberg was never formally charged with sleeping on guard duty, but the suspicions remain. If they were true, they might explain why Ehrenberg never returned to Texas. It might also help explain why James Fannin waited so long on the Plains of Coleto that day.

The sound of the six-pounder also summoned Horton and his thirty or so scouts, but they too found the overwhelming numbers of Urrea's cavalry blocked them from the main column. Unable to reach the Texans, they turned their horses and rode toward Victoria. Fannin was now surrounded without any scouting or surveillance ability.

After detecting the Mexicans, the Texans continued forward but at a leisurely pace. This too has been questioned as if Fannin had intentionally ordered his men not to rush toward the banks of Coleto Creek with its protective trees and crucial water source.

Again, any criticism must be tempered by the fact that Fannin was exercising only minimal authority over these men, who were not committed to the withdrawal in the first place and who felt they could fight and whip the Mexicans any place at any time.

Rather than a tactical blunder on the part of Fannin, the slow movement at this time was probably more correctly the result of the Texans' low regard for the fighting ability of the Mexicans.

As a result, they found themselves trapped in a geologically depressed area of the plain nearly four miles from any water. The low position among the rolling hills north of Goliad meant that the Mexican cavalry and infantry were completely surrounding them from positions elevated six or seven feet above their formation.

Fannin has also been almost universally criticized for halting in this recessed location on the open plains. While a position along the banks of the Coleto Creek, with its water source and tree cover, would obviously have been much more advantageous, the fact that the Texans made their stand from a position lower than the Mexican army was not in itself a tactical mistake.

Fannin, whom nobody accused that day of panic, surely did consider his options after the Mexicans had successfully surrounded him. He could not have known exactly how many Mexican soldiers he was facing nor could he have known prior to this situation that Morales' battalion of Alamo veterans had successfully reinforced Urrea earlier, and the combined force now numbered nearly one thousand men.

Additionally, with Horton and his men headed to Victoria, the Mexican cavalry held uncontested control of the surrounding countryside including access to the crucial water supply.

Fannin, conversely, also held some advantages during the initial contact between the two armies. Ironically, he had become trapped in large part due to wagon problems, and many of those problems stemmed from the fact that the carts were overloaded with guns and ammunition. Now, stranded on the prairie, he found he had an abundance of guns and a reasonable amount of black powder.

But his most important advantage that afternoon was the fact that he had nine brass artillery pieces while the Mexican army, in its rush to overtake the Texans, had left all their cannon behind.

It is not known how much cannon shot and ball Fannin had available that day. Collinsworth had captured a wealth of ordnance and supplies when the Texans had overwhelmed La Bahia the previous fall. Much of the ball had been used to destroy the fortifications but probably was still available for the battlefield. As the Texans had dismantled and destroyed La Bahia and Goliad, the Polish engineers probably collected scrap metal for use as scatter shot. Musket balls had probably been fashioned into grape shot to some extent, and other canister and shrapnel such as metal hinges, chain, glass, and even rock was available. The nine field pieces deployed by the Texans that afternoon were far and away the greatest advantage on the battlefield.

The positioning of artillery was of the utmost importance. While common sense may suggest that high ground is always the best place from which to fire, artillery tactics and strategy no longer adhered strictly to this approach by the 1830s.

Round shot, or iron ball, was most effective when fired at a level trajectory about chest high. Especially at close range, the shot would be propelled through the ranks of charging men creating tremendous casualties and causing panic among the oncoming enemy. After passing through the first ranks, the shot would then bounce across the ground—like a stone skipping on water—and continue tearing off limbs.

If fired from high ground the shot would be more likely to strike the ground at an angle that would result in a high bounce often missing most of the men it was directed toward.

Also, James Fannin's first and successful experience in combat had come in a depressed area along the banks of the San Antonio River beside Mission Concepcion.

So while occupying an elevated position in combat was still considered the more advantageous position, it was no longer deemed absolutely necessary. Not that Fannin had any choice in his position: He did, however, have options available with regards to the placing of his pieces.

With the absence of any natural cover, the Texans were forced to deploy in a four-sided formation—basically a square box—and Fannin ordered the cannon deployed at the four corners of the square.

The Polish engineers were probably given a great deal of latitude in the positioning of the pieces and, if so, they followed generally accepted procedures for that period of history. While deploying cannon directly to the front often addressed the issue of frontal charges, corner positioning allowed the artillerymen an element of leeway in "swinging" the barrels as necessary during the course of the fighting.

Later reports indicate that Fannin ignored the advice of his senior officers such as Shackelford, who were very vocal in their opposition to halting on the prairie. While it is easy to concede that the best strategy would have been to push forward to the nearest water and protective cover, it cannot be determined to what degree that option was open to Fannin that afternoon. With the equipment failures and unruly oxen, a dash to nearby Coleto Creek might have required abandoning the artillery pieces and carts overloaded with guns and ammunition.

That in turn would have left the horseless and basically unarmed Texans with little choice except to continue on foot toward Victoria—a decision that almost certainly would have resulted in their being run down and destroyed in the prairie by the deadly Mexican cavalry units.

Had he not stopped for the hour, or perhaps as long as two hours, it is probable that the army would have reached Coleto

Creek before Urrea's pursuing army could have caught up with him. But again, the negligence on the part of the men in charge of the animals the day previous probably assured that the trip across the prairie on the nineteenth could not be conducted without resting the abused oxen.

With regards to his posting of scouts and guards of his own, Fannin appears to have done what was possible given his limited means—at least with regards to his forward guard. Horton's mounted volunteers were the closest thing to cavalry forces the Texans had that day, and Fannin wisely posted them between the army and their objective of Victoria.

Horton's men also correctly surmised that, if confronted by Mexican cavalry, they would be outnumbered and outmaneuvered so they remained in a group, which limited their ability to scout the countryside in any considerable range. This also resulted in their being separated from Fannin's main force until too late to rejoin them.

The posting of the rear guard was another matter. Fannin, as commander in chief, was negligent in leaving La Bahia without first posting a guard unit to protect his rear. Fannin himself had warned of the untrustworthy locals around Goliad and their spying activities, so he was unable to follow Urrea's advance with any degree of certainty. The recent events involving Grant, King, and Ward, however, should have warned him that the bulk of the Mexican army was very near his position on the morning of March 19.

His posting of the rear guard during the first halt suggests that he was aware there might be Mexican soldiers in pursuit of the column. While the Texans were chronically short of horses—Grant and Johnson after all had been on corralling missions when surprised by the Mexicans—he should have posted some type of rear guard from the very beginning of the evacuation.

Ehrenberg does not explain how he was chosen for guard duty that day, but with nearly three hundred troops including the battle-experienced Greys, Fannin could have chosen a more reliable group than a teenage boy and three of his friends.

And more importantly, they should have been given specific posted orders while they were in the field. Fannin, or the commander he had designated to post the guard, should clearly have ordered them to keep moving, keep scanning the timberlines to the east and west, and to relay messages to him in tandem regarding the sighting or lack of observance of Mexicans.

Regardless of whether the small guard detachment was asleep on duty or merely lax in their assignment, the four were negligent to the point of deserving court-martial charges. Had the guard detachment been doing their job—scouting the ridgelines to the rear of the column—they would have discovered the Mexican advance long before it had become a "long black streak." If notified at the very earliest possible moment, Fannin and the rest of the Texans might well have had time to traverse the three or four miles to Coleto Creek.

But also, if the Texans were really spoiling for a fight and the draft animals were impossible to manage, it still might not have mattered. Later reports suggest that even after the main column observed Mexican soldiers, they continued to march at a normal—even leisurely—pace without apparent concern or alarm.

Estimates as to the number of Mexican soldiers involved at Coleto that afternoon range from highly inflated appraisals of a three-to-one Mexican advantage to later statements that the Texan forces actually outnumbered the Mexicans.

Fannin established his formation with about three hundred men. Urrea later reported that he had only about three hundred forty combined infantry and cavalry, which would have made the forces even in numbers that afternoon. Jose Enrique de la Peña later wrote, "On facing the enemy, however, he [Urrea] had only 260 infantrymen and 80 cavalrymen with which to combat over 400, who had nine artillery pieces and a great advantage over our soldiers in the quality of their ammunition their superior firearms, and their good marksmanship."[5]

Peña continues on to explain that if Fannin had retreated on the seventeenth, General Urrea's forces were so few at that time that the Mexican commander could not have prevented the Texan withdrawal. To stall the Texans, he engaged them in the daylong running battles on the eighteenth while his main forces continued north, and by the nineteenth he had received considerable artillery and about five hundred reinforcements.

He squandered this advantage, however, on that morning when his spies, in the fog, failed to detect the Texan withdrawal from La Bahia. Given the fact that the Texans had pulled off a surprise departure from Goliad despite leisurely cooking and eating breakfast and burning foodstuffs that sent a cloud high into the sky, Fannin probably never realized the advantage fate had dealt him that morning.

Peña also later reported that when Urrea did discover the evacuation, he left his main force with their artillery and pursued the Texans with some of his best cavalry and infantrymen—many of them Alamo veterans. If this were true, it may well have been that the Mexican force surrounding and confronting the Texans on the afternoon of the nineteenth was roughly the same size as the force it was attacking—at least initially.

If so, that might explain the apparent Texan lack of concern in driving to the Coleto Creek. The Texans—including James Fannin—arrogantly underestimated the fighting ability and skill of the Mexican soldiers. And they must have been aware that the Mexicans did not have artillery with them when the battle began.

The Texan superior firepower, including artillery, and the overconfident sense of superiority did not, in reality, however, translate into an advantage over a Mexican force that included experienced and veteran cavalrymen and a hardened cadre of battle-tested Alamo veterans.

Peña also criticizes Fannin for not attempting a "fighting retreat" that afternoon. But Peña could not have known of Fannin's struggle to exercise authority over his men and their opposition to the retreat in the first place.

Nor could he have known the extent of Fannin's problems with his draft animals. Once the fighting did start, the animals were among the first targets of the Mexican sharpshooters, and there is no reason to believe that strategy would not have been followed if the Mexicans were shadowing a Texan "fighting retreat" that day. Because moving his main advantage—the cannon—absolutely required his fatigued and stubborn animals, such a withdrawal under fire would have been impossible.

And Fannin also must have known that the Texan advantage of artillery would quickly be nullified when the Mexican cannon were brought up from the main force.

In fact, once he had confirmed that Fannin and the Texans had left the presidio, Urrea ordered Colonel Garay to send the Mexican artillery and extra ammunition on after his pursuit group, then to move in and take Presidio la Bahia over.[6]

By the time he had overtaken and surrounded Fannin and the Texans that afternoon, however, his artillery pieces had yet to catch up with him. They would not arrive until later that night.

Caught in the open prairie, surrounded, and cut off from Coleto Creek, Fannin ordered the Texans into a square formation and deployed his cannon. The nine pieces of artillery were manned by the Polish artillerymen under the command of Francis Petrusseweiz, but after the departure of the Mexican artillerymen other Texans had trained on the pieces and were at least familiar with the firing drill. Some of the New Orleans Greys had used cannon in combat both during the siege of Bexar and the assault on the central plaza.

Fannin ordered his formation positioned three ranks deep behind what little barricade could be hastily thrown up—mostly supply carts and equipment. The Alabama Red Rovers and Pettus' company of San Antonio Greys formed the front line, and the Mobile Greys were stationed on the right flank. Westover's troops formed the left flank, while Duval's Mustangs and Frazer's Refugio militia deployed to the rear of the square. The artillery was positioned on each corner, and one of the disabled wagons was placed in the center for use as a hospital station.

Ironically, what had led to their encirclement and isolation—the overloaded carts—also gave them their initial advantage since the wagons had been packed with weapons and ammunition. Rifles were plentiful: As many as three guns were issued to each man on the perimeter while other pistols, bayonets, and ammunition were also readily available.

The Texans probably deployed in their formation as the Mexicans completed their encirclement since Urrea immediately attacked with rifle companies to the front and left while cavalry assaulted the rear flank. Urrea's grenadiers directed their assault on the right side of the square directly opposite the Mobile Greys.

The fighting began in early afternoon and lasted until dark, which would have constituted five or six hours of intense and bloody combat that day.

Much of the Texan overconfidence and low opinion of the Mexican fighting ability had been based upon previous Texan victories in skirmishes prior to the Alamo. As early as the Anahuac and Velasco incidents, the Texans had prevailed against seemingly uneven numbers of Mexican soldiers.

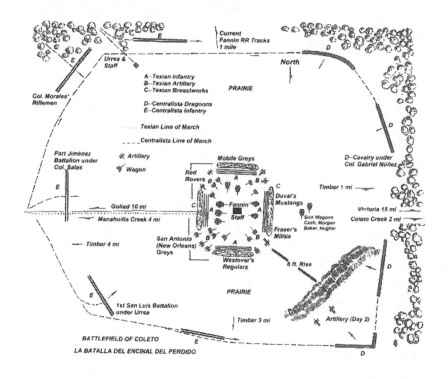

This map of the Coleto battlefield shows that Fannin and the Texans were almost totally surrounded during the half-day fight. The dark square in the middle of the Texan formation represents a disabled wagon that was used as Fannin's command post during the battle. Although seriously wounded, Fannin maintained his command in a manner that drew praise from even his most vehement critics—Mexican and Texan. Map source: O'Connor, Kathryn Stoner, *The Presidio La Bahia del Espiritu Santo de Zuniga 1721 to 1846*, (Austin: Von Boeckmann-Jones Co., 1966).

Collinsworth's bloodless capture of the fort at La Bahia and the considerable Mexican ordnance there seemed to verify Texan superiority in any clash with the Mexican military. The successful resistance with the Gonzales cannon had resulted in a hasty Mexican withdrawal to San Antonio. There the "battle" of Concepcion and Grass Fight had resulted in high profile—if insignificant—Texan military victories. The five-day Battle of Bexar had been the only real military campaign involving strategy and prolonged fighting in Texas prior to Travis' stand at the Alamo.

The Texans clearly won the battle for San Antonio the previous December, but the lessons learned that week had been ignored—or forgotten—quickly in the euphoria of victory. And the main lesson that should have been learned at Bexar was that the Mexican army could, and would, fight and do so effectively and bravely.

The capitulation at San Antonio had nothing to do with inferiority of the Mexican soldiers those five days. Sam Houston understood that, and Fannin almost certainly also must have ascertained the real reason for Cos' surrender. Santa Anna's brother-in-law had been defeated by the siege of the city in which he was deprived of supplies, food, ammunition, and reinforcements. And that siege had succeeded because the Texans had captured Goliad and controlled the supply routes from Copano to Bexar.

And three months later James Fannin, occupying that very same fort at Goliad, failed to realize that the Mexican soldiers surrounding him were not coming from Copano but from Mexico south of the Rio Grande. These soldiers surrounding him at Coleto were also tired, hungry, and in need of reinforcements, but they were in no way comparable to the besieged and starved military garrison the Texans had fought at Bexar.

And even then, at San Antonio, the campaign had stalled and become room-to-room fighting in which the New Orleans Greys, Mississippi volunteers, and Brazoria soldiers had been at an advantage so long as they had protective cover from which to launch their assaults.

On the battlefield of Coleto on March 19, however, there was no such cover, and the superior weapons and firepower of the Texans were effectively countered by the field position from which they were defending themselves. Unlike the Battle of Bexar, Coleto offered neither adobe buildings in which to take cover nor any means of protection for communication or water supply. The only cover on the plains of Coleto that afternoon were the few supply carts and the quickly increasing number of dead animals within the square formation.

And thus James Walker Fannin Jr., on that March 19 afternoon, quickly found himself in formation and in command of a fighting force ready—anxious and eager—to fight. It would appear his stated ambitions since arriving in Texas had finally been realized.

As apparent by his letters to Robinson, however, we know that his ambition had faded and that he was in the process of shedding his command when the events at Goliad engulfed him.

The man in command of the Texan army on the field at Coleto found himself in charge of an army he no longer wanted to lead and in a position he had tried to avoid for six weeks. But the lives and future of his men were at stake, and the situation called for a decisive and courageous leader to step up and assume command. It would be James Fannin's greatest moment in a short and ill-fated Texas military career.

And after that afternoon no man at Coleto or its aftermath—Texan or Mexican—would doubt his personal courage or presence of command under intense and deadly fire.

In the days leading up to the confrontation at Coleto, the New Orleans Greys and Alabama Red Rovers had despised and even defied Fannin as a commander. Duval's Mustangs had defied him and terrorized the remaining Mexicans at Goliad.

Red Rover Joseph G. Ferguson had written of Fannin that "the majority of the soldiers don't like him," and Burr Duval had reported that "Col. Fannin, now in command, is unpopular."

On this afternoon, however, there were no allegations of indecision or affronts to Fannin's personal integrety. On this day the Texans, all of them, followed his commands, and when the day's fighting was over, even the cynical praised his courage.

When the Mexican soldiers advanced on the square formation, Fannin assumed a command position on the right flank. The Mexican assault began as an attack on all four sides of the formation: General Urrea leading members of the San Louis Battalion against the right flank, Colonel Juan Morales commanding rifle companies advancing on the left, Colonel Mariano Salas directing the Jiminez Battalion to the front of the square, and Colonel Gabriel Nunez leading the cavalry against the back of the formation. As the Mexicans advanced, James Fannin ordered that no Texan was to open fire until the command had been given. The Texan volunteers that afternoon did not question his authority and followed his order.

Much has been written about the lack of combat experience and discipline among Fannin's troops garrisoned at Goliad and La Bahia. The lack of supplies—especially clothing—has been well documented and it is easy to envision a ragged band of disorderly malcontents crossing the Coleto plains that March afternoon.

But once in formation and with a battle finally developing with the Mexicans, the Texans that afternoon performed like veteran soldiers.

From about a quarter mile, the Mexican cavalry dismounted and first opened fire without causing any Texan casualties. Fannin's men continued to hold their fire.

The encircling Mexican advance continued, and the second volley of fire on the Texans also proved ineffective. But the range had become close enough that Fannin ordered the men to kneel and squat in the tall grass. Still they held their return fire.

In the absence of Texan response, the Mexican soldiers continued their slow assault and a third round was fired into the formation from about one hundred yards—this time causing a few casualties, with one round destroying the rifle Fannin was holding. He continued to withhold the order to open fire.

Then, as the Mexicans halted to reload their rifles, Fannin issued the firing order. The Texan riflemen simultaneously opened a deadly field of fire as the cannon discharged shot and canister with what Ehrenberg would later call "immediate and horrible" effect.[7]

The devastating counterassault by the Texans resulted in heavy Mexican casualties, however Urrea directed his infantry to charge the formation with fixed bayonets while Nunez' cavalry attacked with lances.

Rotating as many as four muskets, the Texans continued a murderous field of fire while the artillery continued to send shot and canister through the Mexican ranks, literally pulverizing the attackers. Urrea's riflemen finally dropped into the tall grass and began sniping into the Texan square—targeting the Texan artillerymen and the draft animals. But the initial Mexican assault had been repulsed, and the firing lapsed into a brief lull for about a half-hour.

During this period, General Urrea regrouped his four companies and attempted to retrieve the numerous wounded. When he signaled a second assault, the Texans resumed their rotating fire again into the Mexican ranks. One report later stated:

> Their front ranks were so suddenly swept off as almost to form a breastwork sufficient in itself to shield our friends from their assaults. The scene was now dreadful to behold; killed and maimed men and horses were strewn over the plain, the wounded were rending the air with their distressing moans, while a great number of horses without riders were rushing to and from back upon the enemy's lines, increasing the confusion among them: they thus became so entangled, the one with the other, that their retreat resembled the headlong flight of a herd of buffaloes, rather than the retreat of a well-drilled regular army as they were. . . .[8]

Ehrenberg also later described a terrible battlefield scene during this stage of the fighting:

> Frightened by the noise, the horses of the enemy plunged and kicked wildly. Many of the Mexicans were thrown off their saddles, and their riderless horses galloped aimlessly across the field, while wounded men and beasts lying prostrate in the dust were trampled upon by the advancing or retreating cavalry squadrons.[9]

This attack and counterattack scenario continued throughout the afternoon. Volley after volley, the rifle and cannon fire continued to devastate the Mexicans; however, as the afternoon wore on, the Texans also began to accumulate considerable casualties. In the final hour of daylight, Urrea brought up Campeachy Indians to snipe at the Texans from the tall grass surrounding their position.

This tactic proved effective with the Indian sharpshooters wounding at least fifty more Texans before darkness.

Also, toward the end of the afternoon's fighting, the Texans began losing their greatest advantage when their artillery became inoperable. Without water for swabbing, the barrels were becoming clogged and hazardous.

During continuous cannon fire, swabbing with water has some cooling effect on the hot metal, but more importantly, the wet sponges extinguish any lingering smoldering powder residue from the previous firing. At Coleto, as the barrels became clogged with this residue buildup, the danger of new powder charges exploding prematurely became severe.

Also compounding the problem with the cannon was the fact that by late afternoon Petrusseweiz and the Polish cannoneers had all been targeted and killed by the Mexican snipers, and the Texan pieces were being manned by crews formed from footsoldiers. Ehrenberg reported that many of the cannon were being crewed by New Orleans Greys.[10] While the Greys had some artillery experience from the Battle of Bexar, they were not professional artillerymen, and it was obvious that on the following morning the Texans could not use the cannon.

With darkness, the Texan cannon were silenced and the Mexican sharpshooters withdrew out of range since the flash from their rifles gave away their positions and allowed the Texans to effectively pick them off.

In the black of night, the battlefield became quiet and both sides began taking stock of their casualties. Exact numbers for the Mexican wounded and killed are not available, but the totals were considerable.

Inside the makeshift square formation, the Texans had also suffered considerable loss. Dr. Joseph Barnard later wrote, "We had seven men killed and sixty wounded, about forty of whom were disabled."[11]

Among the wounded that afternoon was Colonel James Fannin. After his rifle was shattered by Mexican fire, he had been wounded three times. Ehrenberg later claimed they were "light wounds,"[12] but during the following days Fannin would need assistance in walking and his wounds were severe enough to require considerable medical attention. Barnard later recalled that Fannin was wounded in the thigh.

Shortly after the firing stopped that evening, the brief silence began to be shattered by the cries and moans of the wounded on both sides. The Mexicans could not search the tall grass for their severely wounded since their torches would subject them to the deadly shots of the Texan sharpshooters. The Texan wounded could not be treated for the same reason—the Mexican snipers would target any campfires for the doctors.

The wounded of both sides spent the night without water. While gunshot wounds almost always resulted in pain and high fever, the Texans suffered particularly terrible agony that night. The Mexican army had started using a new ammunition: copper musket balls designed to accelerate the suffering of casualties.

The wounded were also especially vulnerable inside the Texan formation that night. In addition to targeting the artillerymen during the afternoon battle, the Mexicans had also concentrated on killing all the animals inside the square. As a result, Fannin had no way in which to evacuate the wounded.

As the cries of the wounded became a crescendo of pain, other Texans became demoralized by their inability to alleviate the suffering. They too were suffering from the effects of no water and little or no food after a brutal day of transport and fighting.

To further keep the Texans on edge throughout the night, Urrea ordered his buglers to intermittently signal false attacks by calling "Sentinel Alerto!"—the Mexican army assault theme. This, in turn, denied the fatigued Texan defenders any sleep throughout the night.

Although the Mexicans had the Texan defenses surrounded that night, their consolidation of the perimeter was not completely established. Under the cover of darkness, escape by the Texans might have been possible, and later records indicate that many of the Alabama Red Rovers and New Orleans Greys were strongly in favor of such an attempt.

Ehrenberg, who never passed up the opportunity to criticize or blame James Fannin, later accused the colonel for the decision against escaping. Others, however, reported that the decision to remain was made by Fannin and his officers in one of the "elections in camp" that Fannin had so vehemently railed against in his letters to Governor Robinson and the Council.

In the end, however, the consensus was that the wounded would be left to the mercy of the Mexicans, and such abandonment would be unacceptable.

The decision to remain, however, was not unanimous. The New Orleans Greys were particularly vocal in their opposition but in the end opted to stay with the main group. With the decision made to remain in formation, those able to do so began fortifying as best they could. The dead animals were maneuvered into place and knives were used to dig trenches and pile the dirt against the carcasses.

Amidst the cries and moans of the wounded and the false signal charges of the Mexican buglers, a light rain started falling which at first provided relief to the feverish wounded, but the rain failed to provide enough moisture to collect. The Texans continued throughout the night without sufficient water to drink or bathe the wounded, and the temperature plummeted, making all inside the formation even more miserable.

In the Mexican ranks, General Urrea continued to dispatch his cavalry to control the countryside and neutralize Horton and Ward. During the night he received some artillery pieces and a considerable number of reinforcements—fresh troops with ammunition.

Despite the seriousness of their situation, the Texans appeared to be relatively unconcerned about the prospect of another day's fighting as the sun rose. Some of their confidence may have been based upon the anticipation that Horton and his men would return from Victoria with up to five hundred Anglo reinforcements before the fighting resumed. Another consideration may have been that somewhere near them in the darkness were the remains of William Ward's Georgia Battalion that had escaped at Refugio.

The hopelessness of the Texan position was apparent with sunrise. While their cannon were inoperable, Urrea made obvious the arrival of the Mexican pieces. Against effective cannon fire, the carcasses and abandoned wagons sparsely positioned along the Texan perimeter would provide scant defense.

Inside their formation, the Texans were already discussing surrender and the terms they would accept. Urrea wasted little time in the early morning light—firing two or three rounds into the center of Fannin's compound.

Fannin's immediate response—and probably the only option he had left at this time—was to call another "council of war" and confer with his officers. Although some—the Red Rovers and the Greys—advocated fighting on, the majority of Texans inside the square that morning favored negotiations for "honorable" terms of surrender.

Fannin ordered a white flag hoisted, and immediately the Mexicans responded by ceasing fire and dispatching three officers including the English-speaking German colonel of artillery, Juan Holzinger.

Survivor reports in the period immediately following the surrender indicate there was a great deal of confusion about the final terms agreed upon. Fannin appears to have drafted a document that guaranteed they would be considered prisoners of war, that their wounded would receive medical care, and that all prisoners would be paroled back to the United States.

He apparently presented such a document to General Urrea through Holzinger only to have the Mexican commander refuse it outright—insisting instead that the Texans surrender unconditionally.

There was certainly reason for confusion about the negotiations and surrender document: Discussions were conducted in English, Spanish, and German, and the final documents were written in both Spanish and English. But the final signed Spanish copy appears to be consistent and clear:

> Art. 1st. The Mexican troops having placed their artillery at a distance of one hundred and seventy paces and having opened fire, we raised a white flag at once. Colonel Juan Morales Mariano Salas came in company with Lieutenant Colonel Juan Jose Holsinger of the Engineers, and we proposed to them to surrender ourselves at descretion, to which they agreed.
>
> Art. 2nd. That the wounded and their commander Fannin should be treated with all consideration possible, since we propose to surrender all our arms.

Art. 3ʳᵈ. All the detachment shall be treated as prisoners of war and placed at the disposal of the Supreme Government. Camp on the Coleto between Guadalupe and La Bahia, March 20, 1836

> B.C. WALLACE, Major
> J.M. CHADWICK
> J.W. FANNIN, Commander

(Added by Urrea): When the white flag was raised by the enemy, I ordered their leader to be informed that I could have no other agreement than that they should surrender at Discretion, without any other condition, and this was agreed to by the persons stated above; the other petitions, which the subscribers of this surrender make will not be granted. I told them this, and they agreed to it, for I must not, nor can I, grant anything else.[13]

With regards to the issue of whether the surrender was conditional or at discretion, Article 1 very clearly states, "we proposed to them to surrender ourselves *at descretion*, to which they agreed."

Given the fact that Fannin's officers were insisting that the surrender guarantee they be considered prisoners of war, the wounded be provided medical care, and all Texans be paroled to the United States, Fannin himself may have accepted the above terms based upon Urrea's assurance that he would recommend to General Santa Anna approval of those terms and that he was confident of obtaining Santa Anna's approval within a few days.

In addition, Colonel Holzinger mingled among the Texans telling them, "In eight days, home and liberty!"—a statement recalled later by almost every survivor.

The Texan volunteers, therefore, surrendered to the Mexican army, thinking they were to be treated as prisoners of war and paroled to the United States. Dr. Joseph Barnard later recorded:

> . . . After some parley a capitulation with General Urrea was agreed upon, the terms of which were that we should lay down our arms and surrender ourselves as prisoners of war; that we should be treated as such, according

to the usage of civilized nations. That our wounded men should be taken back to Goliad and properly attended to and that all private property should be respected.

These were the terms that Col. Fannin distinctly told his men on his return, had been agreed upon, and which was confirmed by Major Wallace and Captain Dusangue, the interpreter.

. . . We were told that the articles of capitulation were reduced to writing and signed by the commander of each side and one or two of their principal officers; that the writings were in duplicate, and each commander retained a copy.

. . . We were also told, though I cannot vouch for the authority, that as soon as possible we should be sent to New Orleans under parole not to serve any more against Mexico during the war in Texas; but it seemed to be confirmed by an observation of the Mexican Colonel Holzinger, who was to superintend the receiving of our arms.[14]

Captain Jack Shackelford also recorded his observation of the surrender process, which is similar to Barnard's except for Holzinger's alleged promise: "The first words Colonal Holzinger uttered, after a very polite bow, were 'Well, gentleman, in eight days, liberty and home!' I heard this distinctly."[15]

Fannin has been accused of hiding the real terms—*at descretion*—from his men in getting them to accept the surrender. The statements of Barnard and Shackelford suggest there is no proof that Fannin ever falsely promised the men parole, and the documents were also signed and agreed upon by Joseph Chadwick and Benjamin C. Wallace.

Fannin's intentions and his actions in representing the Texans will probably never be established beyond a doubt, but it must also be remembered that he was obligated to act in the best immediate interests of his considerable number of wounded—many of whom had been lying on the cold and damp ground for over twelve hours. Given the fact that he himself was wounded, it is possible that he may have honestly misunderstood the translation.

But he did not clearly relate the terms to his men that morning since the survivors, to a man, would later insist that General Urrea had reneged on his word.

1 O'Connor, Kathryn Stoner, *The Presidio La Bahia del Espiritu Santo de Zuniga, 1721 to 1846* (Austin: Von-Boeckmann-Jones Co., 1966), pg. 128.

2 Charlotte Churchill's 1968 translation of Ehrenberg's diary, *With Milam and Fannin*, does not mention this incident, but a 1993 translation by Dr. Peter Mollenhauer does describe it. His translation can be found in the 1997 book by Natalie Ornish, *Ehrenberg: Goliad Survivor, Old West Explorer* (Dallas: Texas Heritage Press, 1997), pp. 220-1.

3 Duval, *Early Times in Texas*, pg. 63.

4 Pruett, *Goliad Massacre*, pg. 79.

5 de la Peña, Jose Enrique, *With Santa Anna in Texas: A Personal Narrative of the Revolution*, Translated and edited by Carmen Perry (College Station, Texas: Texas A&M University Press, 1975), pg. 72.

6 Pruett, pg. 78

7 Ehrenberg, *With Milam and Fannin*, pg. 172.

8 Pruett, pg. 82

9 Ehrenberg, pg. 172.

10 Ibid., pg. 175.

11 O'Connor, pg. 130.

12 Ehrenberg, pg. 177.

13 O'Connor, pp. 177-8; and Pruett, pp. 89-90.

14 Barnard, J. H., *Dr. J.H. Barnard's Journal*, the *Goliad Advance*, Goliad, Texas, 1912 quoted in Pruett, pp. 91-2.

15 Yoakum, Henderson King, *History of Texas From its First Settlement in 1655 to its Annexation to the United States in 1846 in Two Volumes* (New York: Redfield, 1855), pg. 522-3, quoted in Pruett, pg. 93.

Chapter Twenty-One

Imprisonment

In the various reports that survivors later recorded, James Fannin is hardly mentioned in the events immediately after the capitulation. There are two reasons for this.

Prior to the evacuation of the prisoners, it was agreed that the seriously wounded would be left at the surrender site until carts and wagons could be dispatched to carry them back to Goliad. Fannin, having been wounded three times including a serious thigh wound, remained on the battlefield for two days after the evacuation.

Also, in the days following the surrender, Fannin was isolated from his men, who were understandably preoccupied with their own survival.

The decision to surrender had not been unanimous, and although all the Texans eventually complied, there was initial resistance that bordered on insubordination and threatened the safety of the group inside the square. Much of that resistance came from members of the Alabama Red Rovers and the New Orleans Greys, but in the end, even they stacked their weapons and stood aside as the Mexicans entered their formation.

The situation was tense as many of the Texans, who did not feel defeated, watched the Mexican soldiers inspect their weapons and supplies. The Mexicans, who were understandably tense in this hostile environment, were edgy, and there was a high potential for a violent confrontation.

As the Mexicans were assuming control of the Texan camp, Colonel Horton appeared in the distance with a small group of around forty citizens from Victoria. His appearance represented too little far too late, and all he could do once he recognized the situation was to turn and go back to Victoria.

After the transfer of weapons, the unwounded and walking-wounded prisoners were marched back to Goliad where they crossed the San Antonio River and were deposited in Our Lady of Loreto Chapel inside the presidio.

The chapel, which had been built nearly a century earlier for the Spanish soldiers guarding the nearby Mission Espiritu Santo, was small: about thirty by eighty-five feet with the longer walls facing north and south.

During the events leading up to Fannin's evacuation of La Bahia, the chapel had been stripped of furniture and had served as a storage area. The local citizens had previously removed the wooden icon, and no religious symbols remained save some wooden Stations of the Cross. A small sacristy—measuring about fifteen by twenty feet—was located on one side and had served as a powder magazine.

It was in Our Lady of Loreto chapel inside the fort at La Bahia that nearly 250 Texan prisoners were held—sick, wounded, and starving—for several days without water, food, or medical aid. They were later moved into the open courtyard outside, and James Fannin, himself severely wounded, was placed in isolation inside one of the chapel rooms.

Although tiny by mission standards, the dirt-floored chapel had a vaulted ceiling about forty feet high with three octagonal windows located near the top of the high walls.

Prior to Collinsworth's—and then Fannin's—occupation the chapel had served as the church for the local Mexicans in Goliad. On the night of March 20, 1836, however, it served as a prison.

Nearly two hundred fifty of the Texan prisoners were packed into the tiny building—so overcrowded that many were forced to stand shoulder-to-shoulder and back-to-chest so the wounded could lie on the floor. Many of those casualties had been the result of the copper balls, and the resulting fever and pain immediately created mayhem in the tiny chapel.

Despite the fact they had been without food or water since the morning of the nineteenth, the prisoners were denied any food or medical attention and given no water until the morning of the twenty-first. On that day, a few men were allowed out to make three trips to the river for water.

No food was provided during that second day of imprisonment, and the men finally started protesting until Holzinger provided a small amount of unsalted raw beef, which most of the men ate raw. A few Texans attempted to roast their portions by burning the Stations of the Cross—an act the Mexican captors later labeled as "barbaric."

The night of the twenty-first was later recalled by several survivors as the worst period of their captivity. Air inside the chapel became stifling from body wastes and other odors, and the wounded were in terrible agony with their wounds becoming messy and infected. No additional water was provided and very little water allowed inside from the river.

Tuesday morning, March 22, provided no relief from the miserable conditions. No food was provided for breakfast and only a small, rationed portion of water was allowed inside the chapel. During the day, the wounded from the battlefield were brought to the fort and added to the overcrowded total imprisoned in the church.

Among the wounded returned to La Bahia that day was Colonel James Fannin.

At this time there were approximately fifty-five wounded Texans among the prisoners packed inside the chapel. Wednesday, the twenty-third, brought rain that only increased the humidity and stuffy conditions inside the chapel.

During that day, the third consecutive day inside the church, the Texans were removed from the chapel and placed in the quadrangle along the west wall. The Mexicans then attempted to place their own wounded inside with the Texan wounded but later moved the Texan casualties into one of the stone rooms along the west wall barracks.

It was on this day that Dr. Joseph Barnard reported that he had first made contact with James Fannin:

Wednesday, March 23—My first effort was to see Col. Fannin, and if, by any possibility through him get hold of some of our surgical instruments and hospital dressing for the wounded, we having been robbed of everything of the kind. Most of such articles had belonged to individuals, and Col. Fannin, at my request addressed a note to the Mexican commandant, in which he claimed sundry instruments and other articles, not only as private property according to the terms of the Capitulation, but from the necessity of the surgeons having them for the benefit of the wounded Mexicans as well as of the Americans. The application was of no avail, and I should not mention it except to show that the terms of capitulation had been appealed to once by Col. Fannin, which, of course, he never would have done had there been no capitulation. This day all prisoners, except the wounded, were removed from the church and placed on the west side of the fort. The church still being too small, the American wounded were removed to the cuartels on the west wall.[1]

By March 24, Thursday, many of the Texan wounded still had not had medical attention—five days after sustaining their injuries—but the situation was somewhat improved with the arrival of new Texan prisoners from Tennessee.

Major William Parsons Miller was an Irishman who had immigrated to Texas through Tennessee. Miller had returned to Tennessee as a recruiter for the Texan army and had enrolled a company of men from Nashville. Traveling through New Orleans, the Nashville Battalion had sailed in early March aboard the schooner *William and Frances* for Copano.

After Fannin's surrender, General Urrea had continued expanding his control over the south Texas countryside and had stationed a garrison of sixty soldiers at the coastal port under the command of Colonel Rafael de la Vara prior to Miller's arrival.

Unaware of the events unfolding in Texas during March, the skipper of the *William and Frances* sailed into the port on March 21 and dropped anchor several hundred yards from the shore. The men, who had been confined to the ship for several weeks, took advantage of the arrival by shucking their clothes and plunging into the cooling water. Their swim was interrupted when the Mexican troops appeared. Caught with "their pants down," the men surrendered and were eventually taken to Goliad and imprisoned along with Fannin's men.[2]

The Tennesseans had been captured even before their guns and ammunition had been unloaded from the *William and Frances*, and they were billeted outside the fort in separate quarters and instructed to wear white armbands, which designated them as noncombatants since they had been captured unarmed. Although kept separate from the other Texan prisoners, Miller's men were allowed to tend to the medical needs of the wounded.

Despite the hardships and lack of food, medicine, and water the Texans still held out hope that the worst was almost over. It was, after all, the fifth day since the surrender and Holzinger had promised them they'd leave for home in eight days.

Further boosting their optimism that day was the news from Miller's men that Fannin had gone to Copano with Holzinger to charter the *William and Frances* to return the Texans back to New Orleans.

The prisoners at La Bahia grew even more encouraged on Friday, March 25, when Colonel William Ward and approximately eighty of his Georgia Battalion were reunited with their former comrades. After King's defeat at Refugio, these men had been wandering across the prairies around Goliad into Victoria and back down to Lavaca where they had been captured and returned to La Bahia. And now, like Fannin and his men, they were imprisoned. With the arrivals of Ward and his men and Miller's noncombatants, the total Anglo prisoner count incarcerated at La Bahia now totaled nearly four hundred fifty.

James Fannin arrived back at La Bahia on Saturday, March 26, and was quickly isolated in the sacristy of the chapel with the medical personnel. Barnard later wrote in his diary:

> Saturday, March 26—Col. Fannin with his adjutant, Mr. Chadwick, who had been sent to Copano, returned this day. They were placed in a small room of the church, which had been appropriated to the surgeons and their assistants and guard, rather crowded, to be sure, but we had become accustomed to that. They were in good spirits

and endeavored to cheer us up. They spoke of the kindness with which they had been treated by the Mexican Colonel Holzinger, who went with them, and their hopes of our speedy release. Fannin asked me to dress his wound, and then talked about his wife and children, with much fondness, until a late hour. I must confess that I felt more cheerful this evening than I had before since our surrender. We had reiterated assurance of a speedy release, it is true, by the Mexicans, though we placed but little reliance on them.[3]

While Fannin may have brought back optimism and good spirits to La Bahia, he did not succeed in obtaining a ship for the return of his men to the United States. The captain, fearing a Mexican conspiracy to capture the vessel with its arms and ammunition aboard, hoisted sails, and the *William and Frances* had departed before any negotiations could take place. Still, Fannin had felt, other ships were available and parole would be accomplished soon.

It had been a week since the brutal and bloody battle on the plains of Coleto, and the next morning would be Holzinger's celebrated "eighth day." It would also be Palm Sunday.

But that Saturday the local Mexicans, who were returning to Goliad now that the Texans were captured, were beginning to make demands of the prisoners for their personal property. The prisoners, who as free soldiers at Goliad had been "nearly naked and without provisions," almost certainly had few private possessions remaining. About this time, the fort commandant, Colonel Jose Nicolas de la Portilla, began acting nervous and withdrawn.

As darkness arrived on Saturday, a rumor circulated among the captured Texans in the quadrangle that another ship was now available at Copano and that an evacuation would begin Sunday morning for a march to the port.

This news was received with relief. Someone had managed to keep a flute, and an impromptu songfest was soon underway. "Home, Sweet Home" was a favorite, then it was followed by others of the old songs, with variations and much merrymaking. At last the prisoners turned in, tired and hungry, to be sure, but elated and content.[4]

Inside the chapel sacristy, James Fannin was sharing fond memories of Minerva and his two daughters with Dr. Barnard.

1   O'Connor, *The Presidio La Bahia del Espiritu Santo de Zuniga 1721 to 1846*, pg. 137.

2   Guthrie, *Texas Forgotten Ports*, pg. 17.

3   O'Connor, pg. 138.

4   Pruett, *Goliad Massacre*, pg. 108.

Chapter Twenty-Two

Palm Sunday Massacre

The Sunday morning after the Battle of Coleto had been wet and cold, but one week later Palm Sunday dawned warm and muggy under overcast and cloudy skies.

While James Fannin was kept isolated in the chapel, his men in the courtyard were summoned early and awoke to find the cannon had been repositioned in the courtyard and the Mexican soldiers had donned their parade uniforms.

The rumors of a ship awaiting them at Copano appeared to be true, and Holzinger appeared to be keeping his promise on the eighth day. The Texans were ordered to assemble, and around 8:00 A.M. the orders were issued to begin evacuating La Bahia through the sally port.

The Greys were the first to leave the compound, at the head of approximately three hundred tired, dirty, and starving Texan volunteers. As they left La Bahia in a long double column out through the south entrance of the fort, they were met by even more Mexican soldiers who then formed a single-line escort on each side of them. Directed to the northeast, they marched down the sloping incline outside the fort toward the San Antonio River.

Then they were herded suddenly northward—away from Copano—and some of the Greys realized they were being isolated from the other evacuating Texans.

William Ward's Georgia Battalion and Burr Duval's Kentucky Mustangs were ordered the opposite direction—toward the San Antonio Road on the northwest side of the fort and on the upper ford of the San Antonio River.

The Alabama Red Rovers and Ira Westover's Irish volunteers marched almost directly south out of the sally port on the old San Patricio Road and away from the San Antonio River.

For about fifteen minutes these three groups were marched in different directions until they were well separated from each other. Ehrenberg later recalled the Greys were ordered off the main road and then a command to halt was given, which confused them. They were then told in Spanish to "kneel down"—a command they didn't understand at first. Upon second issuance of the command, the Mexicans raised their rifles into firing position.[1]

They then began hearing volleys of firing from other areas around them and realized, too late, that they were being ambushed. The Mexican soldiers opened fire at point-blank range followed by another volley from a second direction.

To the northwest, John Duval later recalled: "When about a mile above town, a halt was made and the guard on the side next to the river filed around to the opposite side. Hardly had this maneuver been executed, when I heard a heavy firing of musketry in the directions taken by the other two divisions. Some one near me exclaimed 'Boys! they are going to shoot us!' and at the same instant I heard the clicking of musket locks all along the Mexican line. I turned to look, and as I did so, the Mexicans fired upon us, killing probably one hundred out of the one hundred and fifty men in the division."[2]

To the south, the Red Rovers and Westover's men met the same fate on the road to San Patricio. After the initial killing, the Mexicans attacked the wounded and chased down those trying to escape. For nearly an hour, the soldiers and cavalry pursued the wounded survivors, clubbing, stabbing, and shooting those they could find alive. Still, somehow in the smoke, confusion, and bloodshed about thirty men—many of them severely wounded—managed to escape. All but about four of the survivors managed to elude the Mexicans by swimming the San Antonio River and hiding on the northern side of the river.

Fannin remained inside the small room of the chapel and, since he had been isolated from his men since surrender, probably had not been particularly alarmed when the evacuation had begun with his being kept behind. Inside the chapel, however, he must have been aware of the shooting and yelling going on around three sides of the fort that morning.

At La Bahia, Captain Carolino Huerta of the Tres Villas Battalion had been left in charge of the remaining wounded Texans, who were being held in one of the stone buildings along the south wall. After the initial assault on the evacuating prisoners, Huerta ordered the wounded carried into the courtyard.

Joseph Spohn, who spoke Spanish and had been serving as a medic, had been ordered out of the chapel that morning into the columns departing the fort only to be recalled at the last moment. Because his medical skills were useful to the Mexicans he was spared execution, and in surviving, he left us one of the best first-hand accounts of the events inside the presidio that morning. In an interview published in the *New York Evening Star* a few months later, Spohn gave his version of the morning events:

> On Palm Sunday, being the 27th of March, the prisoners were formed into a line, and Mr. Spohn, who was then sleeping in the church, [the hospital] being about 6 o'clock in the morning, was called out and told to form into line; being the last, he fell at the end. They were then marched out of the fort and ranged before the gate, when an officer stepped up and asked Spohn what he was doing there, and ordered him to go back to the hospital where he was wanted, and when on his way was stopped by another officer, who told him to order the assistants to have the wounded brought into the yard: such as could not walk were to be carried out. Being astonished at these preparations, he asked why, when the officer said "Carts were coming to convey them to Copano, the nearest seaport." The orders of the officers were obeyed, and the wounded brought into the yard, and they were full of hope that they were to be shipped to the United States, which had been promised; but their hopes were cruelly blasted when they heard a sudden continued roar of musketry on the outside of the fort, and observed the soldiers' wives leap upon the walls and look towards the spot where the report came from.[3]

Spohn continued in the *Evening Star* interview:

> The wounded were then conscious of what was pass-
> ing, and one of them asked Spohn if he did not think that
> their time was come; and when they became convinced
> from the movements about the fort that they were to be
> shot, greater part of them sat down calmly on their blan-
> kets, resolutely awaiting their miserable fate; some turned
> pale, but not one displayed the least fear or quivering.[4]

And so, as the survivors of the initial assault on the three columns of Texans were being hunted down and killed, the wounded
left inside the fort were placed against the western rock wall of the
barracks in the La Bahia courtyard and summarily executed.

Although Spohn was spared the fate of his comrades that day,
his difficult role during the massacre was not finished. After the
killing of the wounded, only Fannin remained alive, and his execution has probably been the most chronicled death of the Texas
Revolution outside the walls of the Alamo.

Several versions of Fannin's final moments were later recorded,
but only one Anglo eyewitness survived that morning with a first-
hand account. That testimony came from the man who prepped
Fannin for death and comforted him until the moment of his
death—Joseph Spohn.

As reported in the *New York Evening Star* article, Spohn
described the emotional, difficult role he had to perform that
deadly morning:

> . . . . .a Mexican captain of the battalion, called Tres
> Villas, with six soldiers, came up to Spohn, and told him to
> call Col. Fannin, at the same time pointing to a certain part
> of the yard, where he wished him to be taken, Spohn
> asked him if he was going to shoot him, and he coolly
> replied, "Yes."—When Spohn approached Fannin, the
> Colonel asked what was that firing, and when he told him
> the facts he made no observation, but appeared resolute
> and firm, no visible impression on Colonel Fannin, who
> firmly walked to the place pointed out by the Mexican cap-
> tain, placing his arm upon the shoulder of Spohn for

support, being wounded in the right thigh, from which he was very lame.[5]

Some later reports claim that Fannin was told that if he would kneel his life might be spared and he had replied that he had no desire to live after his men had been killed.[6] Spohn does not verify or refute that version.

It was Spohn who served as a crutch to assist Fannin to the chair in which he was to be shot. As he later recalled:

> When Colonel Fannin reached the spot required, the N.W. corner of the fort (in front of the chapel doors and near the water gate), Spohn was ordered to interpret the following sentence: "That for having come with an armed band to commit depredations and revolutionize Texas, the Mexican Government were about to chastise him." As soon as the sentence was interpreted to Fannin, he asked if he could not see the commandant. The officer said he could not, and asked why he wished it. Colonel Fannin then pulled forth a valuable gold watch, he said belonged to his wife, and he wished to present it to the commandant. The captain then said he could not see the commandant, but if he would give him the watch he would thank him—and he repeated in broken English, "tank you—me tank you." Colonel Fannin told him he might have the watch if he would have him buried after he was shot, which the captain said should be done—"*con todas las foralidades necessarias*" (with all necessary formalities)—at the same time smiling and bowing. Col. Fannin then handed him the watch, and pulled out of his right pocket a small bead purse containing doubloons, the clasp of which was bent; he gave this to the officer, at the same time saying that it had saved his life, as the ball that wounded him had lost part of its force by striking the clasp, which it bent and carried with it into the wound; a part of a silk handkerchief which he had in his pocket, and which on drawing out drew forth with it the ball. Out of the left pocket of his overcoat, (being cold weather he had on one of India rubber) he took a piece of canvass containing a

double handful of dollars, which he also gave to the officer.[7]

Spohn was then ordered to take Fannin's handkerchief, fold it,
and tie it over his eyes. Because of nervousness, he had problems
attempting to fold the scarf, and the Mexican captain snatched it
from his hands and ordered Fannin to sit down on a chair that had
been placed in the small courtyard directly in front of the doors of
the chapel. Fannin calmly, but with difficulty because of his thigh
wound, sat in the chair and the captain tied the blindfold over
Fannin's eyes.

Fannin asked Spohn to make one last request of the captain:

> . . . . .tell them not to place their muskets so near as to
> scorch his face with the powder. The officer standing
> behind them after seeing their muskets were brought
> within two feet of his body, drew forth his handkerchief as
> a signal, when they fired, and poor Fannin fell dead on his
> right side of the chair, and from thence rolled into a dry
> ditch, about three feet deep, close by the wall.[8]

Fannin had made three last requests: his watch be properly
placed, he be given a Christian burial, and that he not be shot in
the face. His executioner pocketed his watch, he was shot at close
range in the head, and his body was dumped in a pile with those of
his men.

Approximately three hundred forty Texans were massacred at
and around Presidio La Bahia and Goliad that Palm Sunday morning. Many of them died mercifully quick deaths in the initial
volleys fired into their ranks, but others died slow, agonizing
deaths as they were stabbed, clubbed, and lanced.

For James Walker Fannin Jr., however, death had come quickly
that morning in the courtyard. As his body was drug from the presidio and dumped with those of his men, he suffered the same
ignoble fate of being placed between alternate layers of wood and
human flesh and partially burned. The charred remains were left
exposed to the elements while the vultures and wolves tore their
flesh and gnawed their bones for over two months until they were
finally interred in a mass grave.

But his death was also one of the simplest to define in the bloody conduct of the Texas revolution: Fannin died bravely and honorably. Regardless of the attacks on him in later years, in his death there were no whispered rumors of self-inflicted shots to the forehead at the beginning of battle or surrender begging clemency when the fighting was over.

And death continued to follow Fannin and his men after that Palm Sunday morning. The Mexican professional soldiers and officers were profoundly shocked by the order of Santa Anna to execute unarmed men, and their compliance haunted the military corps of Mexico for years afterward.

The dead Texans that day represented small-town America and many European countries. The town of Courtland, Alabama, lost nearly all its young men that morning as did Bardstown, Kentucky, and other American communities. As soon as the survivors made their reports, newspaper headlines around the world reported the Mexican barbarity and cruelty at Goliad.

In 1940 historian Harbert Davenport described the fatal error of Santa Anna's thinking in ordering the execution of James Fannin and his men that morning at Goliad:

> ... when Fannin's men were captured by Urrea, the first wave of American sympathy for Texas was spent.... The Texan defeat at the Alamo, and the capture of Fannin, had restored the prestige of the Mexican arms. As at no other time during the revolution, Texas was dependent on help from the United States. Had Santa Anna seized the opportunity of Fannin's surrender to dump his men, with Miller's, on the wharves at New Orleans, humiliated, starving, half naked, penniless, homesick, and forlorn, and each with his painful story of Texan mismanagement and Texan neglect, Texas' standing with the American people would have fallen to a new low; and American men, and American money, for the Texan venture would have been scarce indeed. Killing them was exactly the fillip needed to American sympathy and of which the struggling young Republic was then in such dire and desperate need.[9]

But Santa Anna chose instead to adhere to his policy of executing all foreigners under arms, and as a result Fannin and his men joined those of Travis, Bowie, and the Alamo defenders in becoming Texas martyrs.

As darkness settled over Presidio La Bahia and Goliad that night the shooting had stopped. Somewhere, outside the fort, rested Colonel James Walker Fannin's body. Ironically, in death he would achieve for the Texan independence cause what he was unable to achieve during his short life and military command.

Less than four weeks after the Palm Sunday massacre, another battle of the Texas revolution occurred on a plain called San Jacinto. That battle would result in a victory that assured Texas independence. The battle cry that day was "Remember the Alamo"—"Remember Goliad."

1   Ehrenberg, *With Milam and Fannin*, pg. 201.
2   Duval, *Early Times in Texas*, pp. 89-90.
3   O'Connor, *The Presidio La Bahia del Espiritu Santo de Zuniga, 1721 to 1846*, pg. 142.
4   Ibid., pg. 142.
5   Ibid., pg. 143.
6   "James W. Fannin." *Heroes of Texas*. Extract from *Thrall's History of Texas*, The Union National Bank, Houston, Texas, 1929, pg. 3
7   O'Connor, pg. 143.
8   Ibid., pg. 144
9   Davenport, "The Men of Goliad," pg. 5.

Chapter Twenty-Three
Defense of an "Ill-Fated Man"

It is easy to criticize James Walker Fannin Jr., and from the time of his death that Palm Sunday morning there has been no shortage of historians willing to do just that.

His mistakes and shortcomings are obvious: blind ambition, indecision, lack of strategy, underestimation of the enemy, reliance upon "councils of war," and lack of attention to crucial details quickly come to mind.

But to levy these criticisms while taking into account the world and environment in which James Walker Fannin Jr. was functioning—especially during the first three months of 1836—reduces the harshness of those criticisms and even explains some of his actions.

James Fannin was a complicated man. But so were the other Texan leaders during this period—the times and the land seemed to call out to troubled Americans. Travis had his background of marital infidelity and child abandonment as well as accusations of venereal disease and a history of slave trading. Bowie was a slave trader, killer, and a notorious—and mean—drunk. Crockett fled political turmoil and personal debt when he left Tennessee. Houston left behind a history of marital failure, political scandal, and drunkenness when he came to Texas.

Comparatively speaking, James Fannin's character was probably better than many of his contemporaries. A former temperance officer, there are no records of his ever drinking in excess, if at all, while he lived in Texas. He brought debt to Texas with him, but in less than two years his estate at Brazoria was solvent and even profitable. As a married man, there are no suggestions he was anything other than a devoted and loving husband. At various times during his military tenure in Texas he revealed a longing to be reunited with Minerva and his two daughters whom he obviously loved very much.

But like Travis, Bowie, Crockett, and Houston, he had a shadowy part to his past. He was a slave trader and participated in an aspect of the business that even some of his contemporaries despised: the importation of slaves directly from Africa. By contemporary standards he was morally and legally wrong for this, but in 1835 he was just legally wrong. In the prevailing philosophy of Anglo Texas during that period he was simply providing a desperately needed service, but his willingness to deal in human misery for profit does stain his otherwise good character.

By the time Sam Houston had arrived in Texas and assumed the role as commander in chief the first time, he was a veteran of political intrigue in American, Tennessee, and Cherokee affairs. By the time he had campaigned for and obtained his generalship at Washington-on-the-Brazos, Houston had become an honorary Cherokee, taught school, practiced law, sustained wounds at the Battle of Horseshoe Bend, and served as a United States Representative and governor of Tennessee. He had come of age politically by surviving Jacksonian political intrigue in the United States and had been arrested and tried in the House of Representatives for thrashing a fellow representative.

In Texas, he quickly had become involved in the Convention of 1833 in San Felipe. In September 1835 he led a meeting in Nacogdoches to debate the convening of a consultation. He served as a delegate from that settlement to the Consultation of 1835, which deliberated in Columbia in October and at San Felipe in November. The following month he had been appointed major general of the Texas army.

In terms of political experience, intrigue, and savvy, James Fannin was never the match of Sam Houston. But then no white man in Texas—with the possible exception of Bowie—was.

It has been pointed out that despite his abbreviated West Point tenure, Fannin was untrained and inexperienced as a military leader. But Texas was so desperate for *any* men capable of leading troops in battle that even his limited credentials propelled him to the higher echelons of Texan military hierarchy in 1835.

His rapid rise in the military ranks of the Anglo Texans was also propelled by an almost compulsive individual ambition—a personal drive so strong that he could not see that he had overextended himself until it was too late and that he—for better or worse—had become responsible for the lives of nearly five hundred men.

As with any controversial military leader, there is a tendency to examine the background that may have led to his actions on the battlefield. Such has been the case with Custer, Lee, Grant, Sherman, and a host of other commanders.

With James Fannin, however, such an examination is very difficult—made nearly impossible by the censoring scissors of some unknown family member years earlier. It will probably never be known what "peculiar situation" Fannin felt was so important in his background. Perhaps the deleted information pertained to his illegitimate status and how it had affected him as an adult. Perhaps there was some other unknown and unsuspected aspect of his life that was traumatic to him.

But James Fannin has, like the other controversial commanders, been subjected to speculation about his personal ambition and abilities. Harbert Davenport, whose study of Fannin and his men nearly a century after the massacre remains a classic work, speculated as to Fannin's personal and psychological bearing during the revolution.

In a 1932 letter Davenport addressed the question as to why Fannin had remained three weeks at Goliad before finally withdrawing. Fannin "sacrificed himself and his men to his own conception of honor," Davenport concluded.

> When he joined the conspiracy to supplant Houston, he had, in his own mind and to his own conscience, sacrificed his honor as a soldier.
>
> By outraging the accepted standards of decency in opening and copying Governor Smith's letter to Hill; and by violation of Ward's confidence, both of which acts had been severely and publicly denounced by Hill and Ward, he had also transcended his own standards of private conduct.

> Fannin learned on February 5 and afterward that Houston had been right and Fannin wrong in the concept of the war.
>
> Fannin was unwilling to return to the settlements, where also dwelt the ghost of his lost honor. The lives of his young men were his sacrifice.[1]

The letter referred to was the basis of the conflict between Ward and Fannin and Ward's denunciation of Fannin's actions. Davenport's suggestion here is that Fannin, having violated his personal code of honor, felt such a sense of humiliation he sacrificed himself and his men in what was basically a suicide mission at Goliad and Coleto.

John Henry Brown, in 1893, had also speculated that much of Fannin's criticism stemmed from the fact that he had betrayed Houston as commander in chief. "... an *agency* placed James W. Fannin in command of a body of troops independent of the commander in chief, elected unanimously by the representatives of the people in the Consultation,"[2] Brown recorded.

He underlined his point by continuing, "He utterly ignored the fact that the one major-general elected (and major-general was the highest rank yet known to the American people), had been in express terms made (not, as in a large army, the commander of a division or two brigades), but commander in chief of all the forces of Texas. Had he and the council, which subserved his views by indirection and distinct evasion, recognized and in good faith acted in obedience to this great legal fact, he and his noble followers at Goliad would not have surrendered three months later to Urrea, a few days later to be shot dead as so many dogs."[3]

He further stated, "Yet in all this, Col. Fannin was acting under an illegal *agency*, utterly ignoring the rightful Governor and rightful commander in chief."[4]

While Brown was correct in this, he ignored the fact that roughly half of the public officials representing the Anglo settlements were also acting in violation of their own rules and standards. The provisional government of Texas including the executive office was, after all, divided beyond reconciliation. Given the fact that Robinson and the council in session were claiming legitimate authority, Fannin no doubt felt he had the right to accept their offer of leadership.

Marshall de Bruhl is another historian who questioned the legality of Fannin's assuming command at Refugio as Houston departed: "Houston was particularly dismayed by the actions of the ambitious Fannin, who was not a volunteer but a colonel in the regular army and subject to the orders of his commander in chief. By accepting the appointment to head the army, Fannin had betrayed not only his oath but his country."[5]

But personal ambition was rampant throughout the ranks of the Texan soldiers in 1836, and neither Fannin nor Houston were commissioned under any legal document resembling the U.S. Constitution—certainly not the Organic Law adopted on November 13, 1835. Both their claims to authority, after all, were being challenged by Santa Anna as illegal actions.

Fannin was a very unpopular leader. That is an indisputable fact. Brooks and Ferguson verified that fact in letters home during the refortification of La Bahia, and Ehrenberg later spent considerable time in his diary documenting that fact.

But regular army officer popularity among volunteer soldiers was a rarity in Texas during the revolution. At the Alamo, Travis had faced a revolt by the volunteers and acquiesced by allowing free elections: an act that resulted in James Bowie being chosen co-commander of the volunteers. Sam Houston likewise was not popular. Not only were his men threatening to rebel but President David G. Burnet had admonished him: "Sir: The enemy are laughing you to scorn."

The fact that James Fannin was unpopular at Goliad merely reflected the prevailing mood of volunteer soldiers in Texas toward their leaders in 1836.

But that unpopularity, while commonplace in Texas, also worked against virtually every major Anglo military leader. Travis, in sharing command with Bowie, was unable to issue a definitive response to Santa Anna's initial request for surrender at the Alamo. Houston was facing open rebellion as he neared the "fork in the road" on the way to Harrisburg. Fannin was attempting to lead a withdrawal across the Coleto plains of an army that wanted to remain behind and fight.

And that fact alone explains much of what developed in the days immediately preceding the actual evacuation. Fannin's men didn't want to leave La Bahia or retreat to the north. They didn't hurry their preparations the morning of the departure when they had the cover of fog, and they didn't maintain their animals the day before when they were finally getting to at least skirmish with the Mexican cavalry.

As evacuation did finally take place, it was obvious they still were looking for a fight. Instead of loading food, as any soldier should know to do, they instead overloaded their wagons and carts with guns and ammunition. When they became stranded in the open prairie, they chose to remain with those weapons rather than abandon them for the safety of nearby Coleto Creek.

These decisions do not reflect favorably on James Fannin's command during those days, but more accurately they may reflect on his unwillingness—or more probably, inability—to exercise control over headstrong young volunteers, who had not elected him to his command.

As he finally exited the sally port of La Bahia on the morning of March 19, his position was really not unlike that of Sam Houston in the coming weeks: an unpopular leader attempting to coerce a disgruntled cadre of politician/officers under his command.

It was a formula for disaster in both instances. Fate, however, dealt separate hands to Fannin and Houston. While Houston became the "Sword of San Jacinto," Fannin became the "ill-fated man"—a term Houston himself later used to describe the Georgian.[6]

But given these circumstances, Fannin did not violate many established rules of military command during his tenure in south Texas. In his letters to Robinson and Houston, he gave excellent advice as to the situation to the south and the needed responses to counteract it. Granted, the politicians at San Felipe did not have the money, military supplies, or men to comply with Fannin's recommendations, but his advice was nevertheless militarily sound.

Fannin accurately assessed the importance of Goliad and La Bahia initially in the conflict but then refused to acknowledge that the presidio had lost its strategic position after San Antonio had fallen to Santa Anna. He did, however, follow sound strategy by consolidating his troops at Refugio and withdrawing to the fort at La Bahia while leaving behind garrisons at Copano and Refugio. When Copano was abandoned as a port of entry, Fannin correctly advocated restructuring the supply and reinforcement port at Lavaca.

Fannin did not react to events quickly: a fact that has led to charges he was indecisive. The fact remains, however, that he immediately ordered a next-morning departure for the Alamo when he received Travis' request for aid, and he likewise ordered a next-day withdrawal from La Bahia when he received news of King's death south of Goliad. When surrounded on the plains of Coleto, he immediately issued formation orders and established a defensive position. His command problem was not so much of indecision at the time of needed action as it was in his inability to foresee that needed action and prepare for it.

Many of the accusations of indecision on the part of Fannin as a commander center on the period between Houston's first call to evacuate and the final decision to do so on March 19. There are also allegations of incompetence based upon Fannin's decision to divide his command and dispatch the crucial wagons and carts to evacuate the colonists around Refugio.

But as early as November 7, 1835, the delegates of the Consultation had declared the social compact between Santa Anna and the Texans dissolved and had proclaimed the right to act in the interest of the colonists. Although the Consultation was never truly representative of Anglo Texas and seldom even functioned with a quorum, it can be interpreted that their actions did commit to James Fannin and the other military leaders a responsibility to protect the colonists it was claiming to represent.

It must also be remembered that unlike James Grant, Robert Morris, and other adventurers in Texas, James Fannin at least had immigrated to Brazoria prior to the hostilities and had established himself even, at one point, offering to sell his assets to fund the revolution. As such, he may have viewed the colonists around Refugio in a different perspective than those leaders who simply wanted to achieve an independent Texas to develop for themselves.

With regards to his opting to remain on the Coleto battlefield and not attempt an escape through the Mexican lines in the darkness, that decision was not his alone, but another of the "councils of war" that plagued his command. To have made such an attempt would probably only have scattered his men without supplies or arms throughout the countryside to be recaptured by the Mexican cavalry. William Ward and his men suffered such a fate in that very same vicinity.

And then, too, Fannin must have been aware of the political consequences even if such an attempt should succeed and his wounded were left behind at the mercy of the Mexicans, who had just two weeks earlier retaken the Alamo and enforced Santa Anna's "no quarter" policy by taking no prisoners alive.

The concept of a commander leaving his wounded behind on a battlefield in order to escape the enemy would have subjected that leader to censure if not charges of desertion in a time of war. Already U.S. newspapers were probably trumpeting Travis' words of "I shall never surrender or retreat. . . .I am determined to sustain myself as long as possible & die like a soldier who never forgets what is due to his own honor & that of his country VICTORY OR DEATH."

At Coleto, Fannin was aware of Travis' emotional appeal because he had received a similar request from the beleaguered leader including the same message.[7] And he probably could surmise the reaction he would face throughout Texas and the United States if, unlike Travis, he were to abandon his wounded at Coleto and escape.

Yes, it is easy to criticize James Walker Fannin Jr. But the martyrs of the Alamo were already shadowing his every move, and to the north Sam Houston was following a wet and muddy trail to glory. James Fannin, in his last days, was left with a hungry, naked army of malcontents isolated deep in south Texas and pursued by the best general in the Mexican army. It was a formula for disaster.

No military commander should be expected to maintain an army of almost five hundred men with no supplies, food rations, or logistical support. Yet that is exactly what James Fannin faced during 1836. During the time he and his army were positioned at La Bahia, the bickering politicians of the Provisional Government focused their attentions on nonmilitary affairs while the sergeants-at-guard at Goliad posted barefoot men who had subsisted for weeks on unsalted beef and corn.

The provisions lost—and those received—at La Bahia during this period were sent from the United States and not a result of any concerted effort from San Felipe or Washington-on-the-Brazos. Fannin and his men received no supplies, weapons, ammunition, or foodstuffs as a direct result of political action from their own leaders.

Whether it occurred by design or by neglect, Fannin and his men had a valid claim that they were being sacrificed by the politicians sitting safely to the north.

Harbert Davenport, in his 1938 dedicatory address at the monument erected at the site of the grave of Fannin and his men, reflected on Texas' reluctance to embrace James Fannin as a true hero: "Though part of the Texan battle cry at San Jacinto was *Remember Goliad!* (literally, perhaps, *Remember Labadee!*), *Remember the Alamo!* was what the Texans really meant. Forget Goliad! would have been a more correct expression of the mingled shame and pride with which early Texans regarded Fannin's men."[8]

Davenport also touched on another aspect that early Texas historians had tried to circumvent: "And the Texans had, in another sense, a shame-faced feeling that the men of Goliad had let them down. . . . Defeat of the Grant and Johnson parties could be attributed to overwhelming numbers and surprise. But if looked at too closely, the defeat and capture of Colonel Fannin would have to be explained; and the explanation admitted that even Texan valor was not proof against hunger, thirst, and tactical errors, and that Mexicans could be brave. . . . The Texans were glad to bury their recollections of the self-seeking, inefficiency, and almost criminal apathy, which had brought about the sacrifice of Fannin's men, and join in the world-wide expression of indignation and horror arising from Santa Anna's ghastly mistake."[9]

In the end, Sam Houston was right: James Fannin was an "ill-fated man."

1   Barker Texas History Center, University of Texas at Austin, "Letter from Harbert Davenport to Samuel E. Ashbury," College Station, Texas, dated April 7, 1932.

2   Brown, John Henry, *History of Texas from 1685 to 1892 in Two Volumes* (St. Louis: L.E. Daniell, 1893), Vol. I, pg. 436.

3   Ibid., pg. 438.

4   Ibid., pg. 476.

5   de Bruhl, *Sword of San Jacinto*, pg. 178.

6   Ibid., pg. 192.

7   Jenkins, *PTR*, 4:419.

8   Davenport, "The Men of Goliad," pp. 1-2.

9   Ibid., pg. 2.

Chapter Twenty-Four
"Curse the Sluggards For Ever"

In his short life, James Walker Fannin Jr. experienced and witnessed an uncommon measure of tragedy. So many times, even in the darkest of days during the month of March in 1836, he expressed concern for his family should he die in the revolution. Only three weeks before his execution, he wrote Joseph Mims at Brazoria and asked him, "Look to our property—save it for my family, whatever may be my fate."[1]

This particular letter also railed against the apathy of the settlers, which he referred to as being criminal. "If I am lost," he wrote Mims, "be the censure on the right head, and may my wife & children and children's children curse the sluggards for ever." He concluded this short letter with "Inquire of McKinney"—referring to Colonel Thomas McKinney of Velasco.

McKinney's relationship to Fannin at Velasco is sketchy, but it appears that the two did establish a friendship secure enough that Fannin felt comfortable requesting the Velasco businessman watch over Minerva and his two daughters should he not return to Brazoria.

McKinney's great-grandnephew, Reynolds Lowry, wrote in 1953 that "Col. Fannin was a strong personal friend of Thomas F. McKinney and on a certain day he accosted McKinney and said to him: 'I want you to promise me that if anything happens to me you will look after my family.' The promise was made and faithfully kept."[2]

Very little is recorded about Minerva Fort Fannin after the revolution. Sometime before the victory at San Jacinto on April 21 she was reported to be on a steamboat cruise off the Velasco coast when a group of refugees were taken aboard the ship.

Mary Wightman, who with her husband had helped found the seaport community of Matagorda, attempted to escape the Mexican advance by boat with her sister, their slaves, and several neighbors including an orphan girl. One of the ships they boarded was that on which Minerva Fannin was a passenger.

Wightman, who had herself been among Texas' upper society before the revolution, was shocked at the treatment her party received from the other ladies on board—including Mrs. Fannin. Refused food or medical treatment even for the sick children, Wightman later wrote ". . . I had always praised the great courtesy of the southern people, and never in my life had reason to think different till now. I had realized that I could not get a smile from any of the company in the vessel."[3]

She continued, "Mrs. Col. Fannin and children were of the pleasure party. I was pleased with her deportment, knowing that she was probably a widow, and believing that she had been warned not to recognize us as refugees."

It is not known exactly when Minerva Fannin did learn she was a widow. During the period of the Runaway Scrape, she met Laura Harrison Jack, whose husband, William Houston Jack, was also a plantation owner in Velasco. Given the unfolding violent and tragic events occurring throughout south Texas, she was understandably in deep depression and worry, and Mrs. Jack welcomed her and the two children into their house during the early months of 1836.[4]

Many years later Mrs. Jack's granddaughter Betty Ballinger wrote:

> Mrs. Fannin and her daughter, Pinckney, were with my grandmother and her family—on the Neches, where they had taken refuge from the Mexicans in the "Run Away Scrape"—As they sat under a tree, my grandmother reading aloud 'The Lady of the Lake,' Colonel McKinney arrived by boat, and waving his hat said, 'Texas is free!' This was, of course, very shortly after San Jacinto, April 21—He told Mrs. Jack that her husband, Mr. H. Jack was safe, but was obliged to inform Mrs. Fannin of the tragedy of Goliad.[5]

Mrs. Ballinger's rendition of the story, however, contains several historical errors including a statement that the second daughter, Minerva J., was born afterward at the McKinney home.

Although she remained in and around Brazoria in the years after the revolution, little is recorded about Minerva or her children. It appears that both Joseph Mims and Thomas McKinney did keep their promises to James Fannin and that both men cared for his property and his family faithfully in those difficult years.

In the aftermath of Sam Houston's victory at San Jacinto, Santa Anna was held as a prisoner of the Texans and agreed to order the Mexican army to retreat south of the Rio Grande once again.

In June of 1836 General Thomas J. Rusk had been assigned to escort the Mexican army and General Vicente Filisola around Goliad on their journey south. Around June 3 Rusk and his soldiers entered the deserted town of Goliad to find the ghastly remains of Fannin and his men, who, by this time, had been burned, scavenged by wild animals, and left to the elements for nearly six weeks.

Rusk ordered the remains buried and a military funeral conducted on the morning of June 3. The funeral service was to be preceded by a military parade, and Rusk then delivered a short but emotional and powerful eulogy:

> FELLOW SOLDIERS: In the order of Providence we are this day called upon to pay the last sad offices of respect to the remains of the noble and heroic band, who, battling for our sacred rights, have fallen beneath the ruthless hand of a tyrant. Their chivalrous conduct entitles them to the heartfelt gratitude of the people of Texas. Without any further interests in the country than that which all noble hearts feel at the bare mention of liberty, they rallied to our standard. Relinquishing the ease, peace, and comforts of their homes, leaving behind all they held dear, their mothers, sisters, daughters, and wives, they subjected themselves to fatigue and privation, and nobly threw themselves between the people of Texas and the legions of Santa Anna. There, unaided by re-enforcements and far from help and hope, they battled bravely with the minions of a tyrant, ten to one. Surrounded in the open

prairie by this fearful odds, cut off from provisions and even water, they were induced, under the sacred promise of receiving the treatment usual to prisoners of war, to surrender. They were marched back, and for a week treated with the utmost inhumanity and barbarity. They were marched out of yonder fort under the pretense of getting provisions, and it was not until the firing of musketry and the shrieks of the dying, that they were satisfied of their approaching fate. Some endeavored to make their escape, but they were pursued by the ruthless cavalry and most of them cut down with their swords. A small number of them stand by the grave—a bare remnant of that noble band. Our tribune of respect is due to them; it is due to the mothers, sisters and wives who weep their untimely end, that we should mingle our tears with theirs. In that mass of remains and fragments of bones, many a mother might see her son, many a sister her brother, and many a wife her own beloved and affectionate husband. But we have a consolation yet to offer them; their murderers sank in death on the prairies of San Jacinto, under the appalling words, "Remember La Bahia." Many a tender and affectionate woman will remember, with tearful eye, "La Bahia." But we have another consolation to offer. It is, that while liberty has a habitation and a name, their chivalrous deeds will be handed down upon the bright pages of history. We can still offer another consolation: Santa Anna, the mock hero, the blackhearted murderer, is within our grasp. Yea, and there he must remain, tortured with the keen pain of corroding conscience. He must oft remember La Bahia, and while the names of those whom he murdered shall soar to the highest pinnacle of fame, his shall sink down into the lowest depths of infamy and disgrace.[6]

And so on June 3, 1836, James Walker Fannin Jr. and his men were finally given the military burial and obituary they deserved. "... many a mother might see her son, many a sister her brother, and many a wife her own beloved and affectionate husband," Rusk had eulogized. Finally John Sowers Brooks' remains were at rest and he had, as he had promised, not disgraced "the name of a soldier or that of a Virginian." Now, at his home, his mother, father, and sister reflected the sentiments of Rusk's words.

Also in mourning were William Pope Duval at Bardstown, Kentucky, and hundreds of family members of the victims throughout the United States. Present at Rusk's eulogy was Dr. Jack Shackelford who, forced to treat the Mexican wounded inside La Bahia, had endured the sound of the gunshots outside that killed his son and nephew. And at Velasco, Minerva Fannin and her daughters mourned the death of James Fannin.

She did, however, confront the man who had ordered her husband's murder and the massacre of his men. In June of 1836, about the same time General Rusk was eulogizing her husband at Goliad, Santa Anna was being held for shipment to Vera Cruz. Mrs. Fannin and her two daughters were at Velasco when General T.J. Green's Volunteers removed Santa Anna from the boat. Mrs. Fannin "rode a little white pony to the point where Santa Anna was imprisoned and attempted to slay him but was frustrated by a number of soldiers who wanted to take him to Goliad and execute him on the spot where he had ordered Fannin and his men massacred."[7]

After General Green's men had removed him from the ship, he was transferred to the nearby Orozimbo Plantation, owned by James Aeneas Phelps. There, near Velasco, the Mexican president was held from July to November of 1836.

Mrs. Betty Ballinger, whose 1928 letter claimed that Mrs. Fannin had learned of her husband's death from Thomas McKinney, also wrote that "Mrs. Fannin had an interview with Santa Anna who was on the Phelps plantation,"[8] but this is unlikely in the aftermath of the violent confrontation between the two earlier at Velasco.

It appears that after this period, Minerva and her two daughters remained under the care and protection of the families of William Jack and Thomas McKinney. It also appears she had lost contact with her family and James Fannin's family back in the United States.

On December 15, 1836, General Mirabeau Lamar received a letter from Savannah inquiring about the Fannin family and if any provisions for support had been established for the children.[9] Mailed by A. B. Fannin, the writer indicates that the Fannin family members in Georgia were aware of his murder but uninformed about his family and affairs in the aftermath.

Lamar was to receive at least two more letters concerning James Fannin's family, but these correspondence were inquiries about Mrs. Fannin. These letters were from Richard Royster Royall, who the previous December had forwarded Fannin's charges concerning the *Hanna Elizabeth* to fellow Matagorda neighbor Samuel Rhodes Fisher and stirred the controversy that had resulted in Fisher issuing a challenge to Fannin.

Royall's concerns were not Texas politics, however, when he wrote Lamar in May of 1837. Now, it appears, Royall was romantically interested in Minerva Fannin, who had just left Quintana with General Lamar and his wife for a visit in Georgia. "But the Impression strong; will you be Good Enough to ascertain her state of Feelings in Relation to the subject [marriage] in which you will take your time and Exercise your discretion in the manner obtained,"[10] Royall wrote Lamar.

"Could Mrs. F be satisfied with my Person I am confident I can make her Happy and her children under any circumstances should be made equal in advantages to mine—," he continued.

Since the letter was addressed to Lamar at Columbus, Georgia, and Minerva was traveling with the general and his wife, it is almost certain she was aware of Royall's inquiries, but it appears she had no interest. A week later, on May 14, 1837, Royall posted another letter in which he stated, "I should be much Pleased to hear that Mrs Fannin would Return with Genl Lamar and the Lady and that I need not Despair as, I am assured as your Influence can effect I may expect the most favorable Result—."[11]

The "most favorable Result" however appears to have been either a rejection of his proposals or a lack of acknowledgement of them. Many years later Clarence Wharton observed that history and tradition are silent as to whether General Lamar undertook this delicate mission. He also speculated: "We know, however, that some 10 years before he had courted the cousin of Fannin, Martha Low Fannin at Columbus, Ga., and that she had refused his hand and married Doctor Fort. He may well have concluded that he was a failure as a matrimonial agent where the Fannin women were concerned."[12]

Minerva Fannin then disappears again from the history records around Brazoria. Royall's letters were written in May of 1837, and by December of 1839 there are records she had passed away at the home of William Jack in Velasco. In her death, she left Missouri Pinkney and Minerva orphans, and several records suggest that Colonel and Mrs. McKinney assumed responsibility for the girls.

On December 2, 1839, the probate records at Brazoria County show that, at McKinney's request, James Fannin's estate was settled. Some three years after his death his inventory of effects, both real and personal, revealed his estate to include three thousand acres of improved land on the San Bernard River, thirty-nine Negroes, two hundred twenty bales of cotton, sixty head of cattle and farming implements worth an estimated value of $37,090.

James Fannin had come to Texas yearning for material success. After his death, Joseph Mims had in fact protected his interests, and although he never lived to realize it, Fannin had become a wealthy man.

Their contract extended through January 1, 1841, but Mims agreed to the sale of Fannin's property in return for rights to keep and live on the estate. A week after the settlement of the estate, McKinney wrote his old partner Samuel Williams: "I have just returned from Brazoria and have sold the property of Fannin estate for $22,000. Have so arranged as to secure $12,000 for the children poor things. The mother's dying request was that Mrs. Jack would use her influence with me to take charge of them....Will therefore make some provision for the children here."[13]

The two girls lived with McKinney, but the tragedies of the Fannin family did not end with Minerva's death. On November 14, 1847—at the age of eighteen years—Missouri Pinkney passed away at the McKinney home in Galveston.

Several sources state that her sister, Minerva, later attended Rutersville College, but given the fact of her mental and emotional problems that is not likely.

The basis for those stories might have been an article written much later by Mrs. Rebecca J. Fisher in which she stated: "I was a student at Rutersville college and when little Minerva was under the guardianship of Mrs. Robinson...who had her about three years and sent her to school hoping that her clouded intellect might be so brightened and developed that she could be taught to read, and by that means amuse and entertain herself, as it was too well understood that she could never attain to anything beyond, for the vapor which clouded her intellect was too dense and dark ever to be completely removed."[14]

Fisher's article recalled how Minerva, as a small child, had wandered from her care to be found later sitting and playing in a flowerbed. She described James Fannin's younger daughter as having rosy cheeks, light hair, and a luster in her eyes.

Later, the McKinney's moved to Austin and took Minerva with them. But as she became a young woman she became unmanageable, and at McKinney's initiative, the state legislature enacted a special law admitting her as a private patient to the State Insane Asylum at Austin.[15] In return, McKinney remanded to the state assets from Fannin's estate valued at $20,000. For over two decades, Thomas McKinney had kept his promise to James Fannin but, in the end, the only remaining Fannin family member in Texas was committed to the state insane asylum.

Minerva was committed on November 9, 1862—during the Civil War—and remained until she died in that institution on July 21, 1893, at the age of sixty-one years. By that time Thomas McKinney had passed away, and Minerva was scheduled for a pauper's burial in Austin until General W. P. Hardeman paid her funeral expenses.

Eight years earlier, in 1885, the first monument had been established to her father in Goliad. General Rusk had in 1836 arranged a mass burial and military funeral, however the grave had remained unmarked for nearly fifty years. After the revolution the town of Goliad had relocated north of the San Antonio River, and in 1885 a memorial was erected in the new town plaza.

Presiding over the dedication of the marker was William Lockhart Hunter, a former New Orleans Grey who had survived the Goliad Massacre despite being severely wounded that Palm Sunday. Hunter had remained in Goliad after the revolution and become active in Goliad County politics as a judge and state representative. The dedication of the Fannin Memorial in 1885 took place one year before Hunter passed away.

In 1885 a memorial was erected in the new town plaza at Goliad honoring Fannin and his men. Presiding over the dedication of the marker was William Hunter, a former New Orleans Grey who had served under Fannin and survived the Goliad Massacre.

By 1893, with Minerva's death, the Fannin legacy in Texas had ended. Still, no monument, no marker, no memorial had been erected by the state of Texas to James Fannin or his men. Even the exact burial site had been forgotten by the local residents.

Then in 1930 some Goliad Boy Scouts discovered what appeared to be human bone remains, and the community began to develop an interest in locating the actual burial site. By 1932 the University of Texas anthropology department was investigating and located the burial site. In 1936—exactly one hundred years after the massacre and Fannin's murder—money was appropriated for the Texas Centennial, and a massive pink granite monument was dedicated on June 4, 1938.

After Harbert Davenport's address at the dedication ceremonies, James Fannin and his men slowly were forgotten again in the shadow of the construction of the massive five-hundred-seventy-foot monument at San Jacinto and the promotion of the Alamo story.

In June 1836 General Thomas Rusk officiated at a mass burial of
the remains of James Fannin and his men outside Presidio La Bahia.
After a century of obscurity and negligence by the state of
Texas, this granite monument was finally dedicated in 1938.

His family scattered and ignored by the state of Texas and he
and his men relegated to a footnote behind Travis and Houston, it
is as if James Fannin had correctly prophesied his fate when he
exclaimed, "Curse the sluggards for ever."

1   Jenkins, *PTR*, 4:454.

2   Rosenberg Library Archives, Galveston, Texas, "Letter From
    Reynolds Lowry to Mr. C. Lamar Wallis, Librarian," dated
    February 7, 1953.

3   Helm, Mary S., *Scraps of Early Texas History* (Austin B.R. Warner &
    Company, 1884), pg. 14.

4   Brown, John Henry, *History of Texas from 1685 to 1892 in Two
    Volumes*, Vol. I, pg. 659.

5   Rosenberg Library Archives, Galveston, Texas, "Letter From Betty
    Ballinger to Anna McKinley Lowry," dated August 30, 1928.

6   O'Connor, *The Presidio La Bahia*, pp. 158-160.

7   "Wife tried to avenge Fannin," *Goliad Advance Guard*, January 31,
    1985.

8   Rosenberg Library Archives, Galveston, Texas, "Letter From Betty Ballinger to Anna McKinley Lowry," dated August 30, 1928.

9   Lamar Papers, Mirebeau B., Texas State Library, Entry No. 505, pg. 514.

10   Ibid., Entry No. 550, pg. 548.

11   Ibid., Entry No. 552 pg. 551.

12   Wharton, *Remember Goliad*, pg. 28.

13   Rosenberg Library Archives, Galveston, Texas, "Letter From Thomas McKinney to Samuel Williams," dated December 10, 1839.

14   Rosenberg Library Archives, Galveston, Texas, "Col. Fannin's Daughter. The Sad Career of the Unfortunate Lady." Letter to the *Austin Statesman* from Rebecca J. Fisher reprinted in the *Galveston Daily News*, Sunday, November 12, 1893.

15   Rosenberg Library Archives, Galveston, Texas, "Letter From Reynolds Lowry to C. Lamar Wallis, Librarian, Rosenberg Public Library, Galveston," dated February 7, 1953.

Epilogue

Even in death, James Fannin seems to epitomize tragedy. Post revolutionary Texas—as a republic and later as an American state—created larger-than-life martyrs of men like Sam Houston, Stephen Austin, James Bowie, and David Crockett.

Near the San Jacinto battlefield, the city of Houston was created from the swampy coastal lands and became a metropolis named after the hero of San Jacinto. Near the geographical center of the state a political capital was created first named Waterloo then renamed after Stephen Austin. As Texas began to eliminate the Indian threats and expand settlers into the northern and western parts of their territory, counties were named after Bowie, Milam, Crockett, William Cooke, Jack Shackelford, and other patriots of the revolution.

Texas was not as generous in promoting the memory of James Fannin, however. A county was named for him on December 14, 1837, along the Red River border with the Indian Territory now known as Oklahoma. The county seat, however, was created as Bonham—ironically named for the man who reportedly brought Fannin the Goliad evacuation order for which he is so often criticized for refusing.

A community was named for him, but even that act was tainted by the memory of the lost men at Goliad. A small settlement located near the site of the Coleto battle was created around the mid-1800s. Initially, the community was named after James Fannin but with hardly the martyrdom of Houston or Austin—the town was known as "Fanning's Defeat." Ignominiously, even his last name was misspelled with a "g"—the very thing his grandfather had abhorred about the family history when he had dropped the letter. Within a quarter century, however, even that had been diminished when the town became known as Perdido—the Spanish word for "lost." By the 1900s it had been renamed "Fannin" and today has less than one hundred residents.

His native state of Georgia created a county with his name in 1854, carved out of former Cherokee territory in northwest Georgia near Chattanooga. That county seat also, ironically, was named not for the Goliad commander but for a Revolutionary War general.

There are today in Texas three major Texas Revolution-era historic battlefield sites: the San Jacinto Battleground State Historical Park, the Alamo, and the Fannin Battleground State Historical Park.

The Alamo chapel and part of the long barracks have been maintained and operated by the Daughters of the Republic of Texas since 1905. The Alamo is the most visited historic site in Texas with more than 2.5 million visitors each year.

The San Jacinto Park consists of a sprawling eleven-hundred-twenty-acre site with the five-hundred-seventy-foot San Jacinto monument, museum, and park facilities. It is also one of the most heavily visited tourist sites in Texas each year.

One mile south of the community of Fannin on Park Road 27 lies a 13.6-acre park so isolated it cannot be seen from Highway 59. Known as the Fannin Battleground State Historical Park, it is simply a field with restrooms, picnic sites, and a pavilion. In the center of the field a circular hedge surrounds a granite obelisk. This is the state memorial on the assumed site of the location where Fannin negotiated and signed his controversial surrender to General Urrea. The simple but elegant obelisk, about thirty feet tall, contains the following short but very appropriate inscription:

> Victims of treacherys
> Brutal stroke
> They died to break the
> Tyrants yoke.
> Also
> On fames etternal camping ground
> Their silent tents are spread,
> And glory guards with hallowed Round
> The bivouc of these dead.

Unlike the Alamo and San Jacinto monuments, this is a very simple memorial, but despite the misspelled words and grammatical mistakes, the shaft at the Fannin site is just as touching and relevant.

Compared to the monumental markers at the Alamo and San Jacinto, this granite obelisk located at the assumed site of Fannin's surrender after the Battle of Coleto is miniscule and isolated from the public yet it is also simple and elegant. It provides a very quiet and dignified memorial to Fannin and his men, who fought courageously against overwhelming odds.

Nine miles further south, at Goliad, lies the ancient Presidio La Bahia. The massive stone fort was restored in the 1960s through the generosity of Mrs. Kathryn O'Connor to stand as a lasting memorial alongside its sister shrines the Alamo and San Jacinto.

The presidio is a private institution operated under the supervision of the Diocese of Victoria Catholic Church and is considered one of the most authentic restorations of a Spanish-era presidio in the United States. Designed to be a memorial along the lines of the Alamo and San Jacinto, the Presidio La Bahia, however, maintains a separate and special status among Texas Revolution-era historic sites.

Activities and reenactments take place throughout the year at La Bahia, but there are many times, because of the isolated geographic area of Goliad, that a visitor can simply explore the three-and-a-half-acre compound, museum, and chapel at leisure.

At La Bahia there are no 2.5 million-visitor crowds to force you shoulder-to-shoulder to shuffle assembly-line style through Texas history. Photographs are allowed and encouraged. The chapel is still, after two hundred fifty years, reserved for religious services. There are no uniformed security guards watching your every step nor are there uniformed interpreters explaining how you should view the events that happened here.

At Presidio La Bahia, the visitor can leisurely investigate the museum exhibits in the building where Fannin maintained his command while at Goliad; meditate a moment in Our Lady of Loreto Chapel where nearly two hundred fifty starving and sick Texans were held prisoner for three days; linger in the courtyard where James Fannin was murdered; stroll the parade ground where his barefoot army camped in rags; and examine the sally port gates where the Texans were marched out to their execution.

At this restored Spanish fort, James Walker Fannin Jr. and his men are honored and remembered as they should be. Devoid of slide shows and snack bars, this site is a memorial. Several reenactments are held annually, but the most impressive is the annual Palm Sunday observance weekend. Living historians recreate the final days of James Fannin and his men concluded by a very

In this tiny chapel, Fannin's soldiers were imprisoned after the Battle of Coleto. Nearly 250 men, many wounded, were kept for three days without food and very little water. Fannin was himself later imprisoned in a small room to the right while he recovered from his wounds.

In this small courtyard inside the Presidio La Bahia, James Fannin was executed after the massacre of his men on Palm Sunday, 1836.

This Spanish cannon was one of several artillery pieces Fannin alternatively ordered buried then remounted in the chaotic days prior to the evacuation of La Bahia in March of 1836. It was discovered a century later during excavations inside the presidio courtyard and is on display at the fort today.

moving memorial on Palm Sunday morning in which the 1836 funeral speech of General Rusk is again dedicated to the victims.

As one goes from the fort through the sally port gates, the Fannin memorial is about a quarter mile to the left. Located at the site of the 1938 dedication by Harbert Davenport, a large mound of dirt covers the mass grave in which the remains of James Fannin and his men rest where General Rusk honored their memories in 1836. A pink granite monument—miniscule by San Jacinto standards—is appropriately large, simple, and elegant. The names of Fannin and the men who died that Palm Sunday morning are engraved on the base of the memorial.

If recognition and honor seems to have come slowly with time for James Fannin, they have not come at all for his family members. His wife, Minerva, died between 1837 and 1839 at the home of William Jack in Velasco. The location of her remains is unknown. Some reports claim she was interred at the old Velasco city cemetery on the banks of the Brazos River, but if so, there are no markers or monuments—the location is now beneath the loading docks of Dow Chemical's Plant A.

Missouri Pinkney Fannin died at the age of eighteen at the home of Thomas McKinney, and her remains are interred in Galveston at the Trinity Episcopal Cemetery. Located in the far corner, her marker is placed facing away from the cemetery path and almost invisible to visitors.

Fannin's older daughter, Missouri Pinckney, was adopted by Colonel Thomas McKinney of Velasco. She died a decade later and is today interred in Galveston at the Trinity Episcopal Cemetery. Her marker is located in a nondescript area of the cemetery.

Her younger sister, Minerva, died in the state insane asylum at Austin in 1893 and was scheduled for a pauper's grave until

General W. P. Hardeman paid her funeral expenses, and she is today interred in the Texas State Cemetery.

Fannin's daughter, Minerva, died in the state insane asylum at Austin in 1893. She is the only member of the family to be interred in the Texas State Cemetery at Austin.

Joseph Mims continued to live on and operate the Mims-Fannin Plantation at Brazoria for many years. Building a lavish southern plantation-style home, he became wealthy and continued the estate that he and James Fannin had begun to develop. Today the property is maintained by the family of the man who purchased the property from Mims, and a state historical marker honors the site of the original plantation.

Fannin initially emigrated to Texas with his family to become a plantation owner and settled on the banks of the San Bernard River near Brazoria. This marker denotes the location of his home during the brief period before his military service in the Texas Revolution.

The flow of the San Bernard River has changed little since 1834, and the sweeping curve where a giant felled oak formed African Landing is now a residential subdivision with an established bulkhead and pleasure boat docks behind suburban homes.

On the banks of the San Bernard River at Brazoria, African Landing served as the clandestine port of entry for Fannin's slave running operations prior to the Texas Revolution. Today it serves as a recreational bulkhead for a residential subdivision.

Richard Royster Royall, who reported Fannin's accusations concerning the *Hanna Elizabeth* to S. Rhodes Fisher and then after the colonel's murder, courted his widow, is buried just south of Brazoria at the old Matagorda city cemetery. Beside his grave is that of S. Rhodes Fisher, who, after learning of the accusations, challenged Fannin to a duel. In the same cemetery is the final resting place of Fannin's cavalry commander at Coleto—Albert Clinton Horton.

The watch that Fannin handed over to his captors just before his execution was reported to have been exhibited in a Mexican museum, but this claim was never verified and the Mexican government denied the rumor. In 1962 a Miss Annetta Marie Cool passed away in New York City. As her estate was inventoried it was discovered that she had been given several items from a relative named Matilda Fort—of the same family as Fannin's wife, Minerva.

Among those items in Miss Cool's possession at the time of her death was a watch bearing the inscription "Given July 1819 to my grandson James Walker (Fannin), Marion, Ga."[1]

On the silver watchcase is another inscription: "Article taken by captor on execution of Capt. James Walker Fannin. Later obtained by Col. William H. Jack and from whom same was obtained by Dr. Tomlinson Fort." The Dallas Historical Society now exhibits the watch and claims that the officer who ordered Fannin's execution was captured with the watch after the battle of San Jacinto and promptly chastised in the same manner as he had killed Fannin. No reports in the aftermath of San Jacinto, however, verify the collection of the watch—an event that should have been prominent due to the "Remember Goliad" revenge factor during the day's fighting.

The watch, dated 1819—the year before Fannin entered West Point—would have had to be the gift of his maternal grandfather named Walker since James Fannin Sr. had passed away in 1803.

Also included in the items from Miss Cool's estate were Fannin's epaulets from his uniform, his sword and its brass-trimmed leather sheath, and a small painting of what is thought to be a Fannin relative.[2]

Neither source states if the epaulets and sword are thought to be from Fannin's Goliad command or his earlier military days at West Point or with the Georgia militia. Nor is there any explanation as to how, or by whom, the items had been returned to the Fort family.

Today James Fannin is still remembered as the commander who somehow let Texas down—the indecisive leader who was responsible for the deaths of twice the number of casualties at the Alamo and San Jacinto combined. But the facts do not verify these charges.

Speaking of the political division that led to Fannin's defeat, surrender, and murder, Harbert Davenport wrote in 1940: "No Texan can read the records of that fatal month of January without a sickening sense of mortification, shame and wounded pride."[3]

Standing at the site of the mass grave outside La Bahia today, it is easy to wonder if perhaps those words ring just as true now as they did over a half-century ago.

The Dallas Historical Society has on display a watch claimed to be the timepiece Fannin asked his executioners to hold for him just prior to his murder. No reports in the aftermath of San Jacinto, however, verify the collection of the watch—an event that should have been prominent due to the "Remember Goliad" revenge factor during the day's fighting. Also on display are Fannin's uniform epaulets, but it is not known if they are from his Goliad Campaign, Georgia Militia days, or his West Point cadet period.
Photo source: Dallas Historical Society.

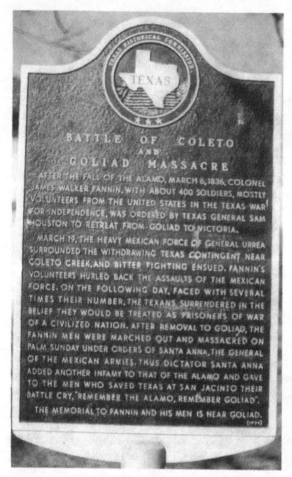

This marker, at the Fannin Battleground State Historical Park, s one of the few state-ponsored plaques dedicated to James Fannin and his conduct during e South Texas campaign in the spring of 1836.

1   Rosenfield, Paul, "Treasure Comes Home," *Dallas Times Herald* Sunday Magazine, March 14, 1963.

2   Harsdorff, Linda, "Fannin's Watch Returns," *The Victoria Advocate*, Sunday, April 10, 1988.

3   Davenport, "Men of Goliad," pg. 7.

Bibliography

Archives

Barker Texas History Center, University of Texas at Austin

Brazoria County (Texas) Clerk's Office, Angleton, Texas, Letters of Credit, Letter Number 29.

Daughters of the Republic of Texas Research Library Archives

Lamar Papers, Mirebeau B., Texas State Library

Rosenberg Library Archives, Galveston Texas

United States Military Academy, *U.S. Military Academy Cadet Application Papers*, 1805-1666

United States Military Academy archives, National Archives Microfilm Publication 2047, *Engineer Department Letters Received Relating to the U. S. Military Academy.*

Journals

Davenport, Harbert, "The Men of Goliad," *The Southwestern Historical Quarterly*, Vol. XLVIII, No. 1, July 1939, pp. 1-40.

Davis, Robert S. Jr., "Goliad and The Georgia Battalion, Georgia Participation in the Texas Revolution 1835-1836," *The Journal of Southwest Georgia History*, Vol. IV, Fall 1986.

Elliott, Claude, "Alabama and the Texas Revolution," *The Southwestern Historical Quarterly*, Vol. L, No. 3, January 1947

Scarborough, Jewel Davis, "The Georgia Battalion in the Texas Revolution: A Critical Study," *The Southwest Historical Quarterly*, Vol. 63, April 1960, pg. 511-532.

Smith, Ruth Cumby, "James W. Fannin, Jr., in the Texas Revolution," *The Southwestern Historical Quarterly*, Vol. XXII, No. 2, October 1919, pp. 79-90.

_____, "James W. Fannin, Jr., in the Texas Revolution," *The Southwestern Historical Quarterly*, Vol. XXIII, No. 3, January 1920, pp. 171-270.

_____, "James W. Fannin, Jr., in the Texas Revolution," *The Southwestern Historical Quarterly*, Vol. XXIII, No. 4, April, 1920, pp. 271-283.

Newspapers

Dallas Times Herald, March 14, 1963
Fort Worth Press, August 13, 1953.
Galveston Daily News, November 12, 1893.
Goliad Advance, Goliad, Texas, 1912
Goliad Advance Guard, January 31, 1985
Houston Chronicle, April 19, 1936
Texas Republican, July 4, 1835, July 18, 1835, September 22, 1835
Victoria Advocate, Sunday, April 10, 1988

Papers

Edward Hanrick to Samuel M. Williams, Williams Papers, Rosenberg Library, Galveston, Texas

James W. Fannin Jr. estate inventory, Record of Wills, Inventories, Etc., Book A, Brazoria County Courthouse, pg. 222, dated December 2, 1839.

"James W. Fannin." *Heroes of Texas*. Extract from *Thrall's History of Texas*, The Union National Bank, Houston, Texas, 1929.

Dissertations

Platter, Allen Andrew, *Educational, Social, and Economic Characteristics of the Plantation Culture of Brazoria County, Texas*, Dissertation Presented to the Faculty of the College of Education, University of Houston, August 1961.

Books

Barker, Eugene C. *The Life of Stephen F. Austin*. Austin: Texas State Historical Association, 1949.

Barr, Alwyn. *Texans in Revolt: The Battle for San Antonio, 1835*. Austin: University of Texas Press, 1990.

Brown, Gary. *Volunteers in the Texas Revolution: The New Orleans Greys*. Plano, Texas: Republic of Texas Press, 1999.

Brown, John Henry. *History of Texas from 1685 to 1892 in Two Volumes*. St. Louis: L.E. Daniell, 1893.

Creighton, James A. *A Narrative History of Brazoria County, Texas*. Waco: Texian Press, 1975.

de Bruhl, Marshall. *Sword of San Jacinto*. New York: Random House, 1993.

de la Peña, Jose Enrique. *With Santa Anna in Texas: A Personal Narrative of the Revolution.* Translated and edited by Carmen Perry. College Station, Texas: Texas A&M University Press, 1975.

Duval, John C. *Early Days in Texas, or, the Adventures of Jack Dobell.* 1892; reprint Lincoln: University of Nebraska Press, 1986.

Ehrenberg, Herman. *With Milam and Fannin* translated by Charlotte Churchill. Austin: The Pemberton Press, 1968.

Guthrie, Keith. *Texas Forgotten Ports,* Volume I and II. Austin, Texas: Eakin Press, 1988 and 1993.

James, Marquis. *The Raven a Biography of Sam Houston.* New York City: Blue Ribbon Books, Inc., 1929.

Jenkins, John H., Ed. *The Papers of the Texas Revolution 1835-1836 in Ten Volumes.* Austin: Presidial Press, 1973.

Hardin, Stephen L. *Texian Iliad: A Military History of the Texas Revolution.* Austin: University of Texas Press, 1994.

Helm, Mary S. *Scraps of Early Texas History.* Austin B.R. Warner & Company, 1884.

Long, Jeff. *Duel of Eagles: The Mexican and U.S. Fight for the Alamo.* New York: William Morrow and Company, Inc., 1990.

New Handbook of Texas in Six Volumes. Austin: The Texas State Historical Association, 1996.

O'Connor, Kathryn Stoner. *The Presidio La Bahia del Espiritu Santo de Zuniga 1721 to 1846.* Austin: Von Boeckmann-Jones Co., 1966.

Ornish, Natalie. *Ehrenberg: Goliad Survivor, Old West Explorer.* Dallas: Texas Heritage Press, 1997.

Pruett, Jakie L., and Everett B. Cole, Sr. *Goliad Massacre.* Austin: Eakin Press, 1985.

Smith, James F. *The 1832 Cherokee Land Lottery of Georgia.* New York: Harper and Brothers, 1838.

Wharton, Clarence. *Remember Goliad.* Glorieta, New Mexico: The Rio Grande Press, Inc., 1931. Reprinted 1968.

Yoakum, Henderson King. *History of Texas From its First Settlement in 1655 to its Annexation to the United States in 1846 in Two Volumes.* New York: Redfield, 1855.

Correspondence

Sheila Biles, Library Technician for Special Collections and Archives Division, United States Military Academy to Gary Brown dated June 14, 1999.

Index